PROFITABLE BUSINESSESS TO START FOR ENTREPRENEURS

(Select and Start your own Profitable Business)

PROFITABLE BUSINESSESS TO START FOR ENTREPRENEURS

(Select and Start your own Profitable Business)

Written By

EIRI Board Of Consultants & Engineers

ENGINEERS INDIA RESEARCH INSTITUTE

4449, Nai Sarak, Main Road, Delhi - 110 006 (INDIA)
Ph. : 91-11-23918117, 23916431, 23840361, 31082370
Fax : 91-11-2391 6431, 2391 8117
* E–Mail : eirisidi@bol.net.in
* Website : www.eiriindia.org

Sole Distributor :
India Institute Of Consultants, 4/27 Roop Nagar, Delhi-07

Printed & Published By

ENGINEERS INDIA RESEARCH INSTITUTE

4449, Nai Sarak, Main Road, Delhi - 110 006 (INDIA)
Ph. : 91-11-23918117, 23916431, 23840361, 31082370
Fax : 91-11-2391 6431, 2391 8117
* E-Mail : eirisidi@bol.net.in
* Website : www.eiriindia.org

Distributed By

Small Industry Research Institute (SIRI)
Indian Institute Of Consultants (IIC)

ISBN : 81-86732-77-2
Printed in New Delhi (INDIA)

Rs. 400

Printed & Published by Sudhir Gupta for "Engineers India Research Institute"
4449, Nai Sarak, Main Road, New Delhi-110 006

Preface

The book **Profitable Businesses to Start for Entrepreneurs** covers almost all the basic and advanced details to setup own Profitable Business. The new edition of the book is covering latest methods including What It Takes to Succeed as an Independent Entrepreneur, Why These Are the Best Businesses, Business Broker, Business Plan Writer, Career Counselor, Janitorial Service, Mailing List Broker, Public Relations, Seminar Producer, Soft Skills Employee Trainer, Temporary Help Service–Professional, Turnkey Office, Daycare Center, Playgym, Supplementary Education and Coaching, Book Packager, Desktop Publisher, Computer Consultant, Computer Repair, Computer Trainer, Database Consultant, Internet Marketing Consultant, Web Services, Recycler, Caterer, Gourmet Food Products Producer, Gourmet Food Store Provider, Juice and Smoothie Bars Owner, Pizza Parlor Owner, Take-Out Restaurateur, Wrap Restaurateur, Adult Day Services Provider, Aerobics/Exercise Instructor, Ambulatory Care Center Provider, Diet Clinic Provider, Medical Transcriptionist, Carpet Cleaner, Drycleaner, Home Decorating Retailer, Kitchen and Bath Designer, Maid Service, Water Conditioning Dealer, Auto Retailer, Beauty Saloon Provider, Vocational School Operator, Wedding Consultant, Real Estate Agent, Children's Clothing Boutique Retailer, Florist, Professional Women's Clothing Retailer, Rubber Stamp Designer, Telemarketer, Trade Show Organizer, Party Planner, Tour Operator, Videographer, Franchising Abroad Regulations on Indian Master Franchisor, 49 Fantastic Money-Spinning Opportunities.

The book has been written for the benefit and to prove an asset and a handy reference guide in the hands of new entrepreneurs and well established businessmen.

Director

ENGINEERS INDIA RESEARCH INSTITUTE

4449, Nai Sarak, Main Road, Delhi - 110 006 (INDIA)

E–Mail : eirisidi@bol.net.in

CONTENTS CUM SUBJECT INDEX

1

What It Takes to Succeed as an Independent Entrepreneur

Every business is nourished by a specific set of skills, of course, and our profiles detail the training and personality traits that each industry requires. However, in general, an entrepreneur needs the following traits:

- Self-confident and assertiveness
- Boldness, courage, optimism, and the willingness to take controlled risks
- A capacity for hard work: discipline, diligence, and perfectionism
- Ambition, persistence, determination, and commitment to a goal
- Leadership ability, decisiveness, efficiency, and the ability to delegate authority
- Team spirit and concern for others
- An ability to solve problems: resourcefulness, inventiveness and organizational aptitude
- Flexibility and adaptability
- Honesty, integrity, and a commitment to high standards of quality
- Street smarts, intelligence, and good judgment

Perhaps most important, you also must love your company. Can you picture yourself in the driver's seat for sixty to eighty hours a week? Will your family and others in your support system back you 100 per cent of the time? "To succeed, pick something you love and are gifted at," suggests Jeannie Gehring, president of Slender Center diet service in Madison, Wiscosin. She, for one, remains "an adolescent in love. I love the advertising, accounting, nutrition, speaking, and counseling aspects of the business. I've never had a day I wasn't roaring to get to work".

Capital

Virtually every entry in this book provides an estimate of start-up costs. Some home-based business can begin with just a few thousand rupees, while others require hundreds of thousands to launch. Of course, the better capitalized business reach profitability faster (and are therefore more fun) than those that squeak by from day to day. When capital is scarce, entrepreneurs use a variety of ploys to hold down initial costs. "Learn to improvise and improve," says Erika Zimmerman, whose Erika's Hair-U-M Inc. beauty shop operates from Darien, Illinois. For example, Dennis Sheaks bought used equipment to outfit Joe Peep's New York Pizza. Donna Porter says some of her best advertising at Playful Parenting of Lancaster (Pennsylvania), a children's gym, comes from enrolling her tots in charity Olympics events. Personal assistant Laura Cribbs made up small candy bouquets to pass out along with her business card. Innumerable sole proprietorships operate from home until it's time to hire a second person. And many businesses hire part-time or commission workers who receive pay only when the work comes in the door.

To be on the safe side, overestimate your expenses and time until breakeven and underestimate your profits. Don't forget to factor in living costs. Most experts suggest socking away enough savings to support your family for a full year, or securing another source of income, such as a working spouse might provide, that can pay the household bills.

An accountant can help you project your business's expenses, revenues, and cash flow. When calculating start-up and operating costs, make sure to include the following: the cost of leasing, buying, renovating, and building your place of business; furniture, equipment, and supplies; gas, electric, water, and telephone utilities; garbage collection, janitorial, maintenance, and extermination; inventory; payroll, professional dues, and continuing education; promotion and advertising; credit card fees; licenses and permits; bad debt; taxes; and insurance.

Funding comes in as many guises as there are businesses. The first place to look, of course, is your own savings. If you can cover only part of your expenses from cashing in your pension plan and raiding your bank book, approach friends and family. Charles Grove, who designs Rs.30 Lac Rs.1 million miniature golf courses, says it's not unusual for a young couple with Rs. 10 Lac to get into the business. "They get their in-laws involved, and a couple of neighbors put up money, which creates a viable financial base to approach the banks. Then the couple sets up a corporate structure with the provision that they can buy the others out."

Small-business owners rarely go beyond family and friends for financing. Commercial banks won't risk lending money to start-ups, although sometimes entrepreneurs can secure personal loans. The Small Business Administration once represented a ready lending source, although its kitty has dwindled in recent years.

Very large (and very promising) start-ups can sometimes approach venture capitalists and limited partners. Occasionally start-ups with massive potential convince investment bankers to float an initial public offering of their stock, enabling them to sell shares to public investors. However, even these funding sources expect the principals to pour substantial home-grown capital into the new business.

To Buy Or Start

Once you determine what sort of business you want, consider whether to buy a company or start from scratch. Both options have advantages and disadvantages: For better or worse, an ongoing business will have all its operating systems in place. You inherit either adept or incompetent employees along with either a ready-made clientele or customers who never seem to pay their bills. If you do your homework well, however, an ongoing business's operating history should give you an idea of future risks and profits.

Ironically, while buying an existing company may be more costly than starting from your own base, you may need less cash initially. Most small-business purchases are leveraged buyouts, meaning the seller accepts a down payment and the buyer pays the remainder of the cost from the business's cash flow over three to five years. Thus, a Rs. 10 Lacs buyout may require just Rs. 3 Lacs in cash.

If you buy a reputable franchise, you eliminate even more of the risk since the parent company guides your every step. Some franchisors offer financing, and sometimes banks will loan against a franchise purchase. However, you not only sacrifice a percentage of your future profits, you also lose a degree of independence when signing on as a franchisee.

Starting from scratch is the scariest option. Those individuals who succeed with their own idea, however, shape every aspect of the business from store decor to corporate structure. Start-up costs are not as high since you pay neither a seller nor a franchisor.

Corporate Structure

For tax and legal purposes, you can set up a business in a number of ways. To limit your personal liability, you can incorporate. While the owner of an unincorporated business accepts complete personal responsibility for all of the business debts and contractual promises, incorporation limits the extent to which creditors can attach a business owner's personal wealth.

Successful businesses pay greater taxes through the incorporation route, however. The corporation is taxed on the business's profits before it pays shareholders the portion of profits (dividends) due them. Shareholders then owe taxes on their personal profits as well.

To avoid the double whammy of paying corporate and personal taxes, ask your advisers about a subchapter S corporation, which is available to certain smaller operations. In such a structure, the corporation channels all profits directly to the shareholders and pays no taxes. Instead, its owners declare their share of the corporation's income on their personal tax returns. Subchapter S corporations thus offer the advantages of limited liability while avoiding the disadvantages of double taxation on corporate profits.

Single-investor operations often opt for a sole proprietorship structure, which cedes the entrepreneur complete control over every aspect of the business. The business pays no corporate tax since all profits are considered personal income. However, sole proprietors also assume complete responsibility for the business's obligations.

In a similar manner, partnerships distribute all the rights and responsibilities of ownership among the shareholders. Each partner reports his or her share of the business's profits as personal income and shares the liability for losses incurred by the business. Limited partnerships provide a variation on the theme; one shareholder (the general partner) assumes unlimited liability for all business obligations as well as the greater portion of control over operations. The investing, or limited, partners share a smaller amount of responsibility, determined by the size of their investment in the business.

Call On The Best

Erika Zimmerman doesn't try to operate Erika's Hair-U-M alone. In addition to top stylists, she hires the best bankers, bookkeepers, and attorneys she can find. "If you try to do your book work on your own, you'll end up a nervous wreck," she says. "Your mind's not on what it should be: running your business."

An experienced lawyer and accountant can advise you on which business structure best meets your needs. They can help you file the necessary documents within the required deadlines and also help you make your way through the paper blizzards precipitated by your trying to obtain licenses, permits, insurance, workers' compensation and sales tax registration, and a federal employer identification number. Professionals can help in tax planning and setting up the best possible accounting systems. The right accountant can show you how, by determining inventory and plant depreciation properly, you can greatly reduce your taxes. But most important, your lawyer and accountant can help you structure a business plan.

The recent rise in PEOs (professional employer organizations) has given paperwork-dreading entrepreneurs another option. PEOs act as human resource departments for small and medium-size businesses, taking over the hassle of personnel, payroll, and so on.

The Business Plan

Brian Ford, audit partner in the Philadelphia office of Arthur Young and coauthor of *The Arthur Young Business Plan Guide* (Eric Siegel, Loren Schultz, and Brian Ford, John Wiley & Sons, New York, 1987, $22.95), admits that many entrepreneurs tackle business-plan writing only to impress financiers. "That's a big mistake," he says, pointing out that a business plan serves as a blueprint for operating a company profitably. "If I had independent means to start my own company, the first thing I'd still do would be to write a business plan." Business plans allow the writer to focus thinking on each aspect of the company's operations, from distribution to competition to marketing. Often entrepreneurs recognize mistakes they've made on paper in time to correct them in practice.

Don't skimp in putting together the business plan. Many plans for even small businesses run 30 to 60 pages or more. The experts say a business plan should contain the following elements:

- A clear, concise statement of your business— its name, address, age, product, goals, financial condition, and prospects.
- A description of the products or services you offer—how they are manufactured or supplied, how they compare to competitors' offerings, and what patents, copyrights, or other protection against competitors you hold.
- An overview of your market—conditions in the industry, the economy, and your region; your competition and future competition; your target customers.
- Your marketing strategy—your pricing, sales, distribution, and customer services; your advertising and promotion plans and how they will increase sales.
- An outline of your company's management—personnel structure, management expertise of yourself and other key employees, business organization, and staffing.
- A statement of your business's sources of financing and plans for repayment of loans.

- A review of your company's financial condition and a preview of its future financial state: start-up costs and breakeven date; past statements (for purchase of an ongoing concern) and projected statements, including balance sheets, profit-and-loss statements, cash-flow charts. Experts recommend monthly or quarterly breakdowns for the first one to two years and quarterly or annual projections through five years.

In addition, if you intend to use the business plan as a document with which to secure financing, your lenders or investors will want to see a two to three-page executive summary at the very top of the business plan. The summary condenses all the information you include in the rest of the plan into a quick-to-read abstract. It concludes with the amount of financing you're seeking and a brief statement of what it will be used for. If this all sounds like too much, then hire a professional business plan writer. Business plan writing has become such a hot profession that this third edition lists it for the first time.

Home

Unless you are a sole proprietor who conducts business from a spare bedroom at home or at the client's premises (for example, a computer trainer or personal chef), you'll need to find an appropriate location and arrange to lease or buy it and to build or renovate the premises. Like all the other aspects of starting a business, construction always takes longer and costs more than projected, so cushion your opening date with a delay in mind. When selecting a site, evaluate the traffic volume and customer accessibility. Check out your neighbors within a several-block radius. While retailers might be hurt by a direct competitor, many storekeepers say complementary businesses build traffic flow.

Ask yourself what your customers expect of you and pick a site with that in mind. Jennifer Kahnweiler, a Cincinnati, Ohio, career counselor, felt the Fortune 500 clients she wanted to land would respond to an upscale image, so she went for premium space. "In the beginning, I took shared offices in an executive suite to cut overhead and tap into clerical services," she says.

While you won't want to pay for surplus space, be sure to find a location that allows for the growth you project. When renting, negotiate to pay only for usable space. (Landlords often charge for square footage under columns and other such nonusable space.) Ask for the right to sublet or sell your lease. Protect yourself against unreasonable rent hikes, and make sure that the lease gives you enough time to establish your business in its location. As a rule, don't commit more than 10 per cent of your projected sales volume to your rental expense.

Help Wanted

When recruiting employees, as when searching for investors, many small companies rely on family. When family members display talent, drive, and desire, merging home and business represents the best of all worlds since you keep profits and goals within the family.

Beware, however. Although your spouse and children might represent a convenient source of help, make sure that each contributes to the business. Countless small businesses have disappeared because they made do with subpar help when they should have hired the best. Businesses that choose professional, loyal, responsible, competent, hardworking, creative employees stand a much greater chance of prospering. Treat your staff with fairness, pay employees well, and reward individual contributions to the business.

Especially in the beginning, absentee management usually proves a disaster, so expect to put your time in on the floor. "You can't hire a manager and expect them to do things like you would," says Dorothy McNish, whose Elecia Michelle Inc. children's clothing boutique operates out of Little Rock, Arkansas. "No employee is as interested in your shop as you are."

On the other hand, if you don't want to spend your entire life locked inside your business, train competent people to handle any emergency and all day-to-day operations. At some point, the owner's best contribution should be managing the big picture. Business schools stress that any entrepreneur who can't leave for six weeks and come back never had a business in the first place.

The Customer Search

Like it or not, every entrepreneur is a salesperson. Starting before you open your doors and continuing throughout the life of your business, you will need to devote a great deal of energy to attracting customers. Each industry requires a different approach. Retailers buy advertising and places of entertainment invite the local media to review their services. Caterers and party planners throw grand-opening galas and invite local businesses that might use their service. Consultants and financial planners cold-call on individuals who would benefit from their expertise. "You can't sit waiting for the touch of Midas," says Erika Zimmerman. "Make things happen. Send brochures. Talk to your local paper and explain that you're just starting out."

No seasoned entrepreneur downplays the importance of ongoing marketing and sales efforts. You may want to hire outside or internal professionals to help in this area. Experienced advertising agencies, public relations firms, and marketing consultants can contribute the extra visibility that will give your business an edge on competition.

Even those small companies that rely on word-of-mouth advertising say it pays to help pass the word along. Some place ads in the Yellow Pages or classifieds in pennysaver newspapers. You might also consider telemarketing and distributing flyers.

The proliferation of the Internet gives entrepreneurs another way to find customers. Daily Soup does 1,000 "Web deliveries" each day. Mailing list broker Mia Clover credits her company's Internet presence with generating 75 per cent of the business contacts for the commercial division. As more and more people jump onto the information superhighway, it's soon going to be de rigeur for a business to have an Internet site.

Call For Help

This book will help you consider what some of the most promising businesses offer in the realms of wealth, excitement, and lifestyle. This book will give you glimpses of what people like and don't like about their chosen fields so that you might envision yourself in a similar company. But don't stop here. Bear in mind the statistics on failure and tap the wealth of help that is available for the asking. Some aid costs money, of course, while other assistance is inexpensive or even free. The libraries are full of information on the specifics of starting a business. Books cover every aspect from writing a business plan to marketing. The larger and smaller accounting firms offer advice in the form of brochures and personal guidance. Don't neglect distributors, suppliers, and others who have a stake in your success. You can also call on the Small Business Administration, local chambers of commerce, industry trade associations and publications, and universities and colleges for help both on starting and running a venture.

Those who start their own business risk failure, of course. On the other hand, if you do succeed, you'll be in control of what management consultant Howard Shenson calls your "des-tiny." Whatever else you experience in the course of running your own business, you'll have the satisfaction of knowing you tried. "Don't be a shoulda, a woulda, a coulda," says Frank Contaldo, who operates Bantam Investment Group, an Elk Grove Village, Illinois, business brokerage firm. "The difference between making a career change to IBM and buying or starting your own business is you're investing in yourself. You'll make the money if you're good at what you do. The glory," he concludes, "goes to the one in the arena."

2

Why These Are the Best Businesses

To be in the Running as a "best" business in this book, a start-up had to promise one of the following products or byproducts (and many promised several):

- Wealth, at least more than an individual with an appropriate background to start a company in a particular field could make working for someone else
- Independence, or the freedom from workplace restrictions
- Fun (or glamour or stimulation or creativity)
- Ease of entry and operations

Who Wants to be Wealthy?

Everyone fantasizes about making millions, and we've included some individuals whose business provide healthy salaries but don't generate real wealth until they are large enough to sell or to take public. Gary Penrod, who grew Building Services Industries into a $12-million-annual-sales janitorial service, enticed a British buyer to spend more than $3 million for his company.

However, while most entrepreneurs expect to make more money than they ever could earn working for a boss, true wealth rarely is the overiding motive for launching a business. For most venturers, starting a company involves creating a job—a dream job.

I Do It My Way

In the course of over three hundred interviews for this book, we heard the recurring theme that independence is the real prize of starting a company. Instead of the nine-to-five drudgery of working for someone else, a business of your own presents a way to control your hours, your environment, and the tasks you perform. We interviewed individuals who said entrepreneurship means never having to say "I'm sorry" to a boss, or never asking for time off in the middle of the week to go skiing or to stay home with a sick child. Founders talked about the joy of making their own decisions: experimenting with a creative merchandising technique, turning down work from unruly clients, working in Palm Springs in the winter and Maine in the summer. "I'm free to make my own mistakes," said one business broker. "I probably make half a dozen bloopers a day—and some are big enough to have gotten me fired if I made them working for someone else. But the creative freedom I have lets me try a lot of unorthodox approaches that work, too. That's why I've about tripled the salary I made before I started my firm."

It's Gotta Be Fun

Founders typically bemoan the long hours, the sacrifices and hard work that goes into turning their start-up into a profitable concern. Then whether we were interviewing someone in the entertainment field ("Whodunit" producer) or in a business where the fun potential is less obvious (temporary-help agencies), entrepreneurs went on to tell us of special compensations: "No two days are ever the same. I'm always doing something new. When I'm at my lowest, something goes right and I experience a real high." Some people were even less restrained in their enthusiasm: "I'm having a ball ! I love the reaction of my customers, my family, my friends." Most of all, they love knowing that they went for it, whether they succeed modestly or spectacularly. " Now, when I'm ninety years old looking back over my life, I'll never have to regret that I didn't try to create my own destiny", said one woman.

Fun, of course, means different things to different people. But realize you'll spend more time with your business (particularly in the start-up years) than with your family, your leisure activities, or your other passions. The experts have good reason to warn against transforming a hobby into a business unless you also have the managerial and organizational expertise to carry it off. However, nobody can make a hateful business successful, at least not in the long run. You've got to love what you do to make it worthwhile.

It's So Easy

Finally, many individuals confine their businesses to just one part of their lives, rather than making them the domineering, overpowering force. These more "holistically" minded people chose operations in which they could either minimize their hours (as, say, artisans or management consultants) or could hire outside managers to run them in their absence. Some entrepreneurs forgo profits to spend more time with family or to pursue hobbies. others see the company's smoothly meshing gears as an opportunity to turn their energies to other start-ups. "This business is simple enough, once I get it rolling, to call in a competent manager," said one entrepreneur. "Sure, I'll check everything closely once a week, but I can use the rest of my time to start the second unit in the chain."

But What Business Will I Start ?

Many individuals aren't really sure what business to start—but they know they're in love with the concept of entrepreneurship. In fact, as the post-World War II baby boomers age, and as women increasingly enter the workforce, this description will fit more and more people as they come to see in entrepreneurship the alternative to scaling the corporate ladder. The higher a person climbs in a corporation, the more heated grows the competition, simply because there are few positions at that level. In 1975, every midcareer vacancy in corporate India had an average of 10 candidates. By 1985, 20 people vied for the same spot, and by 1995, 40 to 60 candidates competed for that vacancy. The answer for increasing numbers of Indians who see their top-management dreams blocked by too many competitors? Instead of slugging it out in a corporation, they're starting their own business.

If you aren'nt positive which business you want to start, don't apologize. As long as you pour the same enthusiasm into a venture once you pick your star, you can be as successful as the individual who always knew which field to enter. However, you may be faced with your own lack of expertise, so you'll probably look for a business that's easy to enter and provides minimum risk. If possible, try on a career before you plunge into entrepreneurship: If you'd like to become a tour operator, take a job with an existing operation for a few months at least. If producing seminars attract you, line up a gig while you're still drawing a paycheck.

The Box Score

A note on the numbers that accompany each chapter: Each figure represents a comfortable average. Just as some start-ups may squeeze by on less initial capitalization and others may require more, revenues, profits, and breakeven time will also vary. "Staffers needed for start-up" represents the minimum to open shop, and entrepreneurs may want to employ more help.

The concept of profits varies from industry to industry as well as geographically. Some companies pay their founders handsome paychecks, leaving practically nothing for profits, while other entrepreneurs forgo salaries almost entirely. We've tried to follow industry norms where possible. For example, most retailers pay themselves Rs.2 Lacs to Rs.5 Lacs a year, leaving profits of just 1to 2 per cent of revenues. On the other hand, particularly in the beginning, sole proprietorships in service businesses typically dispense with salaries and regard everything left after expenses as profit.

3

Business Broker

Job Description: *A business broker matches buyers and sellers of small and medium-size businesses.*

- *Start-up cost as low as Rs. 3 Lac*
- *Potential first-year earnings: Rs 20 Lac*
- *Breakeven time from initial investment: rapid (one year)*
- *Excellent home-based business*
- *No Staffing required*

Frank J. Covich, who consults for individuals who want to become business brokers, under the name Business Activity Alliance, quotes firsthand evidence that his clients have chosen the best of all fields: "Brokers continually see what's for sale in all sorts of industries. It's an amazing thing, but none of the people we've helped get into brokerage leave to enter any of these other businesses." The secret attraction, according to Covich, is that "You can make a lot of money as a business transfer consultant, and, unlike a hardware store or manufacturing business, you don't pay a million rupees ventory and equipment. However, large fees are earned when it's sold."

According to the Department of Commerce, fast-track Indians are an antsy lot: One out of every four Indian businesses changes hands every five years. Enter a new breed of expeditor to match buyers and sellers of small and, increasingly, medium-size business, ranging from card shops to used car dealerships. As a field, business brokerage has been around since the mid-1970s and is still tiny in comparison to its related sibling, real estate, which boasts 150,000 offices nationwide. Tom West, former president of International Business Brokers Association, estimates fewer than 3,400 full-time brokers hang their shingles across the country.

But the money that changes hands in business sales is enormous. Compared with real estate, which counts Rs. 12000 lac in annual sales, all business transfers (including those not sold through brokers) generate Rs. 15000 lac. Estimates on the number of brokered businesses vary widely, but Tom West guesses between 25 and 50 per cent of company sales are handled by brokers. And another thing: Business brokers command 10 to 12 per cent commissions, compared to 6 to 7 per cent real estate agent fees. They still occupy a relatively new niche, however. "One of the biggest negatives we face is people not knowing what business brokerage is," says Leonard Ostroff, who opened The Ostroff Group in Cherry Hill, New Jersey. "I'm looking forward to more competition to help get the world out."

An Opportunity for Professionals

Len Ostroff talked with numerous brokers while shopping for a business he planned to finance with severance pay from a chemical engineering position. He found a wide range of ability among brokers, some of whom he deemed unprofessional. " I had all that money on the line," he says with a grimace, "and no confidence in the brokers I dealt with. There was a real need for somebody to do it right." Ostroff believed he understood how to structure deals that would please both buyer and seller. So, instead of plowing his cash into a buyout of his own, he opened a small office and began brokering.

While they don't necessarily recommend such a seat-of-the-pants approach, Frank and Robert Contaldo managed to get their start without even an office. After selling their chain of three restaurants themselves when they became disillusioned with the brokers they contacted, the brothers launched a franchise they call Bantam Investments Group. With their cars doubling as offices and a part-time employee to answer their home phones, they pounded pavements in search of sellers. They knocked on doors of pizza shops and clothing stores, asking entrepreneurs if they might cosider selling. Once they lined up sellers, they advertised those businesses in newspapers.

Half a dozen years later, with eight salespeople ensconced in comfortable digs in the tiny Chicago suburb of Elk Grove, bantam now sells more dry cleaners and pet shops than any broker in the (Venture Resources) network.

Half A Million

On the upside, the top solo brokerages draw annual commissions in the Rs. 50 Lac to Rs. 1 Cr ballpark, says Tom West, who founded United Business Investments a generation ago and served as president of VR. That top-of-the-line brokerage might split commissions fifty-fifty with salespeople and deduct overhead of about Rs. 2 Lacs a month. That leaves the boss Rs. 80 Lacs as profit—more if he or she brokers some sales personally. For instance, Len Ostroff himself generated two-thirds of the Rs. 1.20 Cr. The Ostroff Group achieved in gross commissions in 1986.

While the majority of brokerages are two- or three-people shops, there is a trend toward multiple offices. Regardless of the number of storefronts, the owner collects half of all fees, so expansion is a nice plan for those who can manage from afar. For example, Ian MacLachlan opened Business Team Inc. in San Jose and added two more California offices within five years, for total gross sales of $12 million and $1 million in commissions, making his company, according to Ian, one of the largest in the country.

Your Resume

Those in the business have a hard time delineating exactly what prepares a person for brokerage. Many states require real estate licenses, but a several-month-long course takes care of that stumbling block. A couple of organizations provide training and support services. The Business Activity Alliance, Frank Covich's outfit, specializes in making business transfer consultants out of professional people, who Frank says are already comfortable with the skills necessary to communicate with business owners. Frank's organization now offers a step-by-step approach to establishing a business transfer consulting practice in association with the Business Activity Alliance. While franchises have no product to sell other than a few weeks of training, some forms, and referral networks, Ian MacLachlan advises those truly unfamiliar with brokerage to buy a franchise. "Some training is better than none at all," he says. He also argues that, since some franchise names carry credibility, you could attract commission-paying customers more quickly than with a sign that reads "John Smith Brokerage." But franchising gets to be expensive if you get too successful. "You don't want to give away another 6 to 8 per cent of your commissions as a franchise fee," says Ian.

Len Ostroff offers would-be brokers the same advice he gives buyers who ask him to find a business in any other field: Go work for an established brokerage before flying solo.

CHARACTER

Good brokers generally share certain character traits. Chief among them :

- ◆ They understand numbers and the law as they apply to business sales. "You have to be able to read a P&L statement—and know that it stands for 'Pretend & Lie,' not 'Profit and Loss,'" says Frank Contaldo.

- They are good salespeople. Much of a broker's time revolves around selling buyers on the merits of particular businesses—and convincing owners to sell.
- Brokers are good negotiators. "You have to deal forcefully with attorneys, accountants, buyers, and sellers," says Tom West.
- They are empathetic. "Somebody wrote a list of the ten most traumatic events in life, and retirement ranked second," says Len Ostroff. "Consider you represent an entrepreneur who built a business over 15 years. He doesn't want the wrong person to take over his baby, and, if you can't justify divesting, he'll never, ever sell."

Finding all these requisites in an employee may rank on the probability scale with finding oil in your backyard, especially considering just a handful of schools offer courses in business brokerage. "Because it's a growth industry, we don't have a large pool of experienced people to draw from," explains Ian MacLachlan. His solution includes ex-CPAs, ex-bankers, and ex-business owners whom he trains in-house. Following the industry norm, all forty of Ian's people operate on a strictly commission basis, which holds down operating costs since you don't have to budget salaries. "We operate more on a partnership basis than as employer/employee," says Ian.

It Comes Down To Selling

Clients fall into two groups: buyers and sellers. Referrals from attorneys and accountants make up sizable portions of both, but you'll spend a great deal of effort coming up with prospects. To track down sellers, "walk, talk, knock, and sell," counsels Frank Contaldo. Although he sees a trend toward telemarketing, Tom West agrees "there's nothing like going to talk to the small-business community. When it's snowing outside, that business owner remembers you when he thinks about chucking it all and moving to Florida."

Lure buyers aboard the easy way: Simply advertise the properties you have to sell. If the particular convenience store they targeted doesn't work out, chances are you have another prospect that might. If not, you can subscribe to business-listing services to come up with likely properties. For a fee, listing networks provide names of franchise and private companies for sale all over the country. In less formal arrangements, brokers who provide leads to colleagues generally split fees.

Most brokers charge 10 to 12 per cent commissions, payable by the seller, with Rs. 1 Lac to Rs. 3 Lac minimums for smaller transactions. Tom West says the average sale involves a Rs. 40 Lac business. Additionally, many brokers handle deals worth millions. "We call them mergers and acquisitions, but it's really the same thing," says Ian MacLachlan. Like many of his colleagues, he is shopping more large deals. "There's truth to the old argument. 'There's no more work in putting together a big deal than a small one,' " says West. And a solid, larger business with better records may be an easier sale. But the best part: The commissions are higher.

Making Matches

Ian MacLachlan finds that about four months elapse between getting a listing and closing the sale. But that's an average. Some listings stay on your files for 18 months, while others sell before you complete the paperwork, particularly if you have a ready stable of buyers. Although MacLachlan concentrates on Indian sellers, Business Team works buyers all over the country, spending Rs. 2 Lac a month to advertise in the local newspapers. For large sales, some brokers contact competitors in a given industry who might buy the particular business they have on the block as a way to expand.

The Perfect Fit

According to Tom West, 90 per cent of buyers who use brokers are first-time owners with zero idea of what particular business they want. The broker becomes an analyst who delves into a buyer's personality in order to find the perfect fit. "People make decisions emotionally," says West, based on the type of lifestyle and environment they want rather than on how much money they can make. For example, because you like gardening you might prefer a flower shop even though you could make more money in a computer-repair business. West recalls the client who answered an ad for a liquor store. "The salesperson found he had six dogs and sold him two pet stores instead."

Frank Contaldo profiles buyers using interview forms made up of fifteen to twenty questions. "We ask why they want to buy a business, who will run it, what are their interests." How much money buyers have in hand ranks close to the bottom of Contaldo's list. "The only way we handle sales is through seller financing," he insists. The buyer puts 25 to 40 per cent down, and the seller takes the rest in monthly instalments that the buyer meets through his new business's cash flow. Buyers like seller financing because they can afford better deals. "The seller makes a lot of money, because he is paid interest," says Contaldo.

Trends

Business brokers predict some fine-tuning of their industry as it matures. The larger acquisitions that brokers now target are attracting large, established real estate and financial specialists. Len Ostroff, for one, happily anticipates this particular trend. "When I'm ready to sell, they'll be ready to buy me out," he grins.

In addition, brokers are becoming both more specialized and more diverse. For example, some are signing up to represent particular franchisors. Others are narrowing their scope to unique niches, such as country inns or professional practices, but aiming for buyers and sellers across the country.

Most of all, business brokerage is becoming more pro-fessional. "Five years ago, there was more of a used-car atmosphere," says Ian macLachan. "A more professional breed of people are coming in, systematizing the business."

4

Business Plan Writer

Job Description: *A business plan writer develops an overall "blueprint" for a new or existing business that includes a five or ten year plan and strategies for such issues as market positioning, competition, reaching target audiences, management structure, start-up capital, and short-and long-term goals.*

- *Start-up as low as Rs. 1.5 Lacs*
- *Potential first-year earnings: Rs. 10 Lacs*
- *Breakeven time from initial investment: rapid (as little as two months)*
- *Excellent business for people with physical disabilities*
- *No staffing required*

One thing that's certain about entrepreneurs: They burn with a passion for their business. scratch the surface of any number of business and underneath you'll find people linked by the common bond of turning their dreams of self-employment into reality. it takes a lot of courage for people to shed the comfortable cocoon of corporate India and reach into the unknown for that gold ring, not knowing if they'll drop it or hold on. It's this blood-quickening sense of risk, the feeling that they're boldly challenging the unknown and winning, that makes entrepreneurs so fervent about their business.

However, this same passion sometimes can make people blind to the nuts-and-bolts needs of their creation. Consumed by the "big-picture" desire to keep their business thriving, entrepreneurs often neglect the "little picture"—the need for vital but necessary tasks such as researching the competition, studying the marketplace, and planning for the future.

That's why a business plan is so important—and why talented business plan writers are in demand.

Who Needs A Map? I know Where I'm Going

Picture this. You're driving down an unfamiliar road. Finally you see a small sign that identifies the road as country highway 537. But when you reach in the glove compartment for your trusty map, it's gone—and you're still hopelessly lost.

That, in essence, is what a company is doing if it's operating without a business plan. Just like a map, aplan guides the way, enabling the company to stay on the main road and not take any detours or ill-advised shortcuts that could lead to disaster.

"A business plan is a written presentation that very carefully explains everything," says business plan writer Donna Barson, founder of Barson Marketing in Manalapan, New Jersey. "it explains the firm, the management team, the products, the services, and the goals. It also has strategies on how to reach those goals."

Business plans have long been fixtures of larger corporations, where they used to be called strategic plans. However, their popularity soared after corporate belt-tightening in the 1980s, when hundreds of thousands of people were "downsized," given early retirement, or simply fired. Too young to retire but too old to start over at an entry-level position in another campany, many laid-off workers struck out on their own and established their own business. Coming from the corporate world, the concept of a business plan was familiar and logical to them. thus, as entrepreneurial start-ups bloomed all across the India, so did the popularity of business plans.

Show Me The money

Business plans have many uses. One, as mentioned above, is to provide a blueprint for a business to follow. Another is to assist the owner/entrepreneur in finding the money to turn dreams into reality. Depending on how elaborate the business/idea is, the amount of money required can range from a small investment to the average salary of a professional athlete. Either way, a sound business plan is vital to an entrepreneur's ability to attract start-up capital.

"In most cases, when you go for financing, you need to have some kind of business plan," says donna Barson. it doesn't matter whether the seed money is coming from a bank, venture capitalist, or rich Aunt Minnie; most financiers want to see a business plan. It assures them that they're not sinking money into a hare-brained venture but rather something that has been logically planned. Think about it: If you wanted to start a business' do you think you'd have better luck in borrowing money if you enthusiastically talked about your idea to a financier or if you presented a carefully written plan explaining why your idea will succeed?

Business plans are also useful in other areas, such as recruitment. If a company is actively trying to bring in outside talent to reach the next level, a business plan is a pivotal document that details the company's operations and defines long-term goals. Not many talented executives are going to risk joining a company in which everything seems to be accomplished by the seat of the pants. Barson noted that some public companies are *required* to have business plans, so that they can show their stockholders and prospective stockholders where the company is heading.

Business Plan Basics

What's in a business plan? That depends on the business. The one constant is that all business plans are not created equal.

A summary business plan (one that essentially summarizes the business's activities and goals) can be as short as 20 to 25 pages. A more advanced plan can exceed 100 pages, not including supporting documentation.

To write a business plan you must be part reporter, part detective, and part psychic. Here's why:

Because some of the data for the business plan comes from interviewing company officers and outside principals such as accountants, you need the information-gathering skills of a reporter. The abilities of a detective come in handy when you dig through public records, financial statements, and other documents to obtain the rest of the information for the plan. A psychic's ability to peer into the future is helpful for one of the most critical parts of the plan—trying to analyze the competition and the marketplace in which the business is competing, and determining what the competitive environment will be like for the company and its products in the upcoming years. "A business plan is composed of three major parts," says Donna Barson. "Marketing and sales, operations/manufacturing, and financial. A business plan writer should have either a marketing, management, or financial background."

Giving Yourself The Business

Start-up costs for a business plan writer are low. A computer and printer are necessities, as are a fax machine and cellular phone. Your computer should have a fast modem for Internet research.

It is recommended that you spend whatever is necessary to obtain a top-quality tape recorder, so that you don't return to your office after interviewing the company CEO only to find that your machine malfunctioned, leaving you with nothing but the depressing hiss of blank tape.

Other start-up expenses include one or more of the books available that provide assistance and guidance for fledgling business plan writers. Business plan software programs also are available.

Another potential initial expense is professional liability insurance. Since a business plan writer is expected to point out future directions and markets for the business to explore, insurance comes in handy if your crystal ball is fuzzy and the business suffers as a result of your recommendations.

Overall, start-up costs can be as low as Rs. 1.50 Lac to become a business plan writer (although the cost of professional liability insurance can raise that figure by several thousand rupees). As for salary, most writers negotiate a fee on a per-project basis. Some charge by the hour, but most business owners reject this method, because it leaves their cost open-ended.

Like other businesses, how much you charge depends on location. If you live in or near a large metropolitan area, you can charge more than if you live in a rural area. It's best to discover through networking or inquiring of other business plan writers what the standard rate is, both per hour and per project, for a business plan in your area, and set your rates accordingly. However, Rs. 1.50 Lac is a typical per-project figure. Thus, if start-up costs are kept to a minimum, it is conceivable that you can break even after finding your first few clients.

How do you find them? By networking, networking, and more networking. As with many other businesses, referrals and word-of-mouth are the best advertisements for a business plan writer. Donna Barson, for instance, joined numerous professional organizations, such as chambers of commerce and economic development groups, from which ultimately came several clients.

"Most chamber of commerce meetings have a 'resource table,'" she said. "It's where members are allowed to display literature about their business."

As with all new businesses, getting that first client is the hardest. However, if all goes well, before long you might be doing a business plan for a growing, dynamic young business–your own.

5

Career Counselor

Job Description: *A career counselor assists clients in defining and understanding career directions and goals.*

- *Start-up cost as low as Rs. 75000/-*
- *Potential first-year earnings: Rs. 12 Lacs*
- *Breakeven time from initial investment: rapid (six weeks to two years)*
- *Ideal home-based business*
- *Excellent opportunity for the disabled*
- *No staffing required*

According to the American Counseling Association, it has become as common for people to seek counseling and advisement for career concerns as it has for them to seek medical help for physical concerns. Betsy Harrison, president of Career Development Corporation, Rochester, NewYork, observes, "our generation places more value on self-worthand challenge—which means we change jobs relatively frequently. Meanwhile, the corporation no longer can guarantee lifetime jobs. These two forces have absolutely turned society upside down." And, in the process, created a whole new field: career counseling.

Effective career counseling is a three-step process:

1. Self-evaluation, in which the counselor helps a client evaluate skills, aptitudes, and interests through tests and discussion.
2. Research into occupations and careers.
3. Preparation for job hunting, including framing the resume and honing interview skills.

In addition, some centers steer clients to industry contacts and even provide access to job listings.

But don't confuse career counseling with employment agencies. "We don't promise a job, even though we have a 98 per cent success ratio," says Susanne Parente, president of the firm bearing her name in Westfield, New Jersey. "We're here to help identify goals and directions."

Who Needs You?

Two types of clients pay your bills: individuals and corporations. "Individuals are primarily professionals making a midlife career switch, people entering retirement, students right out of college, and women returning to the work force," says Jennifer Kahnweiler, of Kahnweiler Associates, a Cincinnati firm. For individuals considering plunging into a new career, Jennifer combines counseling with aptitude tests to help the client decide which avenues to pursue. Then her staff researches the industry to give clients answers to questions they need to get started. What is a typical day like? What skills do you need? What money can you expect? Whom can you contact to tell you more? Who are the prospective employers in this part of the country?

Career counselors command anywhere from Rs.2000 to Rs. 5000 an hour to point individuals in the right direction. Unless the situation teems with some special problems, figure on spending four to eight hour-long session, a fee of Rs.7500 is typical throughout the industry.

Corporation provide bigger bucks than individuals because they buy Rs. 20000 to Rs. 40000 seminars for a group of employees, or they put you on retainer to help a more-or-less steady stream of employees. In a seminar setting, you might talk with employees when layoffs are inevitable. topics include how to write resumes or deal with the depression that typically accompanies the pink slip. The corporation also may pay you to tackle career problems for individuals, particularly in two areas: outplacement (or helping laid-off employees adjust and find a new job) and spouse relocation (or helping the spouse of a new employee find work in the area). In spouse relocation, you may still be paid by the hour, but many outplacement counselors ask for 15 per cent of the employee's last annual salary.

Outplacement

Fired or laid-off employees typically have suffered emotional wear-and tear that counselors address before launching a job search. "People need to understand their anger or frustration," says Kanhweiler, who counts a psychologist among the associates at Kahnweiler Associates. "people who lose jobs often feel a loss of identity," Sue Parente agrees. "We help them put things in perspective. We help them realize they're performing a function— they are not their job."

Such delicate advising explains why the industry's professional societies and those states that require a license say you need a master's degree in counseling psychology in order to call yourself a career counselor.

After you've made what Sue Parente calls, "the warm fuzzy" psychological approaches, you counsel former employees the same way you do others who question their careers. Take spouses, for instance.

Build An Image

Some career counselors start from a home office, particularly if they conduct seminars at many corporations' sites. But you'll probably want to move into an office as soon as you can afford one so you can see individuals more comfortably. Jennifer Kanhnweiler rented an executive suite where she had access to clerical help who type client resumes. "We felt we needed premium space to project a professional image, particularly to corporate clients," says Kahnweiler. She hired an artist to design logo, letterhead, and brochures.

As you grow, you'll need additional counselors. Kahnwelier subcontracts with five independents rather than putting them on salary. That way, she pays them only when she needs them to handle the client load.

Income for solo practitioners generally tops out around Rs. 7.5 Lac, because fees for the most part are hourly. While that's certainly not bad, you can make more by running some group sessions, which pay more than one-on-one counseling. But career counselors expect even more opportunity in the future. "Within five years' anyone who's starting now will have a booming business," predicts Sue Parente. "This is particularly true because we're seeing a market increase in the number of men who relocate when their wives take transfers. They're increasingly asking for spouse location as a legitimate demand. It's a sad comment on society, but may be because they're men, they get it."

6

Janitorial Service

Job Description: A janitorail service cleans commercial buildings. In addition, the company may offer other services such as drapery cleaning and parking lot maintenance.

- *Start-up cost as low as Rs. 1.5 Lacs.*
- *Potential first-year earnings: Rs.8 Lacs.*
- *Breakeven time from initial investment: rapid (one month to two years)*
- *Excellent home-based business opportunity*
- *No staffing required (initially)*

A large interstate chemical conglomerate asked Gary Penrod, a former high school English teacher, to figure out why turnover was so high and the results so inadequate in the company's in-house cleaning department. we're talking hundreds of thousands of square feet of office and industrial space that a couple hundred employees cleaned every night, so the stakes were high. That assignment changed Penrod's life. "I went in with the crews at night. I found people with a second-grade education who were illiterate and knew they had no chance of advancement. There was no upward mobility for these people." It was hardly shocking they couldn't work up enthusiasm for pushing a broom the rest of their lives.

Penrod made two recommendations: Bring in educational consultants to teach the cleaners how to read or disband the in-house janitorial crews in favor of outside contractors whose business involves dealing with consant turnover and low motivation.

The Millionaire Janitor

A few years after making those recommendations, Gary Penrod borrowed Rs. 1 Lac for equipment and payroll and "listened to my own advice.

I started a contract cleaning company." Although it took him a few years to hook his former employer as a client, Penrod offered office cleaning services in two states within the first year. After 14 years, his Building service Industries, Wilmington, Delaware, grossed Rs. 200 million and employed 1,600 in eight states as far-flung as New York and Texas. Penrod sold in the company to a British group for a figure "in excess of Rs.100 million." He also stayed on to help the new owners acquire similar contract cleaning services throughout the United States.

While your business may not burst out of the starting gate quite that fast, there is still real moneymaking potential here. The Building Service Contractors Association International (BSCAI) says that the most significant growth in the U.S. economy between now and the next couple of years will be in service industries, and janitorial service is anticipated to grow faster than virtually every other service category.

Indeed, the commercial cleaning industry has been mopping up in the growth category for years; the number of commercial cleaning franchises rose 38 per cent from 1991 to 1993. (This is on top of 14 per cent average yearly increases from 1984 to 1989). Industry revenues soared as well, leaping from approximately Rs.1400 billion in 1990 to about Rs.2000 billion in 1996.

A Slush Fund

If you plan to start with several contracts, you'll need equipment, marketing, an office, and payroll. (Traditionally, contractors bill on the last day of the month, so plan on meeting weekly payrolls before you ever see a dime of reimbursement.) To do it right, industry experts recommend Rs.10 Lac in seed capital and a similar line of credit to help you grow. Most of that goes for buying heavy-duty equipment. You can also buy existing contractors for about 40 to 50 per cent of their annual revenues.

But you can start for less if you're willing to grow slowly; namely, do all the cleaning and marketing yourself, using a home-based office. Some individuals even start part time, hanging on to daytime jobs and cleaning at night. "I wouldn't rule out what I and hundreds of others did—start with virtually no cash and hang on to make a company work," says Gary Penrod. Franchises start at a few thousand rupees, and many franchisors provide financing. Several even throw in a few contracts to get you started.

In fact, profits are best in those early days because your only expense involve lining up contracts and buying the supplies and equipment you need to clean. Some franchisees claim one-person out fits net 70 per cent of sales (not counting the owner's salary). But you're limited to the few jobs one person can do' so annual revenues may hover around the Rs.10 Lac mark. to expand, add another cleaner, which immediately cuts profits in half. Put on a few staffers and you'll need supervisors, office space, possibly a warehouse, and a sales force to sustain the whole bunch, which explains why the bigger companies are thrilled to pocket Rs.50 out of every Rs.400.

A Clean Sweep

To boost those margins, many contracts add other services, ranging from carpet dyeing to parking lot maintenance. Not only will the additional services improve your bottom line, but many clients like "one-stop shopping." If you clean draperies twice a year, they won't have to hire an outside service.

While you can certainly advertise in the "Business Services" listings of newspaper want ads and in the Yellow Pages, the spoils usually go to the aggressive. "I used to take Sunday afternoon rides looking for real estate signs announcing new buildings, then call on the landlords," recalls Gary Penrod. In other words, dig up potential clients and ask to bid on their cleaning contract.

Make the proposal professional. you might call a building's cotractor to learn what materials it contains. Then contact the chemical manufacturer to find the best way to maintain that particular Ilma-wool-blend carpeting. Show off your expertise by stating how you plan to care for a client's computer room. If you run may be able to polish floors and dust word processors for less than an in-house cleaner because you have trained personnel and buy supplies in bulk.

Once you quit vacuuming yourself, expect labor to eat up about 55 cents of every dollar you bring in. Really efficient firms in nonunion areas usually bid around 60 cents a square foot per year. But before bidding, check out all the variables. "It takes longer to clean 10,000 square feet where 500 people work than the same space with 200 people," says Gary Penrod. "Also determine if the space is carpeted, how old it is, and it's heated and air conditioned. Are you dealing with an insurance office where you'll have to pick lots of staples off the floor or an executive suite that's basically clean?"

Revolving Door Syndrome

Expect your biggest headache to be employee turnover—200 to 300 per cent a year isn't unusual. Cleaning personnel often are transients—students or their parents who quit as soon as school is paid for. Few people see janitorial work as a career, so they lose nothing by quitting when another opportunity arises. "Nobody aspires to be a cleaner," Gary Penrod recognizes. "That's not so much a problem as a fact." The turnover is the reason corporations gave up in-house cleaning in the first place, remember?

You may hold on to people longer if you pay above minimum wage and train for advancement. Recruit employees by offering to transport crews to outlying corporate parks that are far from most employee's homes. Some companies praise the loyalty of disabled and older workers.

High technology may eventually change the way we clean our business. Robots already sweep a few Japanese factories. the steam jets that hospitals use to sterilize operating rooms could be adapted for scouring bathrooms. But those solutions are probably years away from large-scale implementation. Meanwhile, there's still time for entrepreneurs to apply some elebow grease.

7

Mailing List Broker

Job Description: A *mailing list broker performs numerous functions with mailing lists for clients, including researching to find the proper list and maintaining lists.*

- *Low start-up costs (if home-based)*
- *Breakeven time from initial investment: rapid (if home-based)*
- *Home-based business possibility*
- *No staffing required (initially)*

Direct mail. Junk mail.

Call it what you will (and direct marketers *bate* it when you call it "junk" mail), direct mail is one of the most remarkable marketing phenomena of the 20th century. In 1997, Americans spent $244 billion responding to direct mail pitches. That's a lot of cash for something that nobody asked for and that arrived in their mailbox unannounced.

Whether you love it or loathe it, direct mail doesn't appear in your mailbox without an assist from something just as important as the solicitation itself—the mailing list. From the mailing list come the names of people selected to receive the direct mail—names that are geared toward a very specifically targeted solicitation.

The mailing list is often the difference between a successful direct mail campaign and an unsuccessful one. For instance, how many responses would a company that markets rock-and-roll memorabilia get if its catalog was sent only to members of symphonic societies? The obvious answer: not many. As the *Capital* Times of Madison, Wisconsin, says: "The most important element of a successful direct mail campaign is a good target or potential customer list." This is why mailing list companies are in demand—and possibly why you could be too if you started your own mailing list broker service.

Mailbox Mania

Each year, Americans receive an average of 553 pieces of direct mail—a total of 4.5 million tons. It is estimated that every mail—box in the United States is stuffed with 34 pounds of direct mail annually.

Although people moan and groan about receiving junk mail, it's not disappearing anytime soon. Direct mail is popular because it offers several advantages: It's inexpensive compared to other forms of advertising; it allows concentration on targeted markets; it provides for personalized sales pitches; and it has a sense of immediacy about it that prods customers to respond.

Of course, without mailing lists, direct mail is like a racing car without gasoline—a powerful machine standing idle. Mailing lists are the fuel that make direct mail go. Companies that locate mailing lists are called mailing list brokers. It is their job to find the list that best matches the target audience for the solicitation.

In general, there are two mailing list categories: compiled lists (telephone books, associations, or directories) and direct response lists. The direct response list contains people who order through the mail and who past experience shows will respond to direct mail pitches.

Destination Direct

In 1986, R. Mia Glover took a secretarial job with a mailing list company in Crofton, Maryland. It was her first entry into the workforce, and it seemed like a good opportunity to make some money until she got married someday.

"I thought I was going to be a housewife," she says.

Ten years later, believing that the company could be modernized and more aggressive in its pursuit of business, she bought it. Glover changed the name to Destination Direct and revitalized the company with new computer equipment as well as a new outlook. Since its inception Destination Direct skyrocketed from 3 clients to 300, moved from a 900-square-foot facility to a 2,500-square-foot facility, and became one of the leading mailing list brokers on the East Coast.

Destination Direct determines the best target audience for a customer's direct mail campaign and then researches to determine which mailing list(s) are available to fit the targeted criteria. According to Glover, all lists are not created equal; some are outdated or contain errors. Thanks to experience, Destination Direct knows which lists are called the "cleanest" and will meet their client's needs. After they obtain the list, the client either uses it to implement the direct mail campaign or else turns the entire campaign over to Glover, for her company to fulfill (mail out). The company also manages numerous mailing lists, making sure that the data are up to date and organized.

When Glover took over the business, she added an in-house graphic design department as well as copywriters and marketing campaign strategy planners. Her goal was to turn Destination Direct into a one-stop shop for all direct mail needs.

"We wanted to establish a turnkey operation," Glover says, "so that whether clients had never been in the industry before or were long-time industry veterans, we could work for them using a turnkey approach. It's so much easier if you don't have 16 people touching it [the direct mail solicitation]."

To market the company's new image and services, Glover issued press releases, established a website, and used e-mail to alert direct mail marketers about Destination Direct's new services and outlook.

It took about six months for business to begin picking up. However, once it started it didn't stop. Today business has increased at least 50 per cent over what it was when Glover took over. She attributes the rise in business to the Internet. Destination Direct is listed on the top 50 search engines, so that someone looking for a mailing list broker via the Internet almost can't help but find the business. Every time the company's website is updated, Glover has her technical team verify that the business still pops up on those search engines.

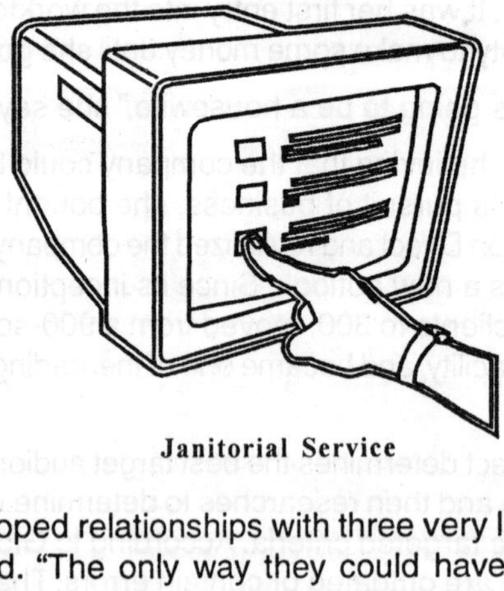

Janitorial Service

"We've developed relationships with three very large public relations agencies," she said. "The only way they could have found us is on the Internet. They contact us all the time for [mailing] lists for their customers."

The Internet has helped the company in other respects, such as regional theaters and charitable organizations. Prior to Glover's takeover, the company's client base had been completely nonprofit. Glover began a commercial division and again used the Internet to get the word out. Today the commerscial division is thriving, with 75 per cent of its business resulting from Internet contacts.

Because of the great success she's had promoting her business over the Internet, Glover only advertises with a small Yellow Pages ad.

Master Of The Lists

If you want to establish your own mailing list broker business, a prerequisite that won't cost anything but is invaluable is industry experience.

"You just can't open a shop," said Glover. "It requires a lot of research. You have to develop a reputation within the industry."

If you've got the experience (or just simply the desire), however, there are two methods worth exploring to establish your business.

The first is to run it as a home-based business in which you primarily obtain, maintain, and sell lists. The only equipment required is computers, fax machines, and so on. Mailing software (at a cost of about Rs. 30000) that complies with everchanging postal regulations is also a requirement. Don't forget about up-front capital, in case you have to prepay for lists before the money starts rolling in. Total start-up costs for this method shouldn't exceed Rs. 2.50 Lacs, and it's possible to recoup your initial investment within one year.

The second method is to establish a turnkey operation. Computers, of course, are still necessary, not only to perform routine office functions but also to direct the printers that produce the actual solicitation materials (letters, forms, and so on). You'll also need a direct addresser (cost approximately Rs.3 Lac to Rs. 4 Lac), which pre-bar codes every piece of mail, and a tabber machine (cost about Rs. 75000), which tabs direct mail in accordance with postal regulations so that it can receive automated rates. If you decide to add graphic design capability, as Glover did, then you need top-of-the-line computers as well, which will add additional equipment expense.

Glover estimates that overall it would take about Rs. 6 Lac of start-up capital to launch a mailing list broker business. "That, and a lot of blood, sweat, and tears." She laughed.

As far as earnings, list fees are given in terms of cost per 1,000 names. The cost per 1,000 for consumer lists (reaching people at their homes) typically ranges between Rs.1000 and Rs. 3500. For business lists (reaching people at their workplace), the rates tend to be higher.

Is E-Mail The Future?

One concern within the direct mail industry is that "direct mail e-mail" might have a negative impact. Glover, however, doesn't buy this.

"A lot of junk mailers have decided e-mail is the better source for their solicitations, but the direct mailers understand that in order to hit a specific market, they really have to use the mail. It's the best medium available. Everyone's got a mailbox," Glover says.

"I think that [direct mail e-mail] is going to separate the true marketers from the fly-by-night marketers. A true marketer knows that they've got to integrate their marketing strategy—the Internet, direct mail, and customer services all have to play a part."

Quite possibly, you might play a part, too—as a mailing list broker. We'll look for your handiwork in our mailboxes.

8

Public Relations

Job Description: Public *relations* means *promoting* a client, *company, product, event, and so on, to the media* in *a variety of ways,* including *press releases,* special events, *and* press *conferences.*

- Start-up cost as low as Rs. 1 Lacs
- *Potential first-year earnings:* 7 Lacs
- *Breakeven* time *from initial investment: rapid (within one year)*
- *Ideal home-based* business
- Excellent *opportunity for people* with *physical* disabilities
- *No staffing required*

When Carol Cone wanted to snare the prestigious McDonald's Restaurant of New England account, she spent almost $40,000 in time and expenses to prove her Boston-based firm had the enthusiasm to sprinkle new glitter on the account that another public relations agency had gripped for 20 years. One of her ploys: a skywriting plane that played off McDonald's advertising theme to splash across the sky: "It's a great time for a great PR agency—Cone & Co." Carol Cone got the job.

Public relations is part showbiz, all right, at least the type of PR that Cone practices. Your job involves carrying a client's message to the media or directly to the public. Sometimes you use quiet press releases and gentle persuasion. Other times you set up special events or other eye-catchers as part of an overall program meant to develop an image or theme that will stick in consumers' minds. One of Cone's more visible programs helped push the Rockport Company from an obscure maker of walking shoes to the acknowledged leader in this burgeoning new field. The program, which included securing an endorsement of its walking shoe by the American Podiatric Medical Association and hiring a medical spokesperson, culminated with one man's walk across America. Rob Sweetgall's 11,208-mile hike grabbed coverage on ABC's *Good Morning America,* in the *Wall Street Journal* and *Parade* magazine, as well as in lots of local spots. Of course, Carol tipped them all off to what a great story an interview with Rob would make.

Investor Relations

On the other end of the PR spectrum sits Robert Amen, of Robert Amen & Associates, Greenwich, Connecticut. His idea the prestigious of razzle-dazzle is a coffee-and-croissant buffet for security analysts at New York's Pierre Hotel. "I consider myself a corporate and investor relations consulting firm," explains Amen. Instead of promoting new consumer products, he reaches institutional investors to talk about a client's stock.

Investor relations is possibly the fastest-growing niche within the swiftly expanding public relations field. The membership of The National Investor Relations Institute has grown over the past seven years and now has more than 2,000 members. The reason: Corporations, skittish over the mass of corporate takeover attempts in the 1980s, are paying more attention to their shareholders, particularly the large shareholders.

Before he set up shop, Bob Amen already had an investor relations background, having worked in that capacity for several corporations as well as with a Wall Street firm that specialized in proxy solicitations. If you enter this PR niche, come equipped with a legal or financial background. "You need contacts in the financial field and financial knowledge," explains Amen, who adds that journalism expertise is handy in other areas of public relations. In addition, if you understand a particular field well and know which publications like which stories, you can turn that experience into PR for your industry. As you grow, increase your knowledge of other industries.

The Accounts

PR agencies generally have two types of clients:

- Project accounts that need to get across a particular message. These relationships last anywhere from a few weeks if all you do is distribute a press release and arrange any follow-up with reporters, to several months if you promote a product roll-out that might involve luncheons and media coverage in several cities. Of course, agencies generally hope the project will lead to the second type of client.
- Retainer accounts that pay a set fee over a longer period. You handle a client's ongoing public relations, which include keeping the media appraised of newsworthy events, and might develop into writing annual reports and employee brochures. "Retainer clients are crucial so you can plan ahead," says Bob Amen. "They

provide cash flow, the continuity that allows you to hire a staff or budget for the future." Robert Amen & Associates' ten retainers provide the bulk of its $750,000 in billings.

To attract those retainers, call on corporations in your areas of expertise and ask to pitch a campaign. Even firms with an in-house PR department may need to farm out particular functions, like developing the West Coast image for a New England-based company.

Don't neglect your company's own PR. Some firms send press releases on new accounts or staff promotions to advertising and industry publications. Success breeds success, so don't be shy about letting others know you landed a big account. You can also host a cocktail party to launch your firm or to celebrate your first anniversary. Invite the press as well as current and potential clients. Also, don't hesitate to network: Meet potential clients through trade organizations or host a seminar on the value of PR. Without being too pushy, let clients know you can perform similar services for their corporate friends. "Some firms in investor relations link with bankers or lawyers," says Amen. "If you handle their PR, they recommend you to their clients."

Making Talent Pay

If you secure enough clients, you can make a good living in PR. Overhead is low: Once you start hiring associates, your biggest expense is for salaries. A solo practitioner can expect to keep the bulk of billings for profit and salary; the owner of a larger firm with many account executives and a lavish office can still earn 10 per cent of the gross as profits in addition to a salary that easily moves into six figures.

In the beginning, many general public relations agencies start at home with a word processor and a telephone. But if image is particularly important, you might need a classy office address. Bob Amen felt he needed an office to attract Fortune 500 clients who might balk at paying high fees to a home-based business. Even so, Amen spent only about $1,000 to set up shop and hire a part-time secretary. You also must pay for your clients' mailings, for phone calls and travel to meet with out-of-town media, and for expenses (such as research) incurred on special projects. But usually you can bill those expenses on top of your fee.

The bigger PR firms gravitate toward larger cities because traditionally that's where the clients are. If you specialize in investor relations, you gain a big edge by locating near New York, since at least 60 per cent of the assets managed by institutional investors congregate on the eastern seaboard. But more general boutiques can round up clients any place businesses need public relations. "If a company deals with press releases that have to be cleared every week or two, it makes sense to be close to the client," says Amen. "You may even have an advantage if you know the local culture and can also deal with the national press in New York and the trade press in Chicago and the entertainment media in Los Angeles."

Most observers expect PR agencies to flourish in the future for two reasons. Corporations increasingly see the value of public relations, even to the point of switching dollars once allocated for advertising to PR. Seventy per cent of Fortune 500 companies surveyed spent over $1 million on public relations in 1997, and 65 per cent increased their public relations budgets during the past five years.

Meanwhile, as contradictory as it seems, those same corporations that can't live without PR are paring their in-house staffs as part of the overall cost-cutting climate. That move leads to the second reason why agencies will flourish. Instead of staffing a PR department, corporations increasingly contract with out-siders to handle their media contacts. According to the U.S. Department of Labor, employment of public relations specialists is expected to increase faster than the average for all occupations through *2006.*

9

Seminar Producer

Job Description: A *seminar producer arranges, and often hosts, seminars for corporations, associations, businesses, and others.*

- *Start-up cost as low as Rs.1.75 Lacs*
- *Potential first-year earnings: Rs. 8 Lacs*
- *Breakeven time from initial investment: rapid (one year)*
- *Ideal home-based business*
- *No staffing needed.*

Case Study : When Jimmy Calano was fired from his job producing seminars, he was indignant. The then 24-year-old had produced seminars since his college days and had no intention of letting some employer knock him out of the business he knew best. Undaunted, Calano hooked up with a partner, 27-year-old Jeff Salzman, who owned a Boulder, Colorado, advertising agency. They then hired their first instructor to do a three-city tour. The seminar was called "Image and Self Projection for Professional Women."

The pair posted "Sold Out" notices on two of those first three seminars and grossed *$220,000* during their first year. But such success is nothing compared to what's happened since. After four years, Boulder-based CareerTrack grossed over *$26* million, primarily on seminars costing clients $48 a shot. Calano and Salzman were soon projecting *$32.5* million in revenues while lining up participants as far away as Australia. In addition to advising young executives on "Stress Management" and "Business Writing," their *60* trainers wax profound on consumer topics such as "How to Find and Keep a Mate."

Okay, class, what lessons do we learn from Jimmy Calano's true-life experience?

A. The seminar business can be cutthroat.

B. The seminar business offers easy entry.

C. The seminar business has a huge and ready market of students.

D. The seminar business can be hugely profitable.

E. All of the above.

If you answered E, take a gold star and enter the wonderful world of seminars.

Thirst

Jimmy Calano knew by instinct what Jack Tumminello, president of The 1st Seminar Service, a Lowell, Massachusetts, seminar broker, confirms through experience: "The thirst for knowledge and know-how is enormous," says Tumminello. "The number of seminars is going to grow."

The 1st Seminar Service makes a living by matching its list of seminar providers with individuals and corporations craving instruction on particular topics. The service estimates some 4,000 "seminarians" discoursed on about 25,000 topics during a typical one-year period. Counting those courses that enjoyed multiple runs, Americans attend 100,000 seminar sessions each year. Counting all forms of in-house training, John Naisbitt writes in *Reinventing the Corporation* that "corporations spend nearly $60 billion a year on education and training ... about the same amount spent on education in the nation's four-year colleges and universities." That's a lot of seminars.

Because the audience is there, and because seminar production is a relatively cheap business to get into, there seems no end to the types of people entering the seminar business: Nonprofit trade associations, such as The American Institute of Electrical Engineers, sponsor curriculums for particular industries; universities experiencing declining student enrolments give courses not only on campus but in cities far from home; and corporations disguise sales calls as seminars, using desktop-publishing workshops to hustle computer software or tax-planning sessions to push municipal bonds.

Even entrepreneurs profess more than one motive: Seminars often generate substantial income, and, if you're a consultant or other professional selling your expertise, they also introduce you to potential clients. Entrepreneurs interviewed for other chapters of this book praised seminars as reputation builders in such varied fields as garden-center retailing and financial planning.

Filling The Classroom

Getting started in the seminar business is dead simple—if you have a course that someone agrees to pay for. Just show up with whatever teaching materials you use, which may be no more than your notes and a gallon of water to keep the vocal cords in working order. Assuming you're a dynamite educator with a hot topic, word-of-mouth can carry you a long way. You may eventually hire an assistant or a whole staff to give similar seminars. Or you may branch out with audio- or videotapes.

But chances are, clients won't drop out of the sky like rain-drops. "We find the biggest problem is not finding people to teach but putting people into their sessions," says Jack Tumminello. "The average marketing cost for producing a seminar is 30 per cent to 60 per cent of sales." The 1st Seminar Service offers one aid. It serves as a clearinghouse for anyone who wants a particular seminar. The service earns a fee from the producer by putting the customer in touch with the right producer.

Seminar Producer

Depending on your topic and your audience, you have several choices on how to market. Newspaper ads and even flyers handed out on the street attract consumers interested in "How to Achieve Happiness in Ten Minutes a Day." You can also try posting notices on the Internet. If you have a very specific but useful topic, cold calls to corporation training managers might be best. You might try direct mail for seminars meant for more general but still targeted groups, such as medical doctors who want to learn the latest malpractice news. But direct mail costs can be stiff—figure $25,000 for a 50,000-piece campaign. Expect to attract no more than 1 per cent of that mailing (500 people), which means each student has to fork over $50 just to pay for the marketing. If you want to pay for the meeting facilities, the instructor, and make a profit, better plan on charging a lot more than that!

Those Who Can't Market, Teach

Or you don't have market at all. Instead, sign on with seminar producers such as Career Track or the American Management Association that contract with instructors. According to Jack Tumminello, depending on which course and how often you teach, an independent instructor can earn $25,000 to $100,000 a year.

The flip side of this suggestion calls for marketeers who don't have specific expertise to sell rather than teach a seminar. The instructor doesn't put up a cent but contributes expertise. The marketeer, or producer, must find the audience and facilities. But, since the instructor is an independent contractor, producers don't worry about payrolls; instead, they just pay the instructor from the proceeds of the seminar. "Usually the organization taking the risk—whoever's doing the marketing—gets the larger percentage of the proceeds," says Tumminello.

The typical provider conducts 8 to 12 programs a year, all focused on an area of expertise. "You can have half a dozen topics that apply to data-processing people, but don't try to address finance people, because then you have to market to a whole new group," advises Jack. But if you build a curriculum for one group, it is hoped that they'll come back for additional seminars over the years.

Of course, CareerTrack provides the exception to that rule, since it markets to everybody in cities of 50,000 or more. Recently it scheduled over 3,000 seminars for a half-million people. Although the courses often enjoy free publicity in newspaper "What's Going On" columns, CareerTrack relies almost exclusively on brochures sent through direct mail to line up participants. "It's not that advertising doesn't work," explains Gillian Goodman, corporate communications specialist. "It's just that direct mail works so well for us."

CareerTrack seminars attract 200 to 500 people per session, often held at a hotel conference room. "The average class is not a workshop," admits Goodman. The company needs the volume to reach breakeven because it charges only $48 per participant.

If your topic is general, such as "Basic Supervision Skills," you may be limited to a gate price of less than $200. But if you have a special expertise in high demand, such as "Robotic Engineering," you can charge $600 to $1,200 for a similar-length program. In this case, the generic seminar needs to draw 50 participants to produce the same revenues as a 10-participant robotics program.

Overhead for a seminar producer can be minimal—an office staff, marketing, a registrar at the course site, and the cost of staging each seminar, including the instructor and renting meeting facilities. Some producers cut deals with hotels and line up accommodations as well. For a busy producer who counts on repeat business, profits can approach 65 per cent of revenues.

In addition to live-instructor courses, technology offers new outlets to the seminar business. CareerTrack sells each of its seminars as four-hour, $39.95 audiotapes meant to turn a commuter's car into a university on wheels. And other companies have gone the step further to videos, which teach everything from "Assertiveness Training" to "Auto Mechanics." Computer-aided instruction teaches children about algebra and professionals about new surgical techniques. The latest-but undoubtedly not the last—frontier: laser videos that allow a student to interact with a taped instructor.

10

Soft Skills Employee Trainer

Job Description: A *"soft skills" employee trainer specializes in teaching business people skills related to human interaction, including stress management, conflict resolution, and team building.*

- *Start-up cost as low as Rs.1.40 Lacs*
- *Potential first-year earnings: Rs.9 Lacs*
- *Breakeven time from initial investment: six months to one year*
- *Ideal home-based business*
- *Excellent opportunity for people with physical disabilities*
- *No staffing required*

It wasn't too long ago that training employees in so-called soft skills—such as how to get along with coworkers and other "people-to-people skills"—was dismissed as too touchy-feely by most of corporate America. Why waste money telling employees to like each other? the business world thought; it didn't matter if employees like each other or not, as long as they do their jobs.

Considered as little more than cogs in a giant machine, employees were left to their own devices in dealing with work-place stress. Ironically, it took the mass corporate downsizings of the late 1980s to awaken companies to the value of their workers. In the aftermath, many of these businesses suffered, as their depleted and exhausted workforce struggled to pick up the slack while being resentful, angry, and contentious. After seeing the negative effects of the layoffs, businesses realized the impact of their workers' "soft skills" on the companies' overall success.

"Employers began to realize [at that time] that employees are part of the productivity chain," says Mark Van Buren, director of Research for the American Society of Training and Development (ASTD). Employees went from being considered a necessary evil to "human capital"—something that no company could afford to squander.

When acts of workplace violence became newspaper headlines, such as the killing of a supervisor by an angry worker who was passed up for promotion, the value of this type of thinking became terribly clear. Suddenly the light bulb is going on: Companies are waking up to the fact that their employees are people, not machines, with all of the problems, worries, and anxieties of human beings everywhere. In this context, spending money on soft skills training seems not foolish but prudent—an insurance policy that may prevent a sudden and terrifying explosion of violence by a distraught employee.

But in order to offer these services to companies, you need trainers. Good trainers became hard to find, as demand for their services skyrocketed. Today numerous sources, including the National Association of the Self-Employed, list "employee trainer" as one of the top-ten high-income businesses that have the best prospects for growth.

Human Capital

Today soft skills training is considered not a frivolous luxury but a benefit, a way for companies to keep employees by offering them classes in such topics as leadership, diversity awareness, and time management. Workers, for their part, realize that they are receiving training that not only helps them in their current positions but also makes them more attractive candidates if they ever decide to test the job market. Thus both sides have their own reasons for embracing training.

The result, as Mark Van Duren points out, is that training is up "across all sizes of companies." And because the ASTD expects training demand to continue to increase, trainers should find themselves with a wide-open market.

Low Barriers

One of the factors that makes employee training such a wise business to start is that it's an inexpensive field to enter. "There are very low barriers to entry," Van Buren notes. Start-up costs are low (typically between $3,000 and $9,000), with most of that going toward standard office equipment: personal computer, software, printer, fax machine, cellular phone, and so on. While a professional office site is useful, it's not necessary; many successful trainers get their start working out of their homes.

For such a small start-up cost, the rewards can be tremendous. The top 2 per cent of personal trainers earn approximately $300,000 annually.

But while money purchases equipment to get you started as an employee trainer, there is one thing that it cannot buy: life experience or, more specifically, how to relate to people and an understanding of how to communicate with them. That, as employee trainer Dee Clarke knows, is something that is earned over time.

Experience Is The Best Teacher

Dee Clarke has headed her own employee training company, the Clarke Training Group, since 1984. She is recognized as one of the best in her profession. Her client list includes some of America's leading companies, including Intel, Chrysler, General Motors, and The Money Store.

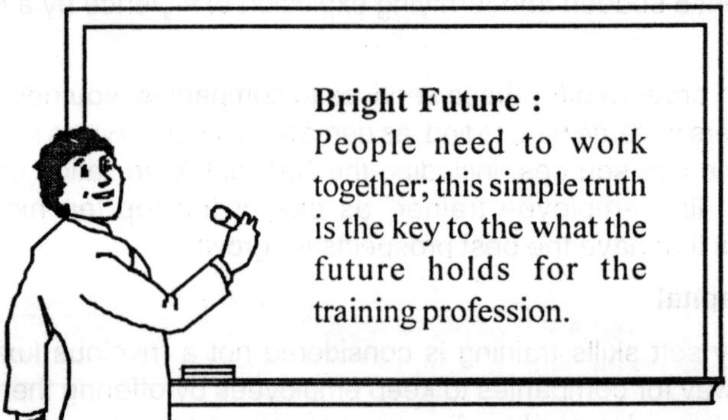

Soft Skills Employee Trainer

Clarke was working as a recruiter in the Minneapolis area when she began teaching a course about sales training ethics at the University of Minnesota. At the same time a company that was familiar with her work needed an employee trainer and asked her to take the position.

This was Clarke's entry into the training world, and she quickly found that she enjoyed it. For a while she kept her recruiting and teaching jobs as well, but thanks to extensive networking, she developed a list of potential employee training clients. In 1984 she entered the field full time.

To grow her business, Clarke avoided spending money on advertising, choosing to focus on networking instead. "People are hiring you," she says, "and they want to get to know you as a person. [When I first started out] I did a lot of networking—finding out which were the most powerful associations in town, such as the chamber of commerce, [and then attending meetings and forming personal relationships with the other members.]"

Another way in which Clarke increased her business was by making cold calls—unsolicited telephone calls to human resource managers at companies, during which she explained her services and inquired if they outsource training.

Her methods paid off. Clarke's business grew at a rate of between 20 and 30 per cent for the first five years, before she cut back on growth to avoid being overwhelmed with work.

Clarke credits her choice of training topics as another big reason for her firm's success. "I chose topics to which I could bring some life experience," she said. "I had been in commission sales, so when I was teaching sales training it was obvious that I was talking about something I had done, not something I just researched and wrote about. People could identify with what I was saying."

Now based in Las Vegas, Clarke says that over the years, companies increasingly come to see the value of soft skills. Just as a business is made up of processes and systems that must mesh seamlessly in order to produce goods and services, it is also composed of people who must work together. With the increasing diversity of today's workforce, such skills as good communications, leadership, and conflict resolution are even more important in smoothing over differences between employees. Workers come from a variety of religious and ethnic backgrounds; an atmosphere of suspicion and anger among employees breeds intolerance, which can easily lead to violence. Soft skills are the way to wipe out that illness before it gets started and affects a business.

"Our tag line is 'If your employees are the engine that drives your business, we have the tools to tune up your workforce,' " says Clarke.

A Fee A Day Is What Clients Pay

Traditionally, soft skills training lasts no more than a full day (as compared to hard skills training, such as how to work a new computer system, that may require much more time). If more time is required, it stretches out over a few weeks.

While lecture plays a part in Dee Clarke's training methods, she notes that years of public school taught most of us how to tune out a teacher. Thus, she relies on hands-on training, such as role-playing, simulations, or a game, that teaches the skills she wants to impart. She also says that people usually make judgments early in the class as to whether the session is worth-while, so that first impressions are very important.

"It's really critical that in those first few minutes they see that you're credible, that you have an upbeat approach, and that you're going to offer them skills that they can actually use," she says.

Usually Clarke charges a daily fee; any external training materials that are required are extra. Fees for employee trainers vary widely, from $1,000 per day (or even less) up to $10,000 per day. You should structure your fees according to how you want your career in this industry to proceed. If it's your desire to establish long-term relationships with numerous clients, it's best to charge less, so that clients believe they're getting value for your services and will not hesitate to call you back.

Another factor in how much to charge is the employee level that you're going to be training. "Companies will pay more to send their executives to training than they will their administrative assistants," notes Clarke.

For beginners, Clarke recommends deciding if you're going to specialize in one particular field (such as the healthcare profession) or be a generalist. Obviously, if you have specialized knowledge of a particular industry, it's best to start out offering soft skills training in that area, because that's where your credibility and experience count the most.

"Credibility is an important thing, because there's a lot of competition in this business, especially at the starting level," she says.

Bright Future

All the indicators point to the fact that soft skills training is going to continue to be a hot profession over the next decade. Even though technology, such as video conferencing, may impact and change the format of such training, the interpersonal skills that trainers teach still need to be delivered in a "hands-on" setting. People need to work together; this simple truth is the key to the what the future holds for the training profession.

11

Temporary Help Service–Professional

Job Description: *A temporary staffing service agency specializes* n providing *professional* employment, such as *lawyers,* physicians, *and so* on.

- *Start-up* cost as *low as Rs. 5 Lacs*
- Potential *first-year* earnings: Rs. 30 Lacs
- Breakeven time *from* initial investment: *rapid (one year)*
- Excellent *opportunity for people* with *physical* disabilities

Like many great ideas, The Lawsmiths struck Eric Walker when he was least expecting it. The engineer was visiting an attorney friend, Robert Webster, when Bob's sister stopped by. "She mentioned she was a lawyer who freelances," recalls Walker. "I asked about temporary agencies, and she said there were none in the legal field.

"If we were doing this story as a comic strip," he continues, "that's where the light bulb would go on." Walker knew temporary-employment services existed not only for clerical workers but also for engineers, nurses, and accountants. After Webster's sister left, the two old friends kept talking, a discussion that led to the formation of The Lawsmiths, a San Francisco—based temporary employment service for lawyers.

A Rose Is A Rose

According to the National Association of Temporary and Staffing Services (NATSS), the technical/professional and medical fields contribute more than 25 per cent of the 2.8 million individuals employed daily in temporary jobs. Niches for accountants, marketing specialists, draftspeople, and other professionals—which barely existed a few years ago—represent the fastest-growing segments of the burgeoning temporary-services industry.

NATSS statistics also reveal more good news for entrepreneurs in this industry. In 1998, staffing companies helped create about 300,000 new jobs in the United States. The entire temporary-help industry has grown at a healthy rate of 9 per cent annually.

Rather than "temp," doctors and clergy prefer the term *locum tenens,* which the dictionary indeed defines as "a substitute physician or clergyman." But, just like a word processor, professional temporaries want to work only three days a week or only during the summer. Most employers won't hire a nuclear plant designer for a day when their own happens to call in sick, but that's part of the beauty of the professional side of the temporary-service industry: Instead of rotating your employees daily, as do clerical agencies, a doctor or lawyer or chief executive stays on the job for weeks at a time. Dr. Alan Kronhaus, an internist who founded Kron Medical Corporation in Chapel Hill, North Carolina, estimates his temps average four weeks on a job, although rare assignments last two and a half years. Longevity on the job eliminates much of a temporary service's expense of employee placement. Another plus to running an agency for professionals is that instead of collecting fees from a hodgepodge of clients, professional services take aim at very specific employers, such as hospitals or financial departments within Fortune 500 firms.

New Math

Like their clerical cousins, most temporary professionals are on the temp service's payroll; the service pays its employees directly and bills clients for work performed by the temp. A difference at this juncture involves basic arithmetic. A top-of-the-line word processor might command $600 a week. Kron Medical charges between $2,000 and $3,900 a week for its doctors, depending on their specialties, which include pediatrics, internal medicine, radiology, and pathology. In turn, the company pays salaries competitive with doctors starting out in group practice, which range from about $60,000 for a family doctor to $135,000 for an anesthesiologist, if he or she works full time—or $1,150 to $2,600 for a 40-hour week.

Okay, you may provide far more aid to professional employees than a clerical firm does, which cuts into profits. For example, Kron Medical covers medical malpractice insurance and pays for air transportation and lodging on assignments, since it places M.D.s all over the country. It even helps them apply for licenses in various states. Nevertheless, Kron's high price tags allow much higher pretax profits than the clerical temp agencies achieve.

Kron Medical, with revenues of $12 million, now bases its 45 full-time staffers in a $4-million building that bears the company's name. But Alan

Kronhaus launched the company from a spare bedroom. Despite modest beginnings, start-up cost $30,000, primarily for payroll until clients reimbursed Kron Medical for the doctors' salaries.

A Start - Up Shortcut

Eric Walker and his partner detoured around the costly start-up phase with two ingenious manoeuvres. The Lawsmiths kept overhead to nil and, more important, signed its lawyers as independent contractors rather than employees. In effect, The Lawsmiths acts as an agent, negotiating an hourly rate with clients and billing for the lawyers. The attorneys wait for payment until The Lawsmiths is paid, and the firm bypasses the cumbersome task of withholding taxes. "This arrangement means we don't have to have a slush fund to pay people before we are paid," says Walker. The entrepreneur warns that establishing your temps as independent contractors is a complicated legal procedure. Some states forbid the arrangement, and the IRS studies the contractor—temp firm relationship closely. "Check with a CPA or attorney who is familiar with recent tax law changes to make sure you meet the federal and state requirements," Walker emphasizes. "Penalties are harrowing—you can end up liable for all the taxes not withheld, even if you can prove the employee paid taxes."

The Lawsmiths' attorneys take home approximately $30 an hour. The firm tacks another $10 to $15 on top of that fee as its cut. Says Eric: "It doesn't take many people working to make a decent income if we get $10 to $15 an hour."

Indeed. At any one hour, about 20 Lawsmiths' lawyers render services to legal departments of large corporations or help sole practitioners whose workloads got out of hand. If 20 people work 40 hours a week, 50 weeks a year, The Lawsmiths accumulates fees of $400,000 to $624,000—after paying the lawyers.

To make things even more attractive, The Lawsmiths claims that expenses total near zero. "Be visible to the rest of the world, but start with as low overhead as possible," counsels Eric Walker. To cut costs, he and his partner work from their homes. In the beginning, a call-forwarding telephone service, costing only $18 a month, gave The Lawsmiths a business phone listing in the Yellow Pages. The partners spent $500 on stationery, business cards, and mailings, plus a similar amount to print a brochure. "Pay a design firm to do your brochure layout right," says Walker. "Don't reek of rinky-dink."

The principals do their own billing and correspondence with a personal computer and use a laser printer. Other expenses include lunches to entertain clients and rent on a conference room several times a month. "Clients never see your place of business since you call on them at their offices," explains

Walker. "But you need a place to interview the temps." The half-hour interviews help weed out perfectly capable lawyers who make lousy temporary attorneys. Experience, top-notch schools, and letters of recommendation can't answer the gut question of who makes a good temporary. "The personality type has to be 'street smart,' he says. "If an employer asks for a quick summary, the temp can't spend days on a long legal treatise." To interview attorneys, The Lawsmiths schedules a dozen interviews in a single day and spends $80 to rent a conference room from a turnkey office concern.

Some states require at least one partner to have a degree in the service you provide. Alan Kronhaus, who still practices one half-day a week, says his medical background helped convince clients he understood the type of doctor they needed. He stresses that dealing with payrolls, billings, and interviewing both clients and professionals requires some business knowledge as well. "If you don't have a business background, team up with someone who does," he advises.

Finding The Clients

Kron Medical mails about 250,000 letters a year to nudge hospitals and group practices to hire its doctors. The company suggests clients might need a fill-in physician until they hire a surgeon or pediatrician full time, or until their own employee recuperates from an illness or injury. Other practices just can't afford a year-round associate when the bulk of their business comes during beach weather or ski season.

Rather than Kron's national focus, The Lawsmiths court a local base of corporations and small legal practices that hire temporaries to ease their workloads. To alert clients to their service, Eric Walker and Bob Webster spend hours calling heads of corporate legal departments. Walker figures he has 30 to 60 seconds to make his initial pitch, merely explaining how the temporary concept works.

"You have to have explanations at your fingertips," he warns. "People say: '$40 an hour amounts to annual salaries of $80,000—I don't pay my full-time employees that.' You have to jump in and invalidate that method of comparison right away. Explain the overhead factor—benefits, vacations, taxes usually amounts to 33 per cent on top of wages. That's a hidden cost that they don't pay temporaries."

Tracking Down The Temps

Temporary services advertise for employees in professional publications. The Lawsmiths averages one resume a day from a one-inch classified ad in the *San Francisco Law Journal.* Walker says many of his firm's regular attorneys have families and don't want to commit to long hours on a continuing basis. Others are sole practitioners who need supplemental income. Kron Medical runs ads in key national medical journals. Many of its temps have just completed medical training and aren't sure where they want to settle or even what specialty they want to practice. Kron offers them an opportunity to sample. Some are part-time physicians, such as the missionary who works in Third World countries half the year.

As temporary help becomes more accepted in the professions, service firms see lots of room for expansion, geographical and otherwise. The Lawsmiths plans offices for Los Angeles and New York, and Alan Kronhaus has far-reaching, if somewhat mysteriously phrased, plans for Kron Medical Corporation: "I'd like to conceive and implement other innovations in the organization and delivery of medical services."

12

Turnkey Office

Job Description: *Turnkey offices, also known as executive suites or business centers, are small furnished offices with shared amenities (conference room, receptionist, and so on) for one or two people that a client rents from you.*

- *Start-up cost as low as Rs. 2.50 Lacs*
- *Potential first-year earnings:* Rs. 10 Lacs
- *Breakeven time from initial investment: six months to two years*
- *No staffing needed*

When Barbara Hildenbrand's boss quit to start his own marketing company, he asked his former secretary to do his typing from her home. "I was out of a job anyway, so I said why not?" she recalls. Soon the boss took office space in an executive suite and began to sell word processing, "which was mainly me typing twelve letters an hour from home."

I Can Do This

Barbara Hildenbrand decided that barely making a living wage for typing day and night made little sense. But her boss had taught her some valuable lessons. As the former secretary helped cope with his start-up details, "I saw the mystique go out of starting a company," she recalls. "I felt this isn't hard, I can do this." He also introduced her to the concept of turnkey offices, also known as executive suites or business centers.

Executive suites are small one-or two-person offices that a tenant rents, complete with receptionist, furniture, common areas such as conference rooms, and optional extras such as world processing services. According to Jane Booras, former executive director of the Executive Suite Network (now the Executive Suite Association), an industry trade association, each of the 2,000 to 3,000 such turnkey offices across the country "generates a generic office environment." One-person proprietorships or branch offices "need space, but not the 1,000 square feet a developer wants to sell."

Intrigued by the concept, Hildenbrand called the real estate offices at Las Colinas, an office-and-residential development under construction near her Irving, Texas, home. "I signed the standard lease for 5,200 square feet at $6,000 a month. I didn't know enough to negotiate. I met with their space planners, and we put in 18 offices."

Hildenbrand had a $72,000 annual commitment—and no-body to pay the rent. It was then she realized she had bought herself not just a typing job but also a sales job. As the building's construction dragged on, she met with prospective tenants in coffee shops and pointed to the hole in the ground that was going to be their office.

A real estate broker saw a tag line on the bottom of the construction sign that advertised executive suites and became her first tenant. The development's real estate office also referred some tenants, and Hildenbrand got another referral from the local chamber of commerce soon after she had joined. But lining up tenants was only one of many challenges. Income also depended on selling her typing and telephone answering services to outside clients. A Yellow Pages ad brought in some business for the answering services, and notices pinned to university bulletin boards generated some typing.

By August, 9 of her 18 offices were rented. Hildenbrand, wearing hats of office manager, receptionist, typist, and space salesperson, had gone through $3,000 in savings, $4,000 from a bank loan against her car, and $4,000 from her parents. "I was so scared I broke out in hives," she recalled, until, somehow, during the last two weeks in August, she rented seven more offices. By year-end, she had hired a receptionist/typist and rented an additional 800 square feet. This time, however, Hildenbrand's real estate client negotiated the lease and got her better terms.

Today, Hildenbrand Associates Inc. operates 47 offices from 11,000 square feet. Rent has escalated to $17,000 a month, and Hildenbrand's payroll covers one part-time and three full-time employees. Revenues topped $380,000 with expenses—including Hildenbrand's own salary—of about $360,000.

The Developer Connections

Barbara Hildenbrand's success story is being duplicated in turnkey offices across the country. "You see basically three scenarios," says Jane Booras. "An entrepreneur takes a lease on anything from 2,000 square feet to a whole floor, then subleases to tenants.

Or developers see executive suites as a way to incubate tenants and bounce them to larger space, so they divide a floor and hire somebody to run them. Or finally, developers contract with secretarial services who run the space on a joint venture basis."

Jane Booras says five offices in a low-rent industrial space might cost as little as $15,000, assuming the telephone system is already in place. You can rent furniture, or even have tenants rent their own if you're on a shoestring. However, larger space in a high-rent district can go for many times that amount. Lease commitments usually run five years, so make sure you have either tenants lined up or a cushion to pay the rent.

Some landlords like the idea of executive suites, gambling that small business tenants will grow and buy larger space in their buildings. Barbara Hildenbrand estimates that former tenants now occupy 35,000 square feet in and around her building. With such trading-up potential in mind, you might talk some developers into favorable rent terms or ask landlords to throw in an extra, such as maintenance.

Whom Will You Rent To ?

Once you have the space, you have to fill it. In addition to tapping real estate and civic contacts, Jane Booras recommends targeted direct mail. "Decide who the best clients are according to your location and expertise," she advises. For example, a downtown executive suite may appeal to financial types or attorneys. Or you might have a word processing system that allows you to write press releases quickly, which might appeal to public relations firms.

Another client source is the Executive Suite Association, which lists members in a directory and provides a toll-free telephone service to companies wishing to locate turnkey office space in distant cities.

Selling turnkey office space differs from selling commercial space, because you're selling your services as well as an address. Point out the benefits. Tenants make no capital investment in furniture or secretarial and reception personnel. Clients can be in business overnight since everything is already in place. They don't have to make long-term commitments. While many executive suites ask for six-month or one-year leases, Barbara Hildenbrand leases month to month and requires no contract. "I found even those companies that sign a lease leave when they're ready." She shrugs. "Also, it's a selling point to say you just have to pay me a month's rent." Those tenants who are branch offices of out-of-town corporations also have to pass leases through legal departments, a procedure that can take as long as the duration of the lease.

Service Menu

When you sell space in an executive suite, you sell convenience. A large menu of services provides two advantages: First, it attracts clients, and, second, it adds profit centers. Barbara Hildenbrand, for example, gets about half her revenues from rent. She prices office space high enough to cover rent on common areas, such as conference rooms, hallways, and the reception area. Secretarial and answering service income, both from tenants and off-premise clients, provides about 12 per cent of revenues. A similar amount comes from Telex and facsimile services. The rest comes from what she calls "miscellaneous": markups on photocopies, postage, and office supplies.

Keep in mind that your biggest expense beyond rent is personnel. Typing is a necessity for your tenants, but you may barely cover a typist's salary from what you can charge. However, you can get better markups on telephone answering services since a receptionist can answer calls for dozens of clients. If you buy a software package to handle your billing, you plight offer to do client billings as well.

By offering a number of special services, your client base encompasses more than your tenants, although they represent your captive audience. Barbara Hildenbrand also offers an incoming mail service for $20 a month to entrepreneurs who want a snazzy business address but operate out of their homes. "One client is an interior designer who needs a place to receive fabric samples and the image our address gives her."

While offering services other than office space boosts income, it also adds an unknown element to your business. You always know how much rent to expect, but you never know how much typing you'll have from week to week. The period between Thanks giving and New Year's may be dead, for example. One solution is to keep your staff lean and hire temporaries for busy periods.

You also sell a tangible ambiance. Hildenbrand points out that clients are typically one-person shops who would miss the social interaction of an office if they didn't talk with other tenants and her staff. I tell the phone room crew to talk with the tenants. If you're not on the phone, talk about the game last night or your vacation. It's not goofing off, it's PR. The tenants don't realize it, but we baby-sit a lot."

Because you "incubate" start-up entrepreneurs until they leave for larger quarters, executive suite managers say they see all sorts of interesting new businesses. Hildenbrand's former boss—the one who introduced her to turnkey offices in the first place—actually took space in her complex. "First he leased my smallest office, then he ended up with two of my largest spaces," she says. "He finally moved out because he needed more space. Then he signed on with my answering services."

13

Daycare Center

Job Description : *A daycare center provides child care during the day, primarily for children of working parents.*

- *Start-up cost as low as Rs. 3 Lacs*
- *Potential first-year earnings: Rs. 6 Lacs*
- *Breakeven time from initial investment: several years*
- *Future growth potential: high*

Society has not experienced such high numbers of mothers in the workforce since Rosie the Riveter went home at the end of World War II. As more women enter the workforce and two-income families become the norm, the dilemma of what to do with children during the day grows more acute. In 1995 the U.S. Census Bureau estimated that 14.6 million preschool children had mothers who were not full-time homemakers. For these parents, daycare is the only acceptable care alternative.

Daycare operators in most parts of the country simply don't worry about advertising to sign up enrollees; many for-profit centers have waiting lists of children clamoring to get in at tuitions ranging from $50 to as much as $200 a week. *Venture Magazine* reported that licensed centers cared for just half of all children needing such supervision. Demand simply outstrips supply. "Some children are signed up months before they are born," reports Jamie MacIntyre-Southworth, whose five Learning Tree schools in Pittsburgh generated revenues of *$800,000* in *1986.* Her schools were so successful, she opened another two facilities.

The Good-Cause Syndrome

If you're successful, you can expect easily to garner 10 per cent pretax profits. Given that norm and the country's demographics, the industry's reputation for lousy profits is downright confusing. Roger Neugebauer, editor of a child care publication aimed at daycare directors, suspects that "the profit motive is not as strong for a daycare operator as someone who is in the business of selling knickknacks." Because "daycare operators may enter the business with a good-cause syndrome," perhaps many fail to stress cost-savings and to pursue opportunities that could add substantially to the bottom line.

Many observers claim anyone who doesn't make a comfortable living from daycare suffers from a lack of business sense. "A lot of elementary school teachers are really dissatisfied with their jobs and think they can just open a daycare center," observes Jamie MacIntyre-Southworth, who taught early-childhood education on the university level before launching the first of her schools.

Although teachers may start the majority of daycare centers, many team with partners who have some business expertise.

Teacher Kay Koulouras, director of Perry Kay Nursery School and Kindergarten in Southfield, Michigan, concentrates on managing her center's 14-person staff and curriculum but turns over business chores to her husband, Perry, who has a management background. This division of labor is one reason Kay says her school has been successful. "My husband takes on most of the bookwork responsibilities," such as filling out federal tax forms, she explains.

Family Affair

Daycare, more than many other businesses, often assumes a family flavor. During various stages in Perry Kay's 25-year history, Kay Koulouras's mother cooked, her mother-in-law watched the grandchildren, her father-in-law did the gardening, and her sons earned allowances for cleaning the facilities. "It's a nice human story," says Koulouras. "But it also helped us cut costs."

The enormous 316-child Council Oaks Learning Campus in the Tulsa suburb of Broken Arrow, Oklahoma, goes a step further in its division of responsibilities by installing a business manager to run each facility. "The education people are free to concentrate on education," says President Jim Seawright, an architect who opted to build the school after a client backed out of the project. Of the narrower range of responsibilities, he says, "The teachers love it. They don't like to worry with the payroll, accounting, scheduling."

The $1.5 million that Jim Seawright's limited partnership raised to open his first school brushes the highest costs of entering daycare. With seed money of $20,000 to $50,000, you can rent and furnish a church basement or renovate a house to accommodate 50 children, which Jamie MacIntyre-Southworth suggests as a threshold for breaking even. To build your own facility, at least quadruple that figure. "A good number of kids is 60 to 80" she says. "Too many facilities with more children are just warehousing." Some operators gain reputation and experience by first offering family care out of their homes.

A Start-Up Quiz

With no national guidelines to follow, you'll run across different requirements for licensing, building codes, and certification depending on your state. Local social or human services divisions of state government can provide legal guidelines for starting a daycare center. In addition, check with one of the 350 early-childhood associations across the country affiliated with the National Association for the Education of Young Children (NAEYC) for more tips on starting a center.

Beyond legal requirements, the entry decisions you face come in great big clumps. In taking the following "test," recognize that not all answers are clear cut. What's right for one neighborhood and one operation may receive failing marks in a different situation. Nevertheless, questions to consider include these:

- Should you apply for government funding? A time-consumsing, laborious process, some warn, but government funding can help you break even faster, particularly if you locate in a disadvantaged area.
- Should you accept babies? Parents of infants literally scurry to find facilities, and you can charge more for little ones than for their older siblings. The downside: Infants suffer higher health risks, and you need a greater staff-to-child ratio to care for non-toilet-trained babies.
- Will purchasing a facility rather than renting pay off in the long run?
- Will serving lunch be worth the extra personnel and insurance costs involved in running a kitchen?
- Should you offer transportation? Many parents view transportation as a big enticement, but keeping vehicles on the road is expensive. Kay Koulouras recalls the emotional relief she felt when Perry Kay dropped its bus service: "I was not comfortable till the last bus came back every day."

The Personnel Dilemma

As with any service company, personnel remains the most costly part of doing business in a daycare center. Kay Koulouras reserves 65 per cent to 70 per cent of her facility's annual budget to meet the payroll costs of her professionals, all trained in early childhood education. No one expects personnel costs to shrink. But operators say daycare has barely explored ways to cut costs and make money through implementing procedures that other industries take for granted. Consider computerizing some administrative functions, for example, or join a central commissary kitchen that services several schools. One dietitian can prepare meals for several schools and scout out discounts for buying in bulk.

In addition, utilize your assets—namely your building and teachers—for longer hours. Offer services beyond baby-sitting. For example, Council Oaks' offerings range from music, dancing, and karate instruction, to scuba diving lessons in the school's indoor-outdoor pool. Parents pay for these ancillary services on top of tuition fees. "If both parents work, their time is limited," explains Jim Seawright. "They just don't have time to take a child for ballet lessons after they come home from daycare. Our job is to cut down on the taxicab effect."

Council Oaks, which accepts kids aged 6 weeks to 12 years, also rents out its gymnasium to neighborhood groups a couple of nights a week. Some operations increase revenue by staying open late for parents who work night shifts. Latchkey of University Place in Tacoma, Washington, attracts some 25 students to a "kids' night out" once every three months. For $10 each, the children attend a Friday night slumber party, complete with popcorn, video cassettes, and dance marathons; the parents get the night off; and the center averages a $150 profit.

Jamie MacIntyre-Southworth looks for her edge by attaching her centers to hospitals, an affiliation that provides many advantages, For one thing, the facilities furnish a ready pool of enrollees: Some 90 per cent of the 400 kids enrolled in Learning Tree schools are offspring of hospital staffers. Perhaps more important, the hospitals help foot the bills in various ways. In addition to outright subsidies or deductions from paychecks of parents who wish to participate, one hospital provides rent-free space and maintenance. "In that center," says Jamie, "we charge parents just $50 a week."

Cashing In On Employer Care

Learning Tree's hospital connection acts as a variation on the theme of employer child care. Once touted as an enlightened employee benefit, daycare programs operated by the boss have not materialized to any serious degree. The Conference Board of New York City recently reported that out of 6 million U.S. businesses, "only 3,000 gave support to employee child-care needs." Working parents should not lose hope, however. The Employee Benefits Research Institute forecasts child care as *the* benefit of the 21st century.

Instead of operating a business they know nothing about however, many employers turn to people like Jamie MacIntyre-Southworth. These corporations subsidize for-profit centers rather than open their own. Barbara Willer, director of information services at NAEYC, calls on-premise employer care just one of many options favored by employers. "In one common situation, various employers form a consortium and contract out child care to a central center," she says.

Start And Sell

In daycare, bigger often means better—or at least more profitable (as long as you don't sacrifice quality for quantity). If you cater to masses of children either in one location or in separate centers, you can buy bulk quantities of everything from crayons to apples to cleaning services. when you employ dozens and collect tuition from hundreds, you need—and can afford— tools like computers for bookkeeping. Economies of scale lead many operators to expand before their first center hits profitability. Jim Seawright says that even before Council Oaks opened, he lined up investors for the second of the 15 to 20 centers, he plans to build. With eager investors waiting, "Financing is just not a problem," he insists.

Despite the advantage of size, daycare remains an industry of small operations. The five existing national chains manage fewer than 15 per cent of all for-profit centers. However, the National Association for Child Care Management singled out an entire midsized segment of new companies, each of which has plans to open anywhere from 75 centers to 2,000. While many of those new facilities will start from the ground up, adding one new center at a time, "there are now a number of entrepreneurs whose game plan is to build up their child care companies to a certain size, then sell," the association reports. In fact, a number of brokers specialize in finding daycare buyers and sellers, a resource you might tap to get in quickly or when it comes time to sell.

Licensing And The Future

Most entrepreneurs expect stricter government guidelines in the future. And, at least publicly, most say that professional operators have nothing to fear. Guidelines are minimums, after all, and many centers set far higher standards than does the government. "We exceed guidelines so far that we won't be affected at all by increased licensing," says Jim Seawright. Jamie MacIntyre-Southworth is more vocal in her support of licensing: "I can take you to five places where people keep half a dozen children in the basement and tell fire department inspectors they are all grandchildren or nephews," she fumes. "Children lose their lives and are damaged emotionally by programs run by individuals who have no understanding of the business."

The national demand for child care seems poised to grow. The Market Compilation and Research Bureau reports that within six months of the birth of their babies, 63 per cent of new mothers currently return to work. As with any other start-up, check out the competition before moving in. If advertising to attract enrollers appears heavy, or if tuitions seem uniformly low, you might want to locate elsewhere.

Barbara Willer at NAEYC has no doubt that in the future greater percentages of parents will choose licensed daycare over other options, such as one parent remaining at home or leaving a child with a relative or neighbor. "The decrease in numbers of babies will be offset by a larger per cent of children in group programs," she predicts. "Economic conditions dictate that both parents work." And, as daycare becomes more commonplace, she suspects parents increasingly value the social experiences daycare provides to their children.

Even the financial community appears impressed with daycare and its potential. *Money* magazine named Kinder-Care Learning Centers, which operates more than 1,000 facilities across the country, as one of the "12 stocks that should stand the test of time."

14

Playgym

Job Description: *A playgym combines play, exercise, and learning with physical activities designed not only to help young children stay in shape but also to help them be more stimulated and aware of the world around them.*

- *Start-up cost as low as Rs. 3.50 Lacs*
- *Potential first-year earnings:* Rs. 2 Lacs
- *Breakeven time from initial investment: six months to several years*

If parachute play doesn't delight you, then the silly pool surely will. These are a couple of favorite activities that Playful Parenting, a Sinking Spring, Pennsylvania, franchise, devised for parents and their six-week- to six-year-old kids.

In Parachute Play, a half-dozen four-year-olds pile into the multicolored parachute while their moms and dads hold the edges high. Giggles turn to uncontrollable, down-in-the-tummy laughter as the parents circle, lifting the parachute to create bubbles that the children scramble to break. Each time a kid tries to climb out, she tumbles back and the laughter reaches higher. (This event teaches concepts of space and volume.)

The Silly Pool: Sometimes bright red Jell-o cubes fill the wading pool. Sometimes it's rice, tortilla flour, or cooked spaghetti. Turn a bunch of one-year-olds loose in the silly pool with plastic utensils to scoop up the "yuk." Then take bets on who has more fun: the babies or their parents. (This event teaches tactile and sensory awareness.)

Tyke - Sized Phys Ed

Playful Parenting is part of a new phenomenon of businesses that offer improved physical fitness for very young children. There have always been Little League and Girl Scouts for boys and girls of grade-school age. But these new programs start with massaging activities for children as young as six weeks. Parents today are open to the idea of child fitness programs because they're worried about warnings that our children spend too much time in front of the tube and because physical education has withered in budget-strapped schools.

Some programs are full-fledged children's gyms, with equipment, activities, and instruction. Sportastiks, a program franchised out of Champaign, Illinois, that takes children age 18 months to 18 years, estimates that 5 per cent of its children are "serious gymnasts," some bound for the Olympics, according to Bev Hayasaki, president of the company and wife of vice president Yoshi Hayasaki— who just happens to be 20-time U.S. national champion in gymnastics.

But rather than train superbabies, most gyms (including Sportastiks) emphasize the fun and learning of physical education. Explains Bill Caplin, proprietor of My Gym Children's Fitness Center, a five-unit chain headquartered in Santa Monica, California: "There's a need for competition, but not in the ages we work with. We lay the foundation for physical education with cooperative sports and games—for instance, two children hold a ball between their tummies in a relay race. They have to learn sharing and working together to make the game work."

Some programs involve parents as equal participants and aim to strengthen the parent-child relationship along with the little one's biceps. This is particularly appealing to working professionals who crave quality time with their children but are a little inhibited about where to start. Gary Siebert, president of Playful Parenting, often recites statistics indicating "the average American mother spends less than four minutes a day playing with her child, and the average American father spends less than thirty seconds a day playing with his child."

All the fitness programs emphasize social and cognitive skills along with the physical ones. "We change the room decor with each five-week session," says Donna Porter, who operates Playful Parenting of Lancaster from the top floor of a Landisville, Pennsylvania, firehouse. "This session, the emphasis is on letters, so we have alphabet designs throughout. When we do the letter 'E,' we pretend we're elephants and swing our 'trunks' during the 'Make Believe' session."

Beverly Hills Or Church Basements

Start-up costs depend on the type of facility. Franchises of Gymboree, Burlingame, California, sometimes set up in churches or Ys where rent is almost negligible. The company's franchise literature says $20,000 will buy you play equipment, insurance, and rights to two franchise locations, Playful Parenting centers range from mall locations, where the rent alone might run $60,000 a year, to franchises in existing daycare centers, where the primary expense is equipment, such as tumbling mats and hoola hoops, Its brochure says to expect to pay $25,000 for equipment and setup and have access to another *$10,000 to $20,000* for advertising, insurance, and working capital.

Bill Caplin chose a Beverly Hills site for his second My Gym. "For us, exposure is important. We're the Cadillac of the children's fitness industry and need to look the part." My Gym spends a lot of money on equipment, as well, ranging from a ceiling mechanism to lower swings and rings to a custom-designed, crawl-through castle. Keep in mind that above all, the exercises have to be safe and fun.

Charging $80 for eight one-hour classes, My Gym targets the higher end of the income spectrum. Says Bill: "We're getting more nannies these days. Both parents are working, and the nannies bring the children for social interaction with other kids."

Operators of less expensive programs agree that the better educated the parents, the more likely they are to enroll their children. "A lot *of* my parents are doctors or schoolteachers, who recognize the value *of* what we do," says Donna Porter, who charges $30 for a five-week session. The lesson: Look for neighborhoods with professional parents.

Be Aggressive

The big challenge is spreading the message that organized fitness programs that combine social and mental games beat taking the kids to the park. If you can't afford advertising, let local reporters know about your program. You may get great publicity through articles describing toddlers who slide, bounce, climb, and crawl. "You have to be pretty aggressive about getting out in the community and making yourself known," says Donna Porter. She calls several families every night, picking numbers from the phone book, to let them know about her center. She also rounds up some of her toddlers and their parents to participate under the Playful Parenting banner in charity events, like the Baby Olympics benefit for the March of Dimes.

Bill Caplin sends mailers to schools and invites parents into My Gym for open houses. "You can also send an instructor to a school with portable equipment," he suggests. Daycare centers looking for ways to entertain their charges might welcome you with open arms.

Such an outreach program also can provide a few extra bucks. You can arrange to visit a daycare facility once a week and give classes all day long to different age groups. Give the center a percentage of the customer fees, and the school director likely will welcome you aboard. You'll probably convert some of those children into regular members at your facility, too.

While classes will provide the bulk of your revenues, use your facilities for such extras as birthday parties and even summer camp. "Business is a little slower in the summer because some people take their children to the pool instead of coming to us," says Porter. On the other hand, "Kids in nursery school come to us only during the summer." Her camps run three hours a day, and parents can sign up for one to four weeks.

For entrepreneurs who really think big, consider what happened with Gymboree. The company generated $10 million through 350 franchise centers. In addition to exercise classes, Gymboree keeps the fun—and revenues—rolling with such extras as videos, books, dolls, clothing, and toys. Twelve years after setting up the first Gymboree class in a San Raphael, California, community center, Fortune Fortune magazine put founder Joan Barnes's net worth at over $2 million.

But before you think big time, you must build a name—and an income—with your gym. Recognize you're dealing with little people who have yet to learn the fine points of walking, much less tumbling, somersaults, or more advanced techniques. Make sure you staff accordingly. Bill Caplin limits My Gym's classes to 15 children and puts 3 teachers on the floor. Donna Porter needs only 1 teacher for about 10 kids since parents participate, spotting for their own children. "But you can't just hire teachers off the street. Both my part-time instructors have degrees in education and experience with handicapped and preschool-age children."

You Gotta Love 'Em

Bill Caplin loves playing with the children. "I was a camp counselor and taught phys ed at a catholic school. But teachers underpaid and not appreciated. So, wanting to combine my love of sports and children, I went to work at a children's gym." After running somebody else's gym for a while, he decided to open his own. Now he owns two My Gym Children's Fitness Centers, a partner owns two, and his brother-in-law runs another—and Bill talks of franchising.

Like so many people who deal with children, Donna Porter acknowledges her satisfaction with her work goes far beyond the $40,000 or so she expects to make in her first year after buying the business from another Playful Parenting franchisee for $30,000. A bookkeeper by training, Donna once ran a daycare program from her home and wanted to work with children again. "But I wanted something people chose to come to, rather than felt they were forced into."

Porter finds a personal fulfilment working with her families. "From the time I was four years old, I always wanted lots of children," she says.

Playful Parenting's franchise brochure quotes President Gary Siebert: "A hundred years from now it will not matter what my bank account was, the sort of house I lived in, or the kind of car I drove—but the world may be different because I was important in the life of a child."

15

Supplementary Education and Coaching

Job Description: *Supplementary education and coaching involves helping students with their studies in a private, non-classroom environment as well as expanding their educational focus and broadening their academic horizons.*

- *Start-up costs as low as Rs. 1.65 Lacs*
- *Potential first-year earnings: Rs. 2.10 Lacs*
- *Breakeven time from initial invesṭmest : sixmonths to several years*
- *No staffing required*

As the quality of education in the Unitd States continues to lag, parents are seeking ways to augment and expand the educational opportunities available to their children. For some parents, that means locating a summer science camp or finding an art appreciation class for kids at the local Y.

Others are focused on goals such as extra coaching in one subject or improving test scores on aptitude tests. Whatever the specific concern, parents looking for extracurricular learning opportunities for their children are creating a new market for teachers and education professionals involved in the educational development of children.

Joan Lamport, founder and co-owner of The Teacher's Room stores, is one teacher-turned-entrepreneur who has brought her considerable skills to that market. In 1979, Lamport and a colleague—both of whom hold master's degrees in the teaching of reading—had grown weary of the layers of bureaucracy in the school system. Since Lamport's work in the schools always had involved making recommendations to teachers about materials to use with students, she was well aware of the suppliers for children's books, music, games, and educational toys. Lamport had also written a textbook called *Teaching Reading* for Macmillan Publishing Company and had designed and sold games and even songs for children prior to deciding to start her own business.

What Lamport had in mind was opening a store where teachers could purchase the books, games, educational toys, and other items that would help them to work more creatively and effectively with their students. After about a year of what she calls "very informal research,' she and her first partner put up about $7,500 each, rented approximately 700 square feet of space in a commercially zoned house and opened The Teacher's Room. They were able to furnish the store with adapted home furniture: A butcher-block kitchen table served as a display area and Lamport's children's old desks took their place in the store too. The bulk of the initial $15,000 investment that she and her partner had put up went into buying stock for the store. in two tile boxes—entering each item as it arrived and then subtracting each item sold every night after the close of business. "Pretty soon," says Lamport, "I was spending two hours every night on inventory!" Word of mouth from their former colleagues and occasional ads in local papers kept business coming their way.

Moving Up

Lamport and her partner were forced to move when their landlord decided to sell the property that housed The Teacher's Room. The two found a storefront space just five blocks away. "My son rented a van and we just packed up and moved," recalls Lamport, who was not thrilled with being forced to move so quickly that they had no time to fix up the new space.

The new move augured well for the success of The Teacher's Room; not only did they retain their former clientele, but their new storefront location drew in street traffic—a new market of parents and children. Lamport, who set up shop without even knowing "what business plans and marketing plans were," welcomed the widening of her market and began to add more games and other items to the stock that she had originally tailored almost exclusively for teachers.

"It was about that time that we decided to turn our informal partnership into a subchapter S corporation."

Growing The Business

The volume of stock in inventory grew steadily in the five years that they, stayed in their first storefront location. Though the business broke even almost from the start, Lamport reports that she was doing about $400,000 a year when they left that location to move to an even larger space. The cash box and bulging file card inventory were beginning to take up more and more of her time—begging a better solution. "One day, a young man I'd taught in school came around selling cash registers. Initially," says Lamport, laughing, "I bought it because I liked him." The purchase did make doing business easier, however, and then one day her son pointed to her inventory system and said, "Hey, Ma, there's something called a computer for things like that." Lamport's son offered to enter all the data on easy-to-use off-the-shelf software, and The Teacher's Room went hightech.

When Lamport's partner decided to return to teaching, Lamport ran her store in White Plains, New York, with part-time help for a year and a half before she found another teacher interested in buying into the business. Since then, Lamport and her partner, Linda Stern Levine, have opened a

second location in Stamford, Connecticut, and installed an entire computer network as they've grown. Today, the White Plains store serves as the central order and receiving station and the two shuttle inventory to Stamford by themselves. Billing, bookkeeping, and inventory run from their computerized point-of-sale terminals. "Now I go home at night and my computers talk to each other !" says Lamport with obvious delight. Both she and her partner make heavy use of fax machines to handle inventory and orders. The store publishes its own catalog of materials for school programs for gifted children—a longtime interest of Lamport's. Levine is about to launch a newsletter of her own, as well.

Well beyond the simple cash box, The Teacher's Room accepts major credit cards and does a substantial catalog business. Just four months after the opening of their second location, Lamport and Levine realized their first million-dollar-sales year.

Today, Lamport sees quite a few stores like hers supported by college and university towns in other parts of the United States. "The two go hand in hand." Teachers and education students as well as the local population support the store, says Lamport. Soon Lamport intends to branch into computer software for children. "If I'd had a business plan," says Joan Lamport as she considers the success of her two stores, "I couldn't have made it turn out better than it has."

Taking The Classroom On The Road

Richard Zoffness and Janet Rogow's Prep Course, Inc., offers an interesting look at how teachers can have their cake and eat it too. Zoffness, a math teacher, and Rogow, an English teacher, both continue to teach full time and love it. They've channeled their considerable entrepreneurial energy into a business that specializes in preparing students to take their SAT exams.

Serious about their business from the start, the two hired a lawyer and formed a subchapter S corporation at the beginning. Later, they hired an accountant to do their books. Zoffness found the inspiration to open the business while teaching an SAT preparation course at a local college. The "inspiration" came when Zoffness took a hard look at how much of the fee for his course went to the college rather than to compensate him. "I thought, 'Anyone can rent classroom space,'" says Zoffness, and after talking over his plan with colleague Janet Rogow and enlisting her as a full partner, the two set out in search of space. Fees for classroom rentals can range anywhere from $600 to $1,400 per semester, depending on the location. They started out renting space in a local high school at night, where they taught two-hour SAT prep classes. Two problems arose in the early days of the business that Zoffness and Rogow have since solved: The rent they paid to the high school was still too high, and the fact that they held only late-afternoon classes kept the two from drawing students who played team sports in the late afternoon and early evening.

Rogow and Zoffness are both adamant that they are in business because they are teachers first, and both were also concerned by the fact that late-afternoon classes were not well timed for students tired from a long day in school. Since their business was new, Zoffness wisely decided to stay in the same market when they moved. "Our reputations as teachers are good in our school community and we didn't want to venture too far outside so early in the game." Eventually they moved their classes to a local community center that offered cheaper rental space and more time. Now The Prep Course, Inc., offers Saturday classes for students involved in sports during the week as well as early-evening courses. The classes, which are limited to 20 students in order to ensure quality education, meet for two and a half hours each, and students improve their SAT scores by an average of 140 points. The fee for each course is $550 for 12 weeks. Despite postal costs for the direct mail campaign Zoffness and Rogow send out twice a year, they've been operating at a nice profit almost from the start, doubling their business in just two years' time.

16

Book Packager

Job Description: *A book packager collects all the necessary elements for a book (idea, writer, designers, and so on) and presents them to a publisher for possible publication.*

- *Start-up cost as low as Rs. 1 Lac*
- *Potential first-year earnings: Rs. 3 Lacs*
- *Breakeven time from initial investment: six months to several years*
- *Excellent opportunity for people with physical disabilities*
- *No staffing required*

Quick, what do the following books have in common? *The Joy of Sex, The Way Things Work,* and *Items from Our Catalog.* Number one, each was a bestseller. Number two, each and every one was created by a book packager.

Book packagers perform many functions, depending on the project, so the definition is still somewhat hazy. But the several hundred independent producers of books (compared with may be 50 a decade ago) do for books what movie producers do for films: Just as independent Hollywood producers hire script writers, actors, and put up part of the capital to entice a major studio to take a film under its wing, book packagers hire writers, contract with designers and editors, and sometimes line up printers to deliver bound books to publishers. In other words, they take an idea for a book and nurture it into something a publisher wants to buy. Packagers deliver to publishers anything from edited manuscripts to camera-ready copy and artwork to finished books. The big difference between packaging and publishing is that packaging leaves distribution to the publishers' massive networks.

From Obscurity To Respectability

Years ago publishers often distrusted packagers as purveyors of slapdash balderdash; today they increasingly welcome book packagers aboard, almost as respected co-publishers. The reason for the 180-degree turn? Unencumbered with bureaucracy, packagers often turn out books faster and cheaper than traditional publishers. The average packager has 5 to 15 books in the works at any one time, while a single editor at a publishing house is responsible for more titles than that. As a packager, you can devote more attention to a project, generally producing books more efficiently and for less than a publisher could.

Packagers are becoming even more important to the book industry as mergers continue to change the face of publishing. Every merger means less staff to handle an increasing load of existing titles, and consequently, fewer people to do the all-important work of securing new titles. Thus publishers are counting on book packagers more than ever today to supply them with fresh ideas, new writers, and potential bestsellers.

Your edge comes by being better equipped to tackle particular projects than anyone else. A number of book packagers specialize in particular areas—and their books on do-it-yourself woodworking or financial management show their expertise. Or you can specialize in books that require sophisticated design and production techniques. If publishers produced such four-color, illustrated books, they likely would need to price the book out of the market just to cover their costs.

Think you might like to enter the world of book packaging? A publishing background makes life a lot easier since, according to *a Publishers Weekly* article, packagers wield "knowledge of almost all facets of publishing: contracts, selling, rights, editing, production, design, finance, etc. The packager completes about 80 per cent of the publishing functions, whereas the in-house editor handles 15 to 20 per cent."

Sue Katz, who launched Sue Katz & Associates Inc. from her New York City home, had worked on both the sales and editorial end with such publishers as Holt, Rinehart & Winston, Bantam, and Scholastic. She also had a master's from Columbia University in business, which proved invaluable in putting together such titles as *Forecasting Revenues and Planning Profits*. "*My* original idea was to do marketing consulting for publishers, but I had a portfolio of ideas for books that I kept coming back to," Katz recalls. In the past, if her employer vetoed an idea, her only route was to drop it. "Now I had a chance to influence those ideas—but I had to get them sold."

Book Packaging For Non-publishers

Even if you haven't spent years in publishing, you might consider entering the field if you have an organized mind, can write a quality book proposal, and have expertise in an area where publishers are clamoring for books. While you provide the specific industry expertise, you'll probably want to enlist a partner who can play all the right notes in the publishing world. And don't restrict your expertise to a single book. "Look at the broad market," advises Sue Katz. "Not just books, but newsletters and audio/visual. For example, a retailer might say, 'Retailing is a very "today" business. May be I could generate a newsletter on hot store designs.' Or, 'I know retailing is taught in schools. What books do they need?'"

Also, take a few courses on publishing procedures and read such industry publications as *Publishers Weekly.* Every publisher treats packagers differently, but boning up on the publishing world at least helps you learn the lingo. Once you can convince publishers you have the know-how, you'll have an easier time selling your wares.

Make An Offer

The first step in selling a book is putting together a proposal. Proposals run 25 to 100 pages or more and include a chapter-by-chapter outline, a sample chapter or two, and a biography of the author. Include any data that will sell the book, initially to the publisher and ultimately at the bookstore. Figures on the success of similar books or on the public's growing interest in a subject help convince a publisher that your project will sell. While too many books on a similar subject suggests a glutted market, beware of the project that has no competition: Perhaps publishers just don't think a book on the subject will sell.

Above all, make your proposal look professional. "Book packagers might spend more money on slicking up the proposal than a writer would," says Sue Katz. "You should have more marketing information. We fuss a fair amount with the presentation."

Katz warns that for every proposal you sell, several others never see a publisher's imprint. Especially in the beginning as you develop a reputation, "you have to be very agile and know the moment to let go." On the other hand, you also have to know when to push an idea. Katz recalls the origins of the *Rock Video Book,* which she ultimately presented in camera-ready form. "The idea was born when I was watching MTV. Soon after, I met a writer who would be perfect: She was rock music critic of *Stereo Music Magazine."* Katz bounced the idea of a book on the new music video phenomenon off an editor she knew at Bantam. Although he expressed interest, he had moved to Simon & Schuster by the time the proposal was ready. Katz had faith, however, that he'd still be interested, and sent him a mock-up of the book (meaning a cover and page layout design) along with the proposal. Simon & Schuster bit-and eventually published the book.

"If you include art, a mock-up could cost $250 to $750," says Katz. If the proposal is never sold, the designer accepts that as a kill fee. However, the designer usually bets that a publisher will buy the book. Then the mock-up fee acts as a down payment on the larger project.

Writers are a different story. In some cases, packagers write the sample chapters themselves. Or you can contract with a freelance author to supply the sample chapters in return for expenses, usually phone bills and possibly travel fees. Like the designers, the writers hope to land a larger contract when a publisher buys the book. Knowing that many proposals never result in contracts, Suee katz usually pays a writer a flat fee to produce sample chapters. "Sometimes it's embrassing how small," she admits.

Once you sell the proposal, writers either sign on for a flat fee or receive a percentage of the advance and royalties. (A 50-50 split between packager and author is common.) You either subcontract other functions, such as editing and proofreading, or perform them in-house.

Royalties

Publishers pay packagers in three stages. First comes the advance—or rather half the advance, since the second instalment comes only after you deliver the completed project. The third stage occurs after the book is in the bookstores, when the royalties start rolling in.

Here's how it works: Let's assume you receive a $20,000 advance against royalties, which means you won't receive any further royalties until your advance is earned out. If the book sells for $20 in the bookstore and you've negotiated a 10 per cent royalty fee, then 10,000 copies must be sold before your royalty payments kick in. In addition to the advance and royalties, many packagers also negotiate a flat production fee, pays for producing mechanicals.

In a variation on the theme, packagers who specialize in books that require production expertise often charge publishers a per unit production cost, much as a printer charges a publisher for books. Say a packager can deliver a full-color book for $3 per unit, using an overseas printer. The packager charges a flat rate of $3.50 per book. To offset these relatively slim profit margins, some packagers retain the right to sell the book in foreign markets. Since they've already paid the expense for color separations, producing the foreign edition costs far less than what a U.S. version costs, assuring higher oversea profits.

How Long Is A Piece Of String?

Packagers try to cover their expense with the advance and production fee and make their profits on royalties. How much can a packager make? "Remember everything you've heard about what writers get paid?" says Sue katz. "Some books get minuscule advances, others get millions. There's just no rule of thumb."

Some packagers expand their base of acting as the middleman between writers and publishers. To increase profits and keep the creative juices flowing, Katz coauthored (as well as packaged) *Having a Love Affair with Your Own Husband (Before Someone Else Does).* Others coventure projects with other book packagers. The approach gains them expertise and valuable publishing contacts while multiplying their projects and visibility. "I did a conventure on *Sports Widow's Revenge*, an event book for wives of sports fanatics," says Sue. "My co-producer was familiar with sports, so I didn't have to research that aspect of the book."

While publishers, with their vast distribution networks, remain the most common source of packager's income, lucrative contracts are to be found elsewhere. You can produce premium editions—a giveaway pamphlet, for example—for a corporation or association related to a particular book. Or you can package books for non-publishing companies such as industry trade associations. Philip Lief, packager of 101 Best Business to Start, finds that packaging books for an association requires just as much work as packaging for a publisher. But, he says, "You're guaranteed the sale of a certain quantity, which takes some of the risk out of the business."

Whether you package books for publishers or private organizations, industry analysts predict that packagers will play an increasingly important role as publishers merge into huge con-glomerates. Publishers suffer from pared-down staffs while their marketing departments demand more "big" books. "Packagers have the opportunity to produce books that are financially successful because we don't have to worry about the financial and editorial constraints that are normally found in a publishing house," explains Philip Lief. Given book packaging's 150 per cent growth rate in the past ten years, chances are there's room for creative entrepreneurs to carve out a niche.

17

Desktop Publisher

Job Description: *A desktop publisher produces a variety of printed material for clients, including newsletters, reports, flyers, and even books, using a personal computer, color printer, and special software.*

- *Start-up cost as low as* Rs. 2 Lacs
- *Potential first-year earnings: Rs. 3 Lacs*
- *Breakeven time from initial investment: rapid (one year or less)*
- *Excellent home-based business*
- *Excellent opportunity for people with physical disabilities*
- *No staffing required*

Malcolm Ross dumped a 20-year career in chemical research to become a desktop publisher. He traded in a monthly paycheck for freelance jobs wherever he could find them. Instead of having the swanky offices and staff backups of a large corporation, he works from his Gaithersburg, Maryland, home and doubles as his own receptionist and typist. He gave up security to enter a field so green most potential clients don't even know they need him.

Although the desktop publishing industry is now booming when Malcolm Ross began he was a pioneer in the industry by producing brochures, advertising, and other company correspondence for corporate clients. Additionally, he also started his own newsletter devoted to desktop publishing, *The Electric Page.* Did he make the right choice? "Oh Lord, yes. I don't want to be a manager again, but I'm growing so fast I'm now looking at premises outside my home." Acknowledging the inevitability of his success, he sighs. "Sooner or later, I guess I'll have to hire some help."

Definition, Please

Desktop publishers are no more than personal computer users who employ very "friendly" technology to compose designs on-screen rather than through paste-up, typesetting, art creation, or the like. Then desktop publishers go one step further by reproducing typeset-quality printouts of what they've envisioned on the screen. While some entrepreneurs use laser printers hooked up to their computers to produce a final copy, others hire a printer to deliver the final step of printing.

Just as you don't have to understand the mechanics of a car to drive one, you don't have to know the first thing about Silicon Valley to stage a desktop operation. But Malcolm Ross explains the process clearly in a monthly newsletter he sends to 1,400 clients or potential clients: "The laser in the printer is made to 'paint' a picture of your computer file on the drum of what is really a photocopying machine, by scanning back and forth at high speed while the drum rotates. Toner, similar to that used in photocopiers, is attracted to or repelled from the image ('painted') or un-imaged areas of the drum. From there the toner is transferred to a piece of paper as it is fed past the rotating drum." To make copies, you take the "camera-ready" image to a printer who runs off duplicates.

Suffice it to say the pseudotypography you produce on $10,000 worth of equipment contained on the top of your desk is professional enough to satisfy most major magazine and book publishers. Unless you scrutinize the type with a jeweler's eye, you probably wouldn't guess that it wasn't typeset.

A Tool Or An End In Itself ?

Desktop publishing is fast finding favor with advertising firms and large corporations to produce everything from company newsletters to menus to advertising flyers. Malcolm Ross pockets two sets of clients: corporations such as Holiday Inn and the World Bank, which hire him as a consultant to guide them through the rudiments of a desktop operation so they can publish in-house; and small businesses, which ask him to design and print brochures, flyers, letterhead, and other material, and for whom he acts as the publisher. "Basically, we're talking about designing direct mail," he explains. "Clients? Drycleaners, church associations, or anyone who needs to get the word out on meetings and services."

Sharon Bobbitt, whose Publications Plus performs similar services from her Evanston, Illinois, home, knows of a dozen the drum of desktop publishers in the Chicago area. Six months into her venture, she had matched the salary she made as AT&T's Chicago manager of public relations. Bobbitt's plans include branching into magazine publishing on her Apple Macintosh. "The machine makes up for my lack of eye-hand coordination," she explains. "Previously, I didn't have the freehand ability to create my own layouts and designs."

Whether you see desktop publishing as a means to another end, such as newsletter publishing, or as the basis of a business, such as designing brochures for local businesses, you probably can get started for less than we indicate here, simply because hardware and software prices continually fall. In addition, the computers simultaneously get easier to use and offer more sophisticated options. You may want to rent an IBM-compatible or Apple PC from a computer-leasing store to see which you like best. Also, you may want to update your equipment in a year or two as manufacturers spring glitzy surprises on the market.

You'll gain expertise daily, so don't let a little thing like computer illiteracy slow you down. A short course on the subject given at a community college might help, but the best thing to do is get in there and practice. Fluency comes within a month or two. "The Macintosh seemed to take my gloves off," says Malcolm Ross. In addition to using it to design flyers for the Main Street florist, he uses his Mac for writing his newsletter, for facsimile transmission, forecasting and spreadsheet analysis, data management, and other aspects of running his own business.

Knock - Knock

If you work from the spare bedroom in your house, how do you let customers know they need you? Ross joined two Maryland chambers of commerce where he "hit people over the head with a two-by-four-anything to let them know I was here." He sends his monthly newsletter to those small and large company contacts he made. *The Electric Page* contains a hodgepodge of desktop publishing news and information on Electro Graphic Services. Ross says on any given issue, anywhere from 0.5 to 5 per cent of newsletter recipients call to ask about his services. Of course, the Internet affords another excellent opportunity for promotion and marketing for your business. Putting up your own web page enables clients to discover you and also to evaluate your work, services, and prices.

Sharon Bobbitt relies on contacts and references. In one coup, she took AT&T work with her when she left her job. "Large companies are downsizing their public relations departments and don't have the staff to take on new chores," she explains. Another early client was the Women's Business Development Center, a non-profit group that advises small business. "It was invaluable to have a real client while I was learning," says Bobbitt. "I didn't charge them much, but I got a lot of referrals through them."

You also might ask printers and office supply stores to refer you to their patrons. Some might prove hostile, particularly small printers that offer similar services. But many may recommend you to clients as a less expensive alternative to typesetting shops.

If you decide to specialize, you may want to advertise directly to businesses in a particular industry. Direct mail or trade publications can alert all the lawyers in North America that you can design their legal forms, for example.

Most desktop publishers begin with a variety of income sources. But Malcolm Ross, who consults as well as publishes, suspects aggressive promoters can take the desktop publishing business in any direction they want. As we said before, the field is growing and changing and it's up to the participants to create the rules—and the opportunities.

18

Computer Consultant

Job Description: *A computer consultant advises clients on computer topics, including what type of system to buy, how to integrate it into the business, and what type of hardware and software to buy.*

- *Start-up cost as low as Rs. 50,000*
- *Potential first-year earnings:* Rs. 3 Lacs
- *Breakeven time from initial investment: very rapid (immediate to one year)*
- *Ideal home-based business*
- *Excellent opportunity for people with physical disabilities*
- *No staffing required*

Peggy Morgan is an entrepreneur with a unique product: gray matter, the unique knowledge she'd accumulated about computers. She'd learned "information systems"— a/k/a computers— on the corporate fast track at Sun Oil and in academia, teaching at Temple University. "I could not have considered starting this business five years earlier because computers were just becoming accessible to smaller businesses. The vast majority of my clients are under $20 million [in sales] and the vaster majority are under $10 million. They just could not have afforded computerization before."

Computers For Everyone

Well, now everyone sees benefits in owning a computer. As the cost of processing vast amounts of data falls and the use of computers as a standard tool of competition rises, far smaller companies than Peggy Morgan's clients latch onto PCs. The most prevalent problem: They often don't know which system best serves their needs or what to do with it once they bring it aboard. Enter the likes of Peggy Morgan and a growing cast of computer specialists. "If a company spends $35,000 or $50,000 for a computer, they might need to spend that much for a professional to develop strategies to use it," Morgan explains. "Many companies can afford that as a one-time fee but can't afford that salary every year."

Computer consultants serve two basic functions:

- They select the appropriate computer system, including which peripherals, networks, and software to buy (a one-time project for a consultant).
- They integrate the computer into day-to-day management (a situation the client may call you back for).

"Essentially", says Morgan, "a computer should make a business so much more productive that it pays for itself. We help people realize the profit potential in computers."

Low Overhead

As a consultant, you don't build any inventory, so you can start inexpensively. Unlike your clients who need more sophisticated hardware,you can start with a personal computer, which you probably already have since you must be a computer expert to consider this sort of business. Since clients expect you to visit their job sites, a spare bedroom or den can provide your office. Your biggest costs will involve marketing. However, the Internet provides a low-cost marketing opportunity.

You have to target appropriate corporate customers and let them know you exist. Like Peggy Morgan, who started Morgan Systems Inc., from her Cherry Hill, New Jersey, home, you'll identify your best prospects as midsize companies. Fortune 500 companies probably will hire an on-staff expert, and start-ups and mom-and-pop businesses can't afford you.

Decide if your expertise cuts across industries: Can you recommend a system as easily for a school as a chemical distributor, or are you more comfortable dealing with a specialty, such as accounting packages for financial departments? Geography must play a role in identifying clients. For example, if your specialty involves robotics, your factory customers may be scattered across the country. However, generalists may have all the business they can handle within commuting distance. Keep in mind that you don't want to eat up your start-up capital with travel expenses.

While your job as a consultant is to complete a specific project, many computer experts forge ongoing relationships with corporations. Many clients find it far cheaper to pay a consulting retainer, good for the few hours a month worth of questions or programing, than to hire a staff person. Set up flexible fee schedules and let clients know how you can help them in day-to-day management.

Network

What computer expertise you don't possess, you can usually buy. Get to know other computer experts around the country and in your area. Many college professors, for example, freelance as consultants. Depending on how much input you provide, either subcontract, by putting the freelancer on your pay-roll, or simply locate the right specialist for your client and fade into the background. Even though you may not receive any remuneration for recommending a specialist, keep in touch with the client. This approach builds goodwill both with clients and with other consultants who may bring you in on cases where *your* experience can shed light.

Those first contracts will be the hardest, because clients want references. However, even after you're consulting to capacity, never forget that new business represents next month's paycheck. "When you start, you market like crazy," recalls Peggy Morgan. "Then you get so busy with one or two clients that you forget that consulting is cyclical. When those jobs come to an end, you're in the hole with nothing. Gradually you learn to say, 'Dumbo, all this comes to an end without bringing in new jobs.'"

Morgan figures she fills only half her week with "billable hours," consulting for clients. She spends up to 15 per cent of her time in administrative functions, such as billing. About the same number of hours is devoted to "practice development"— for example, keeping up with products and researching and lining up seminars that she gives for university classes or for chambers of commerce. Practice development also can provide revenues.

You can make your reputation by writing articles for computer magazines or publications geared to your field of expertise. And if you have a better way to explain, say, a particular software package, consider writing a book. In addition to the royalties or fees, these projects provide dividends when a reader or audience member calls.

Peggy Morgan devotes the other 20 per cent of her time to marketing. "At my strung-out busiest, I still need to court clients," she explains. "If my billable hours fall off, I devote more time to marketing." Morgan stocks a file drawer with folders on prospects she gets from talking to clients or even from the telephone book. She sends brochures and personal notes to the decision maker in charge of computers at each corporation, and follows up with phone calls.

To Grow Or Not To Grow

Many computer consultants choose to stay one-person operations. The whole attraction of consulting, they say, is going solo, leaving the hassles of corporate life. However, an individual consultant is limited to the number of billable hours in a day. The owner of a large computer-consulting firm gets a hefty percentage of the fee generated by each associate. Despite the "user-friendly" movement and the help large computer manufacturers provide, business's growing dependence on number-crunching and computer productivity translates into an increasing demand for computer consultants.

19

Computer Repair

Job Description: *A computer repair technician* fixes *all makes* and models *of personal computers.*

- *Start-up* cost as *low as* Rs. 1 Lac
- *Breakeven time from* initial *investment: rapid* (six *months to one year)*
- Ideal home-based business
- *No staffing required*

Two kinds of people get into the computer repair field: manufacturers and so-called third-party service companies. The biggies like IBM still control the lion's share of the business, but independents are marching away with a larger piece of the growing computer pie every year. The reason is simple enough: The corporations that sign the multimillion-dollar maintenance contracts would rather pay less money for better service—a package entrepreneurs can offer.

You Don't have to Know Computers

Two other kinds of people get into the third-party computer repair field: technicians and everybody else.

"Say you're an IBM service representative," says Joseph O'Donnell, who once was one, before he began running the Mt. Laurel, New Jersey, Office of Service Inc. "If you can offer your clients a better deal [either a less expensive contract or better, quicker service—or both], they may guarantee you won't go out of business." For example, clients who know your work may pay their first six-month contract in advance. Or they may stockpile their own parts so you don't have to buy inventory. Meanwhile, concentrate on signing on more clients until you generate enough contract revenues to support yourself. In any event, you can probably hold start-up below $12,000 by stocking the most necessary parts and operating out of your home.

In addition to the technicians, there is everybody else. "More important than technical knowledge is personality and an orientation to a high level of service," says Joe O'Donnell. Sales types who line up the accounts contribute as much to a computer maintenance business as the repair whizzes, and many entrepreneurs have built fortunes by managing the operating while hiring their technicians.

Besides, computers are increasingly easy to repair, thanks to manufacturer safeguards and software that tells you exactly what's wrong when you insert it in a particular machine. "Instead of diagnostic knowledge, you need logic—if I pop out this board, this will happen," says O'Donnell. "Then you send the old board back to the manufacturer. With a little education, a good business person could be a fairly good technician."

Build And Sell

Most newcomers specialize in a particular type of machine and its peripherals and try to saturate a geographic area. Service Inc., which focuses on IBM machines within a 50-mile radius, develops new accounts through referrals from computer consultants, telemarketing and direct mail (to executives of companies that use computers), and personal contacts gleaned from joining chambers of commerce and computer-user groups.

While several national repair companies exist (including some big enough to go public), as well as companies that tackle most any brand computer on the market, the more common scenario depicts a company growing to local capacity on one manufacturer's computer, then selling. "When you have to subcontract with independents in other areas, you've probably reached $15 million to $20 million in sales," calculates Alan Andrus, a computer consultant. At that point, a company has employees and office expenses that allow pretax profits of 20 per cent of revenues—up to $4 million on $20 million gross. "Those companies at the upper end usually sell for one times annual revenues," Andrus suggests. In other words, if your company grows to $20 million in sales without partners or substantial debt, you might walk away in ten years with $20 million.

The Retainer

Many computer-repair firms service home computers—usually if the customer brings the PC to the shop and leaves it for technicians to work on. Many also charge by the hour for customers who don't want a contract. But the lifeblood of a third-party repair company is the steady cash flow that business contracts bring.

While competition from other independents isn't yet a concern for most entrepreneurs, you still have to give clients reasons to spend $200 to $2,000 every month with "Moe's Computer Repair" instead of with Hewlett-Packard. "You have to know which hot buttons to push," says Joe O'Donnell. Price is one button, as is the immediate and quick service many startups promise. Service Inc. trains its telephone operators as troubleshooters. "Thirty per cent of problems can be fixed over the phone by knowing how to operate the machines," says O'Donnell. "The client has the machine operating immediately."

Pressure From Above ?

As computer sales leveled off, many manufacturers began stepping up their maintenance efforts to bring in revenues. Some third-party firms filed suits against the manufacturers, alleging that the big guys refused to sell them parts and told falsehoods intended to drive them out of business. However, most observers see this adversarial posture as temporary. "If the computer market grows again, the manufacturers will concentrate on pumping out products," says Alan Andrus. In down cycles, customers look for the most inexpensive contract they can find to maintain their products. "The third-party side of the business is almost a recession-proof business," says Andrus.

20

Computer Trainer

Job Description: *A computer trainer teaches clients how to use both computer hardware and software.*

- *Start-up cost as low as* Rs. 1.25 Lacs
- *Potential first-year earnings: Rs. 2 Lacs*
- *Breakeven time from initial investment: extremely rapid (one month to one year)*
- *Ideal home-based business*
- *No staffing required*

In the dinosaur age of computers (circa 1960), virtually every penny that corporate America spent on computers bought hardware and some rudimentary software. Today industry experts estimate that 95 per cent of the money U.S. companies budget for computers goes for salaries. What

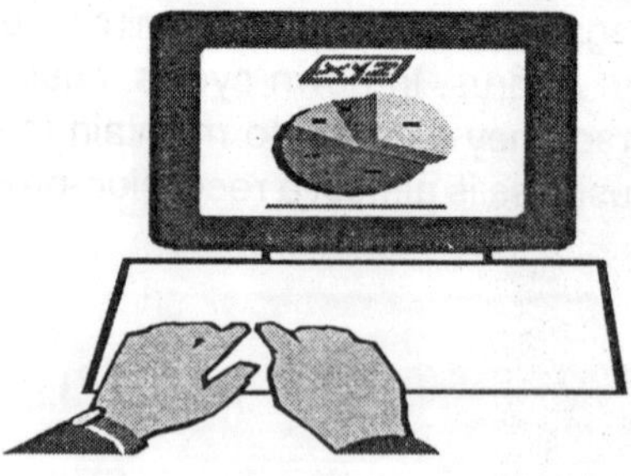

happened? Over the period of swift evolution, the price of hardware fell drastically, placing computers in almost every company. Compared with yesterday's elite circle of computer eggheads who understood the working of every last silicon chip, today's computer users range from secretaries to lawyers.

Despite the proliferation, many nascent computer users would as soon sleep on a bed of nails as sit down at a PC terminal. Enter computer trainers: a growing number of educators who teach everything from basic word processing to intricate manoeuvres around databases. And technology still changes so rapidly that even skilled technicians need constant brush-up courses. "We protect that investment in salaries," explains Lawrence K. Grodman, president of QED Information Sciences Inc., a Wellesley, Massachusetts, firm that trains intermediate and advanced computer users.

The Ways to Go

QED uses the seminar or workshop format, in which an instructor explains computer dos-and-don'ts firsthand to a department of employees. Other trainers range from solo practitioners who teach executives one on one, to video producers with tapes explaining spreadsheet analysis, to software houses distributing disks for operators who use the computer to learn about computing. "We estimate roughly 5 per cent of the amount a company spends on computing should go for training," says Larry Grodman. "For professionals, that works out to about ten days a year."

Don't Byte Off More Than You can Chew

Manufacturers offer some training, and some larger trade schools have entered the business. But there's still plenty of room for the newcomer, especially if you carve out a specialty, such as how to write software or how best to get computers to communicate with each other. "If you try to teach too many things, the cost of marketing and sales can drive you out of business before you ever get started," warns Larry Grodman.

His point is well taken: You must isolate your market and let potential customers know you're in business. You may be lucky enough to line up clients through industry contacts and thereby restrict advertising to word of mouth. If that's the case, you probably can get into business for the pocket money required to set up a home-based office.

However, drumming up clients (a/k/a marketing) costs money. In addition to sending a sales staff on cold calls to corporations, QED mails brochures that resemble university catalogs—and cost as much to produce. (Smaller educators can print an inexpensive flyer that fits in a business-size envelope.) Because QED addresses employees who are already well versed in computing, it advertises in computer trade magazines. However, if you target a more general audience, opt for more general business magazine.

If your scope is more regional, check out the host of local business publications that now blanket large cities. You also can hook up with a community college or seminar producer. In addition to income from tuitions, you make invaluable contacts by teaching classes. If one of your students also works for a corporation, you may find yourself invited to teach the rest of the staff in-house.

How Much Does It Cost ?

Start-up costs also depend on the type of teaching you envision. Shooting and duplicating a video training guide will run at least $10,000, not counting the cost of placing it with users. QED conducts about half its training at "learning centers," or permanent classrooms it operates in a half-dozen cities across the country. "Our people conduct courses for corporate clients on a subscription basis," explains Larry Grodman. "The 165-member companies pay an annual fee that entitles them to blocks of student-days." Tuition varies with how many hours a corporation signs up for, but open enrolment runs about $300 a day. QED charges $2,000 a day to send an instructor to teach in-house, regardless of the number of employees who sign on.

If you instruct at the client's address, overhead is truly minimal. Most of QED's training takes place in the eastern United States because that's where the company concentrates its marketing. But Grodman doesn't think twice if he gets a request to train in Trinidad or Ireland. "We don't open an office, we send a person for a week or two, so it's very inexpensive. We've trained all over the world. How else is a staff in Lagos, Nigeria, going to get training except to contract with a company like ours?"

Accordion - Style Curricula

Once you create a rapport with a client, why not expand your curriculum? If you're competent in data processing, point out that employees could use instruction. If you're weak in an area where a client needs help, offer the course anyway; call in a "guest" lecturer and split the fee. "About two-thirds of our staff are independent contractors," explains Larry Grodman. "Most are private computer consultants who see their relationship with QED as a steady source of income." The flip side of this lesson: Let other training firms know you're available for courses in your specialty.

QED also offers management courses to heads of computer departments. These non-technical seminars have little to do with IBMs. But remember the lesson of the railroad firms that tailed to realize they were transportation companies and missed the opportunities in air travel? In other words, once you are big enough to diversify, recognize you are an educator, not just a computer trainer.

But chances are you will have your hands full teaching just computer courses. As computers continue to filter to increasing numbers of staffers who never touched a keyboard, and as manufacturers dream up one innovation after another for even experienced users, the computer education field presents lifelong opportunity. "It's a dynamic, technical environment that offers no end to growth," says Grodman. "This company I founded can go on long after I'm dead."

21

Database Consultant

Job Description: *A database consultant advises clients on how to manage, update, and maintain their databases.*

- *Start-up cost as low as 1.50 Lacs*
- *Potential first-year earnings: 3 Lacs*
- *Breakeven time from initial investment: extremely rapid (one to six months)*
- *Excellent home-based business*
- *Excellent opportunity for people with physical disabilities*
- *No staffing required*

With corporate offices and small businesses relying on computers for their businesses needs, the market for people with the ability to write custom databases that speed the flow of information continues to expand. While

many people are mystified by the thought of learning to write in the various computer languages used to create databases, entrepreneurs with a knack for computers are stepping in to fill the gap.

When Jane Kelly, a 50 year-old former schoolteacher, brought a $500 Radio Shack computer, she had no prior experience in computing. When she began to experiment with it, she discovered she had an aptitude for computers and began to teach herself how to program in BASIC —just one of the many computer languages available. Shortly thereafter, she struck a deal with an employer to hire her and train her on the job. She attended computer courses and continued to learn on the job until she started to investigate becoming an independent contractor. Kelly sent her resume around while setting up her business as a corporation: JSK Programming Service, Inc. In the interim she worked for Banker's Trust and another client in New York City although her goal was to work from home. Two years later she landed a client big enough to make the move to a home-based business. Kelly continued to learn new computer languages—running through 'X-base" family languages and then D-BASE III and IV before settling on a language called CLIPPER, which she has come to use almost exclusively in her work for clients.

Janice Pauly, founder of JTP Software Service in Ridgefield, Connecticut, was able to pick up computer training through her job at Xerox Corporation. A trainer in the Xerox Fitness Center, Pauly worked with the computer consultants assigned to help her create a database that would track workout periods and employee participation in the fitness center. One day she bought herself a book on programming, and six months later she bought her first Xerox PC for the work she was bringing home at night. Mastering BASIC and then the D-BASE languages, Pauly also settled in with CLIPPER when it came on the market. In 1986, she went out on her own as a sole proprietor in a home-based business.

Finding Clients

Jim Ragsdale, founder of Noteworthy Software, Inc., another successful database entrepreneur, suggests that one way to keep up a steady flow of clients in this business is to work through an agent. He estimates that in his nine years as an independent database consultant, he has discovered between *175* and 180 agencies that place database consultants on temporary assignments in major corporations. In fact, he worked on assignments for Pepsico, American Can, and IBM, among others, before moving his *office* to his home when he found a client big enough to support his start-up. According to Ragsdale, the one drawback of agencies is that they typically take a third of a database consultant's hourly rates-which usually are around *$100* per hour. Today, in addition to working for major corporations, Ragsdale has found a nice niche among smaller businesses in his hometown-among them plumbers and electricians who use his services to create databases for inventory, clients, and billing.

Jane Kelly's clients come to her largely through referrals from her present clients. Currently she's trying to confine her networking to lunches and dinners, leaving her days free for work, thereby raising the number of her billable hours.

Equipping Your Business

All three entrepreneurs agree that the beginning entrepreneur needs a powerful computer, a laser printer, and, if possible, a backup printer as well. A modem is essential for working on-line with a client's computers whenever a visit to the client's

office isn't necessary. In addition, a basic home office setup that includes a computer desk, printer stands, an answering machine, and a good chair for long hours of work are the bare essentials. Some may wish to have more than one computer to work with. Jane Kelly prizes her portable computer and a portable printer for working in client's offices, and the many available laptop computers can easily fill the bill when portability is required. Kelly also highly recommends investing in a media safe to store all the backup disks that contain valuable client data. Kelly says her media safe has saved her many a sleepless night. I know that those disks are protected from fire and humidity.

There's no need to maintain an outside office at the beginning. However, since computers, printers, and other office equipment can encroach on your living space, an outside office is worth considering. Since most database consultants must work on-site in their clients' offices, it's rarely necessary to maintain an outside office for the sake of clients.

Education For The Entrepreneur

Although many entrepreneurs are largely self-taught, Kelly, Pauly, and Ragsdale strongly recommend joining computer users' groups as you study each new language. There are users' groups all over the country for every language and software package on the market, and they offer newcomers valuable networking experience and contacts. On-line bulletin boards—where computer users can write back and forth to each other with questions and solutions—are also a major source of education and information. They are available through most on-line networks. On-line users' groups dedicated to particular languages and software programs are also available. The process of learning to program in new languages in continuous. As new and better software packages come to market, languages draw their own loyal database professionals. For the entrepreneur just starting out, the constant development of new languages and software programs is good news. The personal computer is here to stay. The constant demand for faster ways to process information assures room to grow for database consultants.

22

Internet Marketing Consultant

Job Description: *An Internet marketing consultant advises clients on how to successfully market their business and its products and services on the World Wide Web.*

- *Low Start-up cost*
- *Breakeven time from initial investment:rapid (one year)*
- *Future growth potential: high*
- *Excellent home-based business*
- *Ideal opportunity for people with physical disabilities*
- *No Staffing required*

For years, marketing consultants have used their expertise to help business improve their bottom line by navigating the often-complex waters of the consumer market-place.

Today, however, the proliferation of personal computers in homes and businesses across America gives rise to another new marketing opportunity—the Internet. As more people go online, the tremendous commercial opportunities of the Internet sound a clarion call to American business. Companies are jumping onto the so-called information superhighway as fast as possible, but often they need help understanding this new and often-confusing sales tool. That's when they call on the services of an Internet marketing consultant.

Changing Rules

If the Internet were an animal, it would be a rabbit ... on steroids. That's because it hops around so much, and in such an unpredictable manner, that even the experts don't know which way it's going next.

Although the conventional marketplace is also in a state of constant flux, it tends to change at a more measured and understandable pace. Tried and true methods of selling may have to be altered in the conventional marketplace to fit with modern times, but the point is that they can be altered and will often work.

The Internet, however, throws all rules out the window by constantly reinventing itself. What worked sales-wise on the Internet last month may not work tomorrow or, worse yet, it may be considered tired and stodgy. No one wants her Internet presence to be greeted by yawns and groans, like parents' stories about how tough they had it when they were children. Instead, a company wants its Internet site to have "buzz," to be considered cool and trendy. Unfortunately, since the Internet constantly changes, today's cool site is tomorrow's snoozer. For instance, whereas static informational pages were once acceptable for a company's website, today's sites must be interactive, attention-grabbing, and updated constantly. A company that does not stay current with these developments risks not only falling behind but getting left in the dust by its more Internet-savvy competitors.

The Internet's perpetual evolution wreaks havoc on the old ways of doing business. For business raised on the "old ways", the Internet is a baffling beast—yet one that they dare not ignore. Revenue generated by the Internet is expected to exceed $1.2 trillion by 2002; confusion or not, for most businesses, that figure means it's damn the electronic toepedoes and full speed ahead into the world of e-commerce. Thus businesses leap onto the Internet, often smacking their lips in anticipation of the big bucks, only to watch in dismay as their big new sales venture goes bust. Hits to their site can be measured in the single digits, resulting orders are even lower, and even those people who return usually do so by accident.

What's going wrong? That's for an Internet marketing consultant to discover and fix.

The Write Stuff

Early in 1989, Debra Jason opened her own copywriting business in Boulder, Colorado, specializing in direct marketing. After launching her own website in 1995, Jason added "Internet marketing consultant" to the list of services that she offers. For her, it seemed a logical move.

"I was specializing in direct marketing. The best and most effect websites are direct marketing oriented in terms of style and technique," says Jason. "So it was a natural progression for me to begin writing creative content for website."

To promote this new aspect of her business, Jason wrote articles about web marketing for trade publications. This circulated her name throughout the industry and earned her a reputation as an Internet marketing expert.

"Inevitably, almost every time an article was published, I got an inquiry through my website," she says.

Along with "electronic networking," Jason gave presentations about Internet marketing to various groups and organizations, such as the Boulder chamber of commerce. She also taught classes about marketing (on-line and off) and the Internet at several area colleges.

Her efforts paid off. Today, acting as an Internet marketing consultant constitutes approximately 30 per cent of her business, and she anticipates that it will continue to increase.

Although she is quick to note that she is not a computer expert, her success as a consultant comes from her marketing background. Thanks to her experience, Jason can study a client's website and usually find ways to improve its performance.

"The mistake a lot of people make about having a website is that they don't realize that you have to market it like you market your business," she says. "You don't just put up a website and hope that people will find you."

Jason is extremely knowledgeable about search engines (the services, such as Yahoo, that initially look for user information). Each has its own criteria for determining a site's relevancy and therefore its positioning in the search results. Jason knows how to optimize a site's contents so it is consistent with keywords and phrases in the HTML code and, therefore, shows up early whenever a search engine looks for that particular subject or topic. This is a self-taught skill, and Jason continues to educate herself about the vast and sometimes bewildering world of the Internet.

"I have the basics for what I need to know," says Jason, "and I'm always learning more [by reading books and trade publications and taking classes]."

Electronic Expert?

To be an Internet marketing consultant, you must know marketing. While this doesn't mean that you have to spout marketing theories with every breath, you must know how the complex world of American commerce operates. Why have some products and/or campaigns succeeded and others have failed? What makes a good marketing campaign? What have some companies done to sell their products? At its core, Internet marketing is still marketing.

You also need to know the Internet. While the Internet is too vast and changeable for anyone to really *know* it, you must keep up with the latest trends and developments. What companies are having great success with their websites? What sites are bombing? You also need to keep tabs on new technology and trends, so that you can steer your clients in the appropriate direction. Remember, you are being paid for your expertise.

As Jason has proven, one thing you do not need to have is technical expertise in computing. You should have some basic understanding of HTML code, search engines, and web design, but most often your job will entail simply telling computer experts employed by your clients what to fix, change, or delete. In other circumstances, you can use the services of an independent contractor/computer expert to perform technical services for you.

The main piece of equipment that you need to start an Internet consulting business is a computer with a modem. It must be powerful enough to search the Internet quickly and efficiently and able to download large files and client websites effectively. You'll also need a high-quality color printer to print out this material. To create image files from existing photos, a scanner is also required. Altogether, the total equipment cost for starting a business shouldn't exceed $5,000.

As far as advertising your new business, the best advice is probably to do what Jason did and establish a reputation within the industry. Not only will this prevent large and possibly futile expenditures on advertising, but it will also help you network and make contacts.

Fees for Internet marketing consultants range between $75 and $150 per hour. Since start-up costs are minimal, once you get your business off the ground it should be possible to recoup your starting costs within a year.

Is The Internet In Your Future?

Although there is much debate about the future of Internet sales, businesses are expected to continue trying to understand how to best use the Internet and their website for marketing purposes. That's why the future for Internet marketing consultants looks extremely bright.

'I think that we're at a point where [Internet marketing] is still growing at a rapid speed," says Jason.

May be those two words—"rapid speed"—can also describe your career as an Internet marketing consultant.

23

Web Services

Job Description: *Web services involve the Internet and the World Wide Web, such as designing web pages, building websites, and providing Internet database interactivity.*

- *Extremely low start-up costs*
- *Breakeven time from initial investment:rapid*
- *Future growth potential:high*
- *Ideal home-based business*
- *No staffing required*

What do you think of when you hear the phrase "on the web"?

If you immediately think of being stuck on a giant spiderweb, then skip this section and take a deep breath. You've got a lot of catching to do with the modern world, and you might as well be reested before you start. The Internet has so pervasively invaded the lives of virtually every American over the last decade that it's hard to imagine a time it didn't exist.

American business has been profoundly affected by the arrival of the Internet age. Suddenly the old rules of commerce have gone out the window, replaced by a brave new world in which the rules seem as ephemeral as the electronic images whizzing through cyberspace. Many businesses require or want a presence on the World Wide Web (WWW). Anyone who performs web services is in extremely high demand—a fact that probably will not change in the foreseeable future.

Hyperlinks Makes It Happen

As the Internet evolves, it's become clear that the World Wide Web is the place to be for business. Nicknamed the "web" because it encompasses many sites linked together, the web is the user-friendly part of the Internet.

Users travel to various sites without having to know or understand how to operate the complicated software that runs the Internet. Instead, by clicking on simply worded hyperlinks, users happily zip from one site to the other while all of the computer wizardry that makes the trip possible speeds by unnoticed in the background.

Like any new technological innovation, it took a while for the Internet to become part of American life. However, as more and more people went "on-line" and began using the Web for everything from researching a term paper to planning a vacation, American businesses realized it's where they need to be. After all, the web seemed like a businessperson's dream: a sales tool available for consumers 24 hours a day, 7 days a week. But who was going to put these businesses on the web? That's where webmasters and web designers come in. People skilled in the art of building websites, placing them onto the Internet, and maintaining them suddenly are in demand.

Initially, the functions of a webmaster and web designer often were split. A web designer builds the site, while the web-master maintains it. However, nothing stays the same in the computer world for long. Today it is common to combine both functions.

As the Internet grows and matures, it is evolving into more of an interactive medium; instead of being content just to have a page or site filled with information, businesses want their consumers to interact with their site. They want their clients to have the ability to order merchandise and material from it, they want to know which areas of their site people visit, they want to recognize return customers, and so on. To get these results, they turn to a web services business—such as DataDrive.

Master Of The Web

It was 1991 when graduate student Alan D. Thornhill began noticing the embryonic Internet.

"I started paying attention to what was going on with hyper-text and data exchange," he says. Faced with a need to send large amounts of data to colleagues, Thornhill began experimenting with early servers such as Gopher. In 1993 he launched his first web server using bits and pieces of software he pieced together, since there wasn't an easy way to get onto the still-developing Internet at the time. Still, he saw the potential that the Internet held.

"I was waiting tables at the time to survive, and I realized that I could make a lot more money consulting on the Internet than I could waiting tables," he says.

Thornhill began consulting with companies and individuals that wanted to put themselves onto the Internet. In 1996 he moved to Houston, took an academic position at Rice University, and launched DataDrive as a Web services company. Today DataDrive (www.datadrive.com) supports the WWW presence of approximately 120 clients.

Although Thornhill started out as primarily a designer of websites, the advent of more powerful and easy-to-understand software meant that anyone could build a site. Thus he positioned DataDrive as a company that provides a variety of web services. Among the company's services are web page construction, web-optimized image and graphics creation, and securing/establishing a presence on a web server.

DataDrive's specialty is providing database interactivity, which means building websites that actually can deal with and react to a client's needs, rather than just being a static document. Thornhill feels that this is the future of the Internet.

"This is where the Internet must go if it's going to survive," he says. "It has to interact with the user, because people get bored with static pages that don't change. A website has to adapt to a user, and those are the type [of sites] that we build."

Although his company is located on the Internet, one of the most pervasive advertising/marketing vehicles ever devised in the modern age, Thornhill says old-fashioned referrals and word of mouth caused DataDrive's client list to swell. Today his company is so successful that it serves clients all over the world.

"It's all I can do to keep [the client roster] reigned in," says Thornhill.

Spinning Your Own Web

Thanks to the dramatic drop in the cost of computer hardware, starting your own web services business is extremely inexpensive. For $3,000 you can buy a sufficiently powerful computer and software to begin designing web pages. Even better, some web software is available for free directly off the Internet, or else as shareware, which means that you pay just a small fee if you utilize it.

Since this is an ideal home-based business, the expense of finding and renting a commercial location is eliminated. In addition, any computer that's powerful enough to design websites certainly is going to be sufficient to serve your other business needs such as bookkeeping, which excludes the need to buy a separate system just for those purposes.

"The real expense is in having a machine connected to the Internet 24 hours per day, 7 days per week," says Thornhill. "You have to have a server connected to the Internet." One way to cut that cost is to buy the services from a company that specializes in maintaining continuous contact with the Internet.

Even with these costs, however, it is possible to begin a web services business for under $7,500. Your start-up cost can be recouped rapidly once you obtain paying clients. If you consult, the standard fee ranges from $ 100 to $150. As for project fees, DataDrive uses a three-tiered rate schedule that is representative of the industry in general: $2,000 to $4,000 for basic services, such as setting up a no-frills" website; $8,000 to $15,000 for establishing a more sophisticated site with some interactivity; and $20,000 to $40,000 for having a completely interactive site. The majority of DataDrive's projects fall within the $8,000 to $15,000 range.

Are You "Web" Worthy ?

Obviously, in order to start a web services business, you must understand computers and the Internet right down to the last byte. Since you will be interacting with clients and trying to understand their needs, as well, you also must be adept at dealing with a diverse group of business people. Often they come to you not knowing what they want, and need you to guide them.

"You have to understand your client's needs, even if they don't," says Thornhill.

As with all businesses, the more you put into a Web services firm, the more you earn. Since credibility is important in this field, Thornhill advises anyone starting out to do a few non-paying jobs in order to build a reputation.

"That's what DataDrive did early on," he says. "They [the clients] couldn't afford much, but I saw a real opportunity to make a big splash on the Internet with their project. Thus I was able to build my portfolio and able to sell myself to others and find paying clients."

Once you have paying clients, however, it's possible to make a six-figure income if you want to invest the time and effort. The Internet has become an integral part of American commerce. Businesses are searching for those who know how to make it speak their language, as well.

24

Recycler

Job Description: *A recycler collects paper, glass, aluminum, and other waste materials and recycles them for profit.*

- *Start-up cost as low as Rs.35,000*
- *Potential first year earnings:* Rs. 80,000
- *Breakeven time from initial investment: rapid (as little as six months)*
- *Ideal home-based business*
- *No staffing required*

Looking for a venture in a relatively new field, with low start-up costs and an infinite supply of raw materials? As added incentives, throw in the documented support of the American public and the knowledge that your involvement in this enterprise will contribute to an ever-growing global battle against pollution. If your interest is piqued, then recycling may be the business for you.

According to the Council for Solid Waste Solutions, each American now discards over four pounds of waste each day—as a country, we throw away about 180 million tons of solid waste each year. We used to thoughtlessly toss out empty jars and cans. But as landfill space has become alarmingly scarce, and increased public awareness has led many communities to disavow noxious methods of waste disposal such as incineration, the search for disposal alternatives has set the stage for the emergence of the environment-friendly recycling industry.

"Recycling," as we have come to know it, is an umbrella term for a set of procedures and techniques that bestow new life on used manufactured products such as glass, paper, and cans. This broad perception of the field underscores the vast range of opportunities that are available to entrepreneurs on all levels. While the beginning business person probably will discover that industrial aluminum recycling is not viable as a low-cost start-up, the more rudimentary phases of recycling, consisting of collection and redemption, offer a solid and accessible starting point from which to form a company.

Redeeming Activities

As a result of losing a bet, Guy Polhemus spent four weekends working in a New York City soup kitchen in 1984. With a B.A. in mass communications from Emerson College in Boston and a background in film production and media consulting, Polhemus was not exactly primed for a transformative experience. However, his direct confrontation with the profound daily problems of the homeless affected him deeply. During those weekends, he saw thousands of homeless people benefiting from New York State's "bottle law," which requires consumers to pay a five-cent deposit on purchased containers, to be refunded by the bottler upon return. Polhemus observed that consumers and collectors who hauled their containers to local supermarkets faced long hostile waits before they received their refunds. Prompted by his desire to exploit the inadequacy of these existing structures, Polhemus decided that a redemption center catering to homeless collectors would comply with the "bottle hill," aid the environment, and provide job opportunities for the homeless as well. Within three years, Polhemus set up WE CAN, a not-for-profit organization based in midtown Manhattan.

Polhemus's story is flecked with small miracles, such as his stumbling upon a rent-free 10,000-square-foot vacant lot when he searched for start-up space, and the initial foundation support he captured, thanks to a healthy dose of publicity. Yet, while his company is philanthropically oriented, its growth and success are due to the type of savvy management to which any organization should aspire. Polhemus started collecting containers with $7,000, a staff consisting of 3 homeless people, and incorporation papers drawn up on a pro bono basis by the law firm of Milbank, Tweed, Hadley & McCloy. Today WE CAN have four redemption centers, employs 100 people, and has paid out over $5 million in nickel deposits.

The redemption centers work on a very simple basis. WE CAN pay collectors a nickel for each container they bring in. The returned containers are accumulated on the grounds of the redemption center, where employees separate them by brand. No distinctions are made according to color or size, nor are labels removed. Then trucks from various bottling companies arrive regularly to cart off the latest stockpiles of the city's plastic, glass, and aluminum containers. Bottlers are required by state law to buy back used containers and to pay an additional handling fee of one and a half cents per container to the redemption center. As the Glass Packaging

Institute notes, approximately 30 per cent of all glass containers now contain recycled material (known as "cullet"), so it is clear that bottlers are responding to both government mandate and the public's mounting concern.

Collection Boxes

In addition to the redemption centers, WE CAN operate the Collection Network, which places collection boxes in offices throughout the city, enabling organizations that participate to "comply with local recycling laws while helping poor and homeless New Yorkers." Companies fill the three-feet-tall boxes with non-breakable "empties," and WE CAN pick up the discarded material on a scheduled basis. The proceeds from the "donated" containers offset the operating costs of the redemption centers and pay the salaries of the formerly homeless employees. Simply put, diversification has allowed Guy Polhemus's dream of recycling to become a triumphant reality.

While WE CAN operate on a not-for-profit basis, there is certainly money to be made in the collection and redemption of beverage containers. The key to succeeding in this business is to find an area that has yet to be tapped by collectors or redemption centers and to get the word out once you open up shop. Although it would seem as if recyclers would fare best in densely populated areas, the Aluminum Recycling Association notes that the abundance of storage space enjoyed by the rural entrepreneur results in higher rates of recycling away from the cities.

WE CAN's Collection Network gets its goods for free, as participating businesses reap benefits such as a lower volume of garbage to be taken away by private carters, tax deductions, and a reputation for environmental and social concern. On the entrepreneurial side, private collectors usually pay a flat fee, such as $20 per ton of glass bottles, for the right to place a receptacle on the property of a participating establishment, and then arrange for regular pickup. Profit emerges from the sale of collected containers to recycling companies. In the case of glass, collectors can sell their amassed goods to recycling companies for as much as $90 per ton. If you consider the volume of glass waiting to be harvested from universities, restaurants, and hotels, the potential for success is clear. According to the Glass Packaging Institute, just 35 per cent of all glass bottles and jars sold in the United States were recycled in 1997. Glass is easiest to sell; aluminum cans pose more of a problem, mostly because of the intense competition generated by a preponderance of existing redemption centers.

Diversity is another key to cracking this business. As the field has grown, many entrepreneurs have developed multimaterial recycling operations, centers where consumers can bring all of their recyclable plastic, glass, and aluminum materials; receive refunds when appropriate; and rid themselves of unwanted, space-consuming trash without filling up another landfill. With persistence and a smart marketing approach, a collector of discarded Coke cans can become an emperor of trash.

Paper : Reams Of Possibility

According to research by Franklin Associates, Ltd., 33.9 per cent of the garbage filling up our nation's landfills is composed of glass, metal, and plastic materials, while paper waste products rest in 34.1 per cent of the available space. This incredible volume of discarded paper pours out of businesses, which daily generate enough paper to circle Earth 20 times, says the National Recycling Coalition, Inc, a washington-based alliance of businesses, individuals, and environmental organizations. While the recycling of paper causes the quality of its components to deteriorate slightly, it is important to note that one ton of recycled paper (whose composition meets the EPA's standard of at least 50 per cent waste material) saves 17 trees. Clearly, paper recycling makes good sense and good business. If paper is your material of choice, the best prospects for profit lie in collecting high-quality papers from businesses and selling products made from recycled paper.

The United States is the largest consumer of paper in the world. Unfortunately, paper recycling is proceeding very slowly. In 1985, about 20 per cent of all paper products were recycled. By 1995, that figure had increased to only 27 per cent. This paper has to get to the companies that will turn it into pulp, filter it of its contaminants, de-ink it, mix it with virgin material, refine it, and press it into usable form. Collecting newspaper is not often a viable possibility for the low-level entrepreneur, as large refuse companies have pounced on collection opportunities that evolved from the enactment of curbside recycling laws in many states. The best way to start out in paper is to look away from the sidewalks and focus on your area's office buildings.

Be Creative

In soliciting clients, use common sense. Look for businesses that probably have a high volume of waste, such as print or copy shops, or offices where many computers are in use. Corporate settings will demand that you be extremely persuasive, because a contract with you requires the initiation of an office wide recycling program. According to the San Francisco Recycling Program, collectors of office-generated paper usually require 500 to 1,000 pounds of paper for a pickup, so clients will need to know that you can be relied on to facilitate the flow of waste products from desktop to truck. Some collectors, such as Vangel Paper Co. in Baltimore, pay clients as much as $50 per ton for High-grade paper, while others, such as

Newhallville Recycling, Inc., in New Haven, Connecticut, get it for free—it all depends on the level of competition in your area. As the price of paper can waiver dramatically, you'll have to convince your clients that the quality of your service will not be affected by market fluctuations.

Use a little ingenuity—produce desktop boxes for all of your clients' employees and central storage bins to be placed next to computer clusters and photocopying machines. Another possibility is to rent large storage receptacles to your clients, to be situated in an outdoor spot easily accessed by your trucks. Again, this centralizes the collection process and offers another opportunity for your start-up to generate revenue.

At the most basic level, you will need a truck, a telephone, a method of promoting your business, and boxes in which your clients can accumulate paper. A somewhat more sophisticated start-up might involve the purchase of scales, shredding equipment and a baler, warehouse space, and even facilities for expansion into non-paper materials. Above all, explore the rates at which paper mills are willing to purchase discarded high-grade paper—you should always be able to get more for this than for waste paper or newsprint.

The recycling of paper can be justified commercially only if goods made from recycled paper are marketable. Bountiful opportunities await the paper recycler with a proclivity for retailing. Gift bags, greeting cards, envelopes, and animal bedding are just some of the examples of items in demand. Whether sold out of a mail-order catalog or a storefront operation, products made of recycled paper often are expensive to produce, so it is imperative that you choose merchandise whose cost is not prohibitive.

Americans finally have begun to recognize the damage inflicted by a century of unchecked pollution. If we are to make a serious commitment to repair the environment over the coming decades, then surely recyclers will lead the way. An understanding of the opportunities combined with an entrepreneurial spirit will yield results in this growing field. As Guy Pollhemus puts it, a recycler is on the right track if he or she "sees a need, addresses that need, and still manages to survive!"

25

Caterer

Job Description: *A caterer provides food for corporate* occasions, *private parties, weddings, and other large gatherings.*

- *Start-up* costs as *low as Rs. 1.50 Lacs*
- *Potential first-year earnings: Rs. 2 Lacs*
- *Breakeven* time *from* initial *investment: one year or longer*
- *No staffing required*

Ginger Swallow's Creative Cuisine catered three parties in the Houston area in every week during her second year of operation, but she'd rather do just five events a year. In fact, "One bash a year would be fine—as long as it's the right bash." Her definition of the "right bash" owes more to economies of scale than snobbery. "I want to feed parties of 30,000 ... 40,000 ... 50,000 people." At $50 a head, revenues mount quickly. Ginger's single-person shop hasn't reached those heights yet, but the effervescent hostess has catered someTexas-size shindigs. For example, she has done six parties for between 1,500 and 2,500 people, and booked two more affairs at $110,000 and $140,000.

The best part of it all, Ginger admits in an undertone, "I usually keep two-thirds of the revenues as profits. That's what's left after I pay for food, help, and transportation."

The Sweetness Of The Bottom Line

Two-thirds?? That's pretax profits of $66,666 on a $100,000 dinner! These figures aren't so hard to believe when you realize that Ginger Swallow employs tactics that keep her overhead to zip, which gives her a richer bottom line than the average caterer. For example, her house serves as an office and she hires employees and even a kitchen in a nearby bankrupt restaurant only on days she actually caters events. But even operators who invest in $50,000 kitchens and full-time chefs, even those who spend heavily to promote their service to corporate clientele, allow that catering profits are the best in the $354 billion restaurant industry. "Once you deal with enough masses, your profits can be 25 per cent of revenues. In some cases, you'll do 50 per cent," says Frank Spinarski. With those figures in mind, he left a swank hotel chain where he was director of catering to launch The Aristocrats catering outfit in Huntington Beach, California.

Those figures, however, may grossly underrepresent the industry since many home-based caterers don't even list in the phone book. Ginger Swallow shuns a phone listing, reasoning that anybody hosting hundreds of people will hire by reputation, not by Yellow Pages. "I don't want the kind of occasional business that such advertising would bring," she insists. "I want to be known as the caterer in the Dallas area to come to for large bashes."

Sandwiches By Contract

But extravaganzas are certainly not the only route to the catering hall of fame. If you can carve out a reputation in any one area, you can do quite nicely. For example, anyone connected with the wedding business in the Washington area knows Love at First Bite. Consultant Jay Treadwell recommends lining up six-month contracts with corporations, a move that brings in continual business from executives who don't have time to go out to lunch.

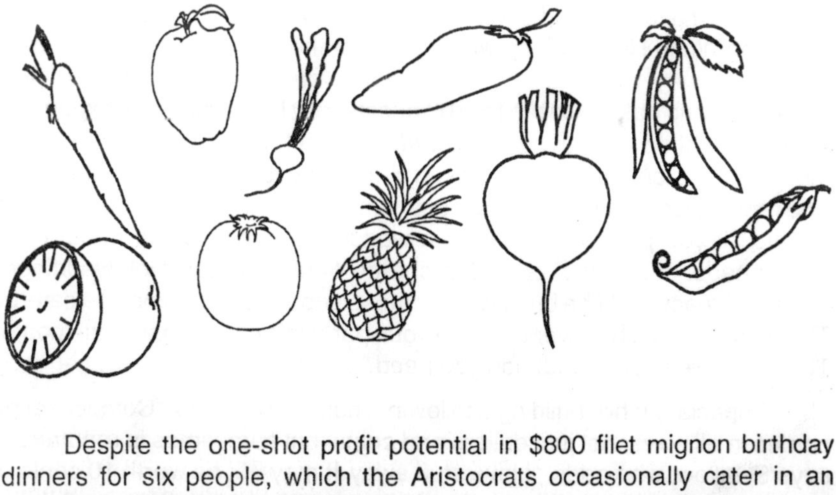

Despite the one-shot profit potential in $800 filet mignon birthday dinners for six people, which the Aristocrats occasionally cater in an individual's home, Frank Spinarski says, "Corporate is where the bread and butter is." Not only do they throw bigger and more expensive parties, corporations party more often.

To tap that corporate sector, Frank Spinarski took along a client list of 8,000 area corporations when he left his former position at the hotel chain. (You also can find corporate names through chambers of commerce and on the Internet.) "We called everyone on that list to see if their company used caterers," he recalls. "Probably 1,000 people in the country consistently use caterers. We call every one of them regularly, asking 'When will you use us?'" Such cold calls bring in meager business at first, but once the corporations hear of the other fantastic parties you host, they start responding positively. Frank says that now of the 30 contacts he makes during a typical week, 6 or 7 book parties.

Make Them talk About You

Word of mouth is undoubtedly worth more to caterers than to restaurateurs. Anxious brides or corporations throwing parties for new product send-offs "are not going to risk embarrassment by trying an unknown caterer," says Jay Treadwell. "They ask for recommendations." Your reputation as a fabulous restaurant chef may be recommendation enough. Ginger Swallow worked as corporate chef for a wealthy Texas real estate couple famous for their flamboyant soirees. All the banks and real estate brokers and corporate execs knew Swallow because they'd attended her parties.

But those entering the field with less visible credentials say there are as many ways to create reputation as there are parties to throw. "Build a party into your start-up costs," recommends Jay Treadwell, who was formerly the general manager of Ridgewell Caterers, the Washington giant that regularly feeds the White House along with the rest of the Capitol Hill soci-ety. Make that give-away party an impressive showcase for your talents. Beef Wellington and baked Alaska for 100 guests may be prohibitively expensive, but you might do something special with cocktails and canapes. Spend the money for an ice carving or a baked Brie that your guests will remember. And rent the local museum garden or another enticing locale to lure influential people. "If you plan to specialize in weddings, invite florists, department store heads, musicians, people in charge of places that book weddings," explains Treadwell. "The bride will ask those people to recommend a caterer. The answer might be 'I went to a fabulous party this caterer gave last month.' That's all the recommendation you need."

Especially while building a following, don't cut corners. "Compensation comes in all ways, not just dollars and cents, but sometimes in reputation," says Swallow, who adds, "I give stuff away. It may not be worth 10 cents of my time to add edible flowers, but it's a way to sell my company." If you can't get a client to pay for the frills but enough influential guests are attending, you may wish to add carved pineapples anyway. Look at it this way: Such extra attention is cheaper and more effective than advertising

To Buy or Rent

Unlike many other businesses, you can start as big or as small in catering as your pocketbook allows, because you can buy your own elaborate facilities or rent just about anything you need. Jay Treadwell figures $100 per square foot will outfit an institutional kitchen. (Caterers do most actual cooking on-site, either with equipment they bring or facilities supplied by the clients. But you need a kitchen for "prep work," such as cutting vegetables.) Heavy-volume jobs require a truck and temperature-controlled holding cabinets. You either rent china, linens, and other staples, or buy them outright and keep the cut that otherwise would go to the rental agency.

Anticipating monthly revenues of $50,000 (after nine months in business, they are halfway there), Frank Spinarski and his partners invested $50,000 in their kitchen and hired a full-time chef and secretary. But you can get by with far less. Ginger Swallow catered her first $22,000 party using her own pots and pans and rented kitchen space. She invested $5,000 of her $15,000 profits from that first affair in equipment meant to enhance her signature. For example, "I hired carpenters to make a huge, fancy cheese board shaped like a cowboy boot" to serve 40-pound blocks of cheddar at Tex-Mex barbecues.

While you can certainly administrate from a spare bedroom, consider Health Department regulations before actually cooking from home. You're legally considered a restaurant when you cater. But many places rent their kitchens. Some large city restaurants advertise their facilities for caterer use. In addition, don't forget church or school kitchens. "If you offer something special, like cooking a treat for the kids, you might get a good deal on using the school kitchen after hours," says Jay Treadwell.

As for personnel, a freelance legion makes its living by working for caterers. Ask party planners or banquet managers to recommend servers or ice carvers. Says Ginger Swallow: "If I go to a restaurant and see somebody I like, I approach them—the chef, the bartender...."

Who Does It

Restaurateurs are the most obvious converts to catering, but marketing types who hire culinary experts are sprinkled throughout the field. Jay Treadwell warns against underestimating the business aspects of catering. "The restaurant business is 70 per cent food-oriented, with the rest going for service, organization, etc. Those figures flip-flop in catering; 30 per cent food and the rest delivery, transporting the food, lining up rental equipment, juggling personnel." In catering, organization counts.

Another handy trait is a smooth manner. On one hand, you must deal professionally with corporate clients and party planners who expect a receipt for every shrimp. But you also must assure parents of the bride that you'll be on time and everything will be beautiful for the special day.

You don't have to limit your business to gastronomy. Ridgewell Caterers, with expected annual revenues of between $15 million and $17 million, was begun in 1928 by the cook of the French Embassy and the butler of the British Embassy to supply all the accoutrements, such as china. Party rentals are still a big part of the business. Ridgewell's, now headed by identical twin brothers Jeff and Bruce Ellis (grandsons of the founders, who fell in love and were married), did not build its kitchen until 1970. "People like one-stop shopping," says Jay Treadwell. "You can rent items from a rental store, but act as a coordinator on flowers, tents, whatever. In all likelihood, it's a profit center for the caterer and a relief for the client."

Never lose sight of the fact that people come to a caterer for the unusual. If they want the restrictions of a set menu, they would go to a restaurant. "Outline menu possibilities, but leave the impression that you can do anything," advises Jay.

And make suggestions. Ginger Swallow recalls an aviation company that requested a Tex-Mex picnic for 1,200. Instead, "I suggested an international theme, and we ended up with cuisine from six countries, including a luau with a huge pig in honey sauce and steaks branded with the company's logo. My fee went from $5,000 to $35,000." The meeting planner moved the party into an airplane hangar and added a band, Vegas tables; and a limousine containing a Joan Collins look-alike; his fee leaped from $3,500 to $10,000. The client? "They were ecstatic," says Ginger. "They threw a party everybody remembers."

26

Gourmet Food Products Producer

Job Description: *A gourmet good products producer develops speciality food items for the consumer market.*

- *Start-up cost as low as Rs. 1.25 Lac*
- *Potential first-year earnings: Rs. 1.50 Lac*
- *Breakeven time from initial investment: rapid (six months to one year)*
- *Ideal home-based business*
- *Excellent opportunity for people with physical disabilities*
- *No staffing required*

Duggan and Robert Peak were setting up their booth at the San Francisco Food & Wine Show when the enormity of what they were doing hit Duggan, a former which range from a Poppy Perfect salad dressing to a cucumber dill vinegar. "Robert had left this prosperous advertising agency and we had just left this prosperous advertising agency and we had moved to Oregon, hundreds of miles away from my restaurant contacts in southern California." She looked over at their baby, whom they had smuggled into the show, hoping the officials wouldn't notice and throw them out. "It felt like opening night, and I was scared. I looked at Robert and said, 'My God, look what we've done.'"

As the doors opened at 9:00 .A.M., throngs of wholesale buyers from department and specialty stores clogged the aisles, leaving Duggan Peak no more time to worry. The couple had transformed their booth into a pastel kitchen. The look, unusual in contrast to the sterility of most booths, attracted crowds right away. Robert had created progressive packaging in airy grays and pinks, a memorable departure from the home-spun cliches of most specialty foods—the burgundy bonnet topping the jar of marmalade. And

Duggan had tasted every oil, vinegar, and salad dressing in California when concocting an all-natural, really different taste. By 10:30, Robert was discussing terms with the buyer from Nieman-Marcus when Duggan felt someone grab her hand. "You don't want to go exclusive with Nieman-Marcus," he said. "I'm from Macy's."

"We thought we'd be okay if we sold 2,000 cases during our first year," recalls Robert. "We sold that many our first show." During their start-up year, the couple hit sales of $1 million—and profits of $420,000. Within two years, sales had tripled as Duggan's Own grew from 14 products to 59.

You've Gotta be Special

First the bad news: For every Robert and Duggan Peak success story, failures in the specialty food business abound. Your family recipe has got to be really special to compete with giant conglomerates that unleash entire research and development (R&D) departments on $4 mustards. "Individuality is really important," says Robert. "Do some research to come up with something unique either in the packaging or product." adds Morris Kushmer, a consultant who has introduced to America more than 600 items during his career, including the first cappuccino mix and the first crouton: "If you can get the customer to pick up and read your lable, you're half way home."

A tip on the label: In addition to conveying a quality image, many food manufactures add a recipe either on the packaging or tied around the bottle's neck. After all, the more customers use your marinade, the sooner they will be back for more.

Landing On The Shelves

The first customer you must sell is the merchant. In the old days, food entrepreneurs sold to local clientele and watched their distribution expands as their fame slowly grew. "We used to take new products to the corner grocery to get an idea of how they would sell," says Morris Kushner. that approach is increasingly difficult as supermarket chains muscle corner groceries out of extistence. Some specially food stores still take samples on consignment, but many supermarket chains now charge a "slotting fee" of several thousand dollars to introduce new products. In the United States, the specially food market is estimted at $13 billion.

Now for the good news: Kushnar adds to that picture: "When I first started, specially products looked at 5 per cent of the population. Now we can target 18 to 20 per cent—that's the number of families with gross incomes of $35,000 or more. The first thing they can afford is good food."

Supporting Cast

This new interest in top-of-the-line consumables has catalyzed an entire industry to help entrepreneurs introduce the latest in shiitake mushrooms and coriander marinades. Perhaps the most important new aid is the growth of trade shows: These allow mom-and-pop operations to go national (or international) immediately by attracting the attention of department and specialty stores that buy in bulk. Although specialty food shows have been around for a generation, recently their popularity has exploded. The International Fancy Food & Confection shows, sponsored by the National Association for the Specialty Food Trade, attract from 15,000 to 30,000 attendees from specialty food, wine, gift, and department stores as well as restaurants, mail order, and other related businesses. The Peaks attended nine shows in one year, including jaunts to Tokyo, Paris, and West Germany. "Shows literally showcase your products," explains Morris Kushner. "Brokers and distributors will see your products and latch on to you."

Food brokers do not take title to your herbal cheese sticks but merely act as your sales representative with accounts all over the country. For enticing retailers to buy your products, brokers receive 2.5 to 5 per cent commissions. You handle the shipping and accounts receivable. Food distributors go a couple of steps further for their 25 to 30 per cent fees. They act as middlemen by actually buying your product and shipping it to retailers they sign up.

Someone's In The Kitchen

Two avenues exist to produce the products: You can do it yourself or hire a copacker. Duggan and Robert Peak chose the initially more expensive route of operating their own factory. "To hold our overhead low, we moved from Los Angeles to Oregon," says Robert. The manufacturing plant they rented included acreage where they grow basil, tarragon, thyme, and marjoram to supplement herbs grown by local farmers. The couple's first $5,000 went for show fees and labels for their sample jars in the San Francisco show. Then they proceeded to invest $75,000 from savings to meet those increasing orders. "During our first six months, every time we got a check from a client, we would rush to the bank and get cash for more inventory," recalls Robert.

The Peaks chose to manufacture their products so they could control quality. More commonly, entrepreneurs manufacture through copackers who agree to maintain high standards by ad-hering strictly to recipes supplied by the food's creators. "You take the recipe to someone who produces it under your label," explains Morris Kushner. "A copacker buys vinegar and oils in tankfuls for all their customers, so volume provides savings."

As a rule of thumb, expect to "keystone" your products—double the cost of producing the item to wholesalers, who then tack on another 50 per cent at the shelf. For example, if your overhead, including food and packaging, labor, rent, and delivery, amounts to $1 per jar of wild mushroom pate, charge wholesalers $2 and consumers $3. "That strategy should cover all the essentials and leave a few pennies for advertising and new-product development," says Kushner. Costs should fall as your volume increases; some overhead items, such as rent, remain stable no matter how many cases you churn out a day, and bulk buying actually lessens per-unit food costs. "Volume production will bring the $1 cost down to may be 87 cents, which allows you to give a product a shot with a coupon or a ribbon on the top of the jar after a few months," says Kushner.

Keep Those Products Coming

Savings also frees up cash for new-product R&D. "Nowadays, you don't stand a chance with one item," warns Kushner. "You have to build an image with pizza, onion, avocado—all the salad dressing flavors under one label."

Specialty food retailers and suppliers deal regularly with cottage manufacturers, so don't try to pretend you have General Food's resources. Buyers want assurances you can deliver as promised and suppliers want to know you can pay on time—so don't make promises you can't keep. Possibly because they projected a professional image in their packaging and with their factory, Robert and Duggan Peak had no trouble lining up suppliers. "People gave us credit—vinegar and olive oil companies put us on net days," says Duggan, still amazed. "Some shipped their first order COD, then established a line of credit."

Retailers likewise were helpful. "Our first orders were all prepaid or COD," says Robert. "Some larger orders can't do that, but department-store buyers said they knew we were just starting and offered to pay us the day after they got the goods."

Today Duggan laughs recalling her anxiety at the first show. "But you know, this was supposed to be a kind of early retirement for us," she says. (Duggan is in her early 30s, Robert is in his mid-30s.) "Everything happened so fast. We were bitten by success."

27

Gourmet Food Store Provider

Job Description: *A gourmet food store locates and sells specialty, bard-to-find, and unusual/exotic food items.*

- *Start-up cost as low as Rs.80000*
- *Potential first-year earnings:* Rs.15000 *per month*
- *Breakeven time from initial investment: six months to several years*
- *Ideal home-based business*
- *Excellent opportunity for people with physical disabilities*
- *No staffing required (initially)*

Walking through the big burgundy barn that houses Expression unltd offers quite a sensory experience. More than 100 varieties of crackers line its shelves, as well as 126 jams, 45 mustards, and spices from unpronounceable regions. The bright colors of 38 flavors of jelly beans vie with the warm earth tones of 23 whole-bean coffees in burlap sacks. The take-out food section sends odors wafting through the aisles. Generous samples of goat cheese and Swiss vegetable pate mean nobody leaves Expression hungry. Located on a remote country road in the Wachung Mountains of Warren, New Jersey, 40 miles from New York City, the store sells one ton of cheese every three days.

"Six or eight years ago, specialty food stores didn't exist," says Elaine Yannuzzi, who owns what many consider the ultimate in specialty food stores. "Meats were available in old fashioned German delis, and you could get a dozen of the more pedestrian cheeses at the supermarket. But nothing like this existed."

Expression Through Food

In fact, Expression unltd. began without a single food item in sight.

"Things were different in 1970; a woman expressed her-self through her children and her home," explains Elaine Yannuzzi, who stocked the original Expression with a stitchery department, children's toy area, decorating section, and gourmet cookware corner. In the mid- 1970s, she added cheese to complement the cookware, and soon inserted other gourmet items. Today, all the old departments except cookware are gone, and cheese represents 30 per cent of the store's sales. Revenues now amount to millions, and, with the addition of take-out foods, sales jumped by at least one-third. (See "Take-out Restaurateur," page 126.)

Nobody knows the true size of the gourmet or specialty food market, because an exact definition of specialty foods doesn't exist. Is the Brie that you could buy only in specialty cheese shops a decade ago still considered a specialty food even though you now can choose from a half-dozen Brie brands at the supermarket? But, as an indication of the industry's growth, the National Association for the Specialty Food Trade (NASFT) estimates that the specialty food market is at least $13 billion in the United States.

Why We Experiment

The reasons for Americans' new taste for gourmet foods include

- Increasing popularity of home entertaining
- Less time for food preparation coupled with higher incomes (well over half of all homemakers also work)
- Improved refrigeration and transportation that provides fresh, exotic fruits and vegetables year round
- Increased preference for "all-natural" foods made without preservatives, salt, or sugar
- Availability of hundreds of new products that are expanding Americans' diet to include salmon pate and radicchio

However, along with this heightened receptivity to specialty foods comes new competition. In addition to increasing numbers of specialty food boutiques, every supermarket in the country now has its gourmet food selection. To bring customers through your doors, you must create an experience they just can't get in a fluorescent-lit supermarket that stocks dogfood and detergent along with the arugula and extra virgin olive oil.

If your start-up budget is skinny, you can open a 1,000-square-foot true specialty store: just teas or cheeses. Carry only a handful of companion items, such as biscuits or balsamic-flavored vinegar. By addressing such a narrow market, you become known to the area's aficionados. You may eventually send out a catalog to attract mail-order customers for your chocolate truffles or whole-fruit jellies.

A Generalist In Speciality Foods

Rather than creating a niche in a particular food category, Expression unltd. goes to the opposite extreme by providing the last word in specialty food shopping. Although Elaine Yannuzzi earns 80 per cent of her sales from just 20 per cent of her products, she carries thousands of items to create an atmosphere that brings customers from a 100-square-mile radius. "We carry a line of Indonesian spices that may be 50 people travel from around the area to get at Expression. We do special orders on really odd items," she says.

To choose which items to stock, Yannuzzi shops the massive Fancy Food & Confection Shows twice annually. The show's 2,200 booths "overwhelm a person just starting out," she warns, "but I assure you [choosing a product mix] really does become manageable after a few years." Her first criterion in deciding whether to stock a particular item involves taste. "A specialty mustard sells for $3.50 to $5.00, compared with 79 cents in the supermarket. The taste has to say 'Oh, wow!' "

She continues, "If price is very much out of line, we'll still stock a superb product, but in lesser quantity till we see how it sells."

365 Turns A Year

Because specialty foods retailers look for fast inventory turnover, you don't have to pile up debt to stock your store. "You don't bring in a spring line of sportswear that takes three months to turn," points out Elaine. "Try for weekly or biweekly turns on jarred foods and daily turns on prepared foods." Use proceeds from this month's sales to buy next month's. Stash additional funds for prime buying times, such as before Christmas.

Of course, to get such fast turnover, location is crucial. A specialty food store's 40 per cent margins, while vastly superior to the 10 per cent margins a supermarket copes with, just don't support mall locations. But try to get the most visible spot your pocketbook allows. Expression unltd. broke this cardinal rule; Elaine Yannuzzi located her shop in a building she already owned because it needed a tenant—even though she was miles from nowhere. After struggling a few years, she overcame the disadvantage of her remote site; now, during Christmas season, Expression needs a police officer to direct traffic out of its back-roads parking lot. "But 'location, location, location' is a good rule," she admits. "Rules make life easier."

To combat its isolation, Expression advertises weekly in New Jersey's largest newspaper as well as in other papers less frequently. In addition, the store employs a full-time public relations manager to call on caterers, corporate customers, restaurants, and other clients who get discounts for buying in bulk.

Sampling Boards

Once you get customers into the store, you still have to sell the foods. Because many of your items are unusual, they can be intimidating. (Question: Does blackberry sauce go over ice cream or lamb? Answer: Both.) The 35 year-round and 60 holiday time Expression employees taste each new item and learn about its origins so they can answer customer questions. To provide customers with a firsthand experience, the store gives away 350 pounds of cheese, chicken salad with water chestnuts, and chutney a week in samples. On weekends, one employee does nothing but refurbish the sampling boards. Elaine Yannuzzi asks manufacturers to provide as many free samples as possible, arguing that a smear of basil mustard on a pretzel can sell a whole jar. Even with help from food packagers, she still spends $150,000 a year on freebies.

Specialty food stores walk a thin line between offering the foods that customers know they want and exposing them to an ever-increasing number of new treats. A specialty food customer is almost by definition, adventurous: Your job is to create an atmosphere conducive to experimenting. "Even though an item may be unknown to a customer, they are secure because they know we select with care and feeling," says Yannuzzi. "Specialty food stores sell confidence. We sell a spiritual thing lingering behind the products."

28

Juice and Smoothie Bars Owner

Job Description: *Juice/smoothie bars owner serves freshly squeezed concoctions made with fruits and vegetables as well as smoothies, which are fruit-based drinks comprised of fruit, ice cream and/or yogurt, and other ingredients.*

- *Start-up cost: Rs. 5 Lacs*
- *Potential first-year earnings: Rs. 4 Lacs*
- *Breakeven time from initial investment: rapid (as little as one year)*
- *Future growth potential: high*
- *Health-oriented business that appeals to consumer's desires for nutritious meals*

What's the latest, hippest trend in beverages?

If you said "coffee bars," go to the rear of the class and repeat "what's In/What's Out 101." Coffee bars are yesterday's news. Today the juice/smoothie bar is America's choice for liquid refreshment. The exploding popularity of juice/smoothie bars led *Entrepreneur magazine* to label them one of the "hottest business" of 1998. "juice bars continue to pack a hefty punch in the beverage world," said the magazine.

But *Entreprenuer* wasn't alone in pointing out the juice/smoothie trend. "All Hollywood seems to be juicing now," proclaimed *Los Angeles magazine* in January 1998, summing up Tinseltown's fondness for juice drinks and juice bars. But it isn't only celebrities who are wetting their palates this way. According to one source, the American juice market rang up approximately $2.8 billion in annual sales by the close of the 1990s. Clearly, this is an excellent field to "squeeze" into.

Healthy Habit

What are the reasons behind the explosion in juice/smoothie bars?

A primary force driving this market is health. No matter how you foam it, top it, or flavour it, coffee is never going to be as healthful as juice. Heightened awareness about the health danger of coffeine has also led concern about coffee drinking.

Health-conscious consumers, however, consider juice drinks nutritious. Besieged by news reports touting the advantages of consuming more fruits and vegetables, people are searching for fast ways to get their "five a day" servings of both. Knocking back several juice drinks daily seems to be the perfect solution. As an article in the *Toronto Star* said: "Most Canadians have trouble consuming the five to ten servings of fruit and vegetables that [a Canadian health agency] recommends we eat every day. [But] drinks just one cup of juice a day counts as two servings of vegetables and fruit."

Many people head to their local juice bar to get the nutrients they need instead of relying only on regular meals. Fruit juices, for instance, are a great source of vitamin C. Vegetable juices, such as carrot juice contains flavonoids that produce an anticlotting effect and are good for your heart. It also contains resveratrol, which helps lower LDL,or "bad," cholesterol.

It's not only the United States that has embraced the juice bar concept. In October 1998 the British newspaper *The Daily Telegraph* reported that "a whole host of juice bars has recently opened on this side of the pond."

Real Smooth

Smoothies—blend juice concoctions of fruit, nonfat frozen yogurt, sorbet, and juice—are popular offerings of many juice bars. In fact, some juice bars feature smoothies over standard juice drinks.

It isn't hard to guess where the emphasis lies at a retail establishment called Smoothieville. Located in Chapel Hill, North Carolina, Smoothieville opened in October 1996 by brothers Jim and Robert Millican.

"We were both in sales," says Robert, "and we had a hard time finding healthy ways to eat in hurry."

Realizing that a lot of other people were in the same situation, the brothers—who had always wanted to be in business together—searched for a field that was in the early stages of development but yet still offered long-term growth potential. The two looked at many different businesses; the one that kept popping up was juice/smoothie bars.

"We saw how popular smoothie and juice bars are on the West Coast," says Jim. "Comparisons were being drawn with the smoothie business now to where [frozen] yogurt was 20 years ago."

Aware that the juice/smoothie bar concept was beginning to migrate east, the brothers decided to open their own business. Besides being native North Carolinians, they chose Chapel Hill because of its progressive outlook. (It's the home of the University of North Carolina.) They knew a contemporary mind-set was essential to their chance of succeeding with such a new, innovative food product.

Without downplaying the healthy aspects of smoothies, the Millicans positioned the product as a tasty meal replacement. In advertisements on local AM radio as well as in personal appearances before civic and professional groups, the brothers sought to educate the public about the great taste and health benefits of smoothies, and why they are a preferable meal alternative.

Their target efforts paid off. Business boomed from the start, even though they opened in crisp weather October with essentially a cold beverage product. Sales were so strong, increasing at an annual rate of approximately 25 per cent, that the brothers opened a second location in Durham, North Carolina, in 1998.

One factor the Millicans believe has contributed to their success is using whole fruit, pure juices, natural sweeteners, and non-fat dairy products rather than sherbets or yogurts that may contain sugar. When customers see their smoothie being made, they know they're getting a unique-tasting product that is also extremely healthy. If customers don't want any of the 15 varieties that are on the Smoothieville menu (all with unusual, fun names such as "Hairy Dog" and "Bluezilla"), they can order their own combination of ingredients.

"We get a big crowd for breakfast; people take it on their commute to work," says Jim. "The same for lunch." This illustrates that the Millicans' strategy of positioning smoothies as meal replacements has made an impact.

Prices at Smoothieville range from $2.80 to $3.85. The cost depends on the ingredients in each drink. It takes ten employees to run a store effectively, with two or three working each shift.

Blending Your Way To Success

As you might expect, it takes more than a blender and a handful of fruits and vegetables to begin a juice/smoothie bar business.

Since this obviously isn't a home-based business, you need a retail location. Add that cost to an equipment investment that can easily reach (and even surpass) $50,000 due to the large amount of specialized equipment that must be purchased (refrigeration units, countertops, blenders, and so on). Other expenses include staff salaries, an advertising budget, and supplies (cups, spoons, napkins, and the like). Overall, the minimum investment to begin operating a juice/smoothie bar is approximately $100,000.

Annual income for this type of business depends on numerous factors, including location, competition, and expenses. However, it is possible to make $100,000 in your first year, which means you could recoup your initial investment in 12 months.

A variable expense with this business is food. Obviously, a juice/smoothie bar is particularly vulnerable to sudden fluctuations in the cost of fruits and vegetables due to weather, insects, and other causes. While Smoothieville has managed to hold the line and not raise prices in response to unexpected increases in the cost of fruit, the Millican brothers constantly study the market and are kept aware of any possible shortages/price increases from their suppliers.

One way to help keep profits smooth is to diversify your menu. Some juice/smoothie bars offer sandwiches, healthful snacks, and other items. On the menu at Smoothieville is coffee, mainly because the Millicans wanted to be able to offer a hot drink during cold-weather months. Eventually, the brothers anticipate offering sandwiches as well.

One important factor the Millicans believe has helped them become successful is that they keep the experience at Smoothieville fun. The Millicans maintain a good relationship with their customers, even to the point of posting pictures of "frequent smoothers" on the Smoothieville website.

Frivolous Fad Or Favorite Food?

The $64,000 question for juice/smoothie bars is whether they have the staying power to survive in the highly competitive food industry. After all, the retail food establishment is littered with the bones of concepts such as frozen yogurt that seemed so sturdy at the beginning, only to wilt when consumers moved on to the next big thing.

Experts think that juice/smoothie bars will escape that fate, mainly because of their healthful reputation. As people seek ways to eat and drink more nutritiously yet still retain their busy lifestyle, they seem likely to turn to a glass of "liquid fruit or vegetables" as a perfect alternative to fast food.

Another factor that may help juice/smoothie bars prosper is that the market is still largely untapped. The Millicans estimate that only 25 to 30 per cent of their potential customer base knows what smoothies are; that means that nearly 75 per cent of their potential customers have yet to learn about their product.

"For that reason it [the market] is still on the upswing. It's still growing," says Jim Millican.

29

Pizza Parlor Owner

Job Description: *A pizza parlor owner cooks and serves pizza and other Italian-style foods.*

- *Start-up cost as low as Rs. 3 Lacs*
- *Potential first-year earnings: Rs. 3.50 Lacs*
- *Breakeven time from initial investment: one to four years*

Here's a statistic bound to please pepperoni producers everywhere: Approximately 10 per cent of all U.S. restaurants serve pizza. Americans were estimated to have gobbled up $22.5 billion worth of these tasty, round, tomato and cheese creations in 1998. To put it another way, people in the United States consume about 100 acres of pizza each day—and we show no signs of stopping. According toTechnomic Inc., a Chicago restaurant consulting and research firm, pizza sales are estimated to grow at a yearly rate of 4.5 per cent between 1998 and 2003. With approximately one out of four belonging to a franchise, the rest range from elaborate shops (such as the one topped by a Leaning Tower of Pisa emblazoned with "PIZZA" in two-foot-high letters, which grossed an astounding $2.25 million in one year) to tiny take-outs that provide 40 per cent profits to moms and pops.

A Slice of Americana

The credit for the insatiable pizza hunger lies both with a better product and with today's lifestyles. "Fifteen years ago, pizza was greasy kids' stuff," says Paula Werne of *Pizza Today.* "High school kids liked it, but their mothers didn't. Today we're rid of the grease and have turned pizza into a healthy food with the four different food groups—milk (cheese), bread (crust), vegetables (toppings like spinach and tomato sauce), and protein (sausage and pepperoni)."

Product improvements made pizza acceptable; product convenience made pizza flourish. Unlike other fast-food customers, pizza eaters call ahead for take-out, or have Domino's deliver it to the door in less time than it takes to bake a pizza at home. "Families are converting that one night a week they used to go to McDonald's into a night at home with take-out and the VCR," says Dennis Sheaks, who attributes 46 per cent of Joe Peep's N.Y. Pizza's orders—and 57 per cent of its dollar sales—to delivery. And never mind what Burger King says, pizza operators invented "have-it-your-way fast food. Want a slice instead of a 17-inch pie? No problem. Hold the anchovies, add extra cheese? Sure thing.

Not A Lot Of Dough

Pizza restaurants are like a raw canvas: You can create anything you want on the basic concept, ranging from an inexpensive take-out to an elaborate chain. If you want to start small, you can set up a two-oven take-

out operation in a reasonable location for $50,000 or less, compared with ten times that figure for most fast food franchises or a sit-down restaurant. The difference boils down to the degree of difficulty involved in the operations. Pizzerias sell simple products (even those that add antipastos and sandwiches) that require little expertise, equipment, or decor.

Dennis and Diane Sheaks bought used equipment when they moved Joe Peep's N.Y. Pizza into larger quarters in North Hollywood, California, ten months after buying the restaurant for $70,000. "Toasters or automobiles have lots of moving parts to wear out," says Dennis, "but an oven is just a big insulated box with gas controls. Ovens are like wrenches—they never wear out."

The functional, unassuming look the Sheaks chose for Joe Peep's not only kept opening costs to $80,000 (including renovation to add plumbing) but also created a "fun atmosphere" that involves customers, says Dennis. "The kitchen is separated from the order area only by a low-level counter. The customers watch their pizza being made."

As for ambiance, you can install Tiffany-like lamps and stained glass or go for a minimal look. Dennis Sheaks invites customers to scribble graffiti on the walls—anything that has to do with Joe Peep's or pizza—during the 20-minute wait while their order cooks. "People stand on each other's shoulders or bring in a friend who's never been here before to show what they wrote in the past. It's a form of entertainment."

Because they require little space, pizzerias sometimes can afford expensive mall locations or retrofit buildings other restaurants would shun. For example, some gas stations abandoned during the oil crisis of the 1970s were reborn as pizzerias.

Delivery doesn't have to be expensive, either. If you don't want to spring for your own vans, hire drivers with their own cars and insurance and reimburse them on a per-mile basis.

Stand Out

Despite the presence of national chains, independents do quite well in the pizza business. However, if you choose to go it alone, recognize you'll never match Pizza Hut's advertising budget. Therefore, you have to have something going for you: location, product, price, or atmosphere. Dennis Sheaks offers a top-notch pizza at a premium price. "Domino's large pizza costs just 75 per cent of Joe Peep's biggest size," says Dennis. "But Joe Peep's is twice as big. If you don't give value, gear for low income people who only have $4 to spend anyway, or very high-end customers, looking for an avant-garde style."

Let's assume you and your spouse run your pizzeria with two employees and operate with a 30 per cent food cost and average strip-shopping-center rents. If you gross $200,000 a year, $80,000 or so will find its way into your pockets.

In a different scenario, you might shoot for the heights. As Dennis Sheaks sees it, if you don't mind plowing hours and profits back into operations, there's plenty of room for expansion. For himself, he envisions a ten-unit Joe Peep's chain, possibly followed by franchising. His first step is to perfect a pilot restaurant. And the Sheaks are well on their way to that goal: Joe Peep's grossed $750,000 in its second year under the couple's management, compared with just $200,000 when they bought the restaurant.

Joe Peep's still sells the same secret-recipe pizza that had already earned the restaurant a loyal customer base. The difference, says Sheaks, boils down to marketing.

"The first thing we did was capture on our computer the name and address of everyone who came into the restaurant," he explains. "Then we created a VIPeeper Club." (To join, all you have to do is sign up.) Each month, Joe Peep's sends discount coupons or announcements of "members-only" parties to 16,000 members. While the mailings cost $2,500 a month, that's far below the thousands more it would cost to reach those people by television or even newspaper.

Joe Peep's also proclaims it will deliver "anywhere in the world, except South Africa." Dennis warns this is an expensive strategy, because for every driver he sends on a 15-mile journey, additional employees must handle local deliveries. But he's thinking ahead. "We've already got customers 10 miles away from this store. I'll open my second store on the periphery of my customer base. Those existing customers will establish the new store through word-of-mouth advertising."

That second store is the second step in a pizza empire, says Sheaks, who holds an MBA and ran his own management consulting firm before buying Joe Peep's. As he points out, "I figure I'm more qualified than Ray Kroc was when he started McDonald's."

30

Take-Out Restaurateur

Job Description: *A take-out restaurateur prepares and* sells *a wide variety of food that* customers usually *take home to eat.*

- *Start-up cost as low as* Rs. 2 Lacs
- *Potential first-year* earnings: Rs. 4 Lacs
- *Breakeven* time *from* initial investment: six months *to two years*
- Item: A National Restaurant Association (NRA) study once asked how often Americans purchased take-out foods. Eight out of ten people said they purchased a take-out meal or snack at least once a year, and seven out of ten respondents from households where the female head worked full time said they bought take-out more than twice a month.
- Item: A Louis Harris poll found Americans' leisure time declined by eight hours over a recent ten-year period. "Juggling careers and families means little time is left for leisure activities," observes an NRA publication. "Consequently, many consumers look for ways to 'expand' their time" with such tricks as buying prepared meals.
- Item : With the introduction of such fascinating toys as videocassette recorders and compact discs, the home has evolved into the prime entertainment center of the 1990s. And many homes also have microwave ovens that heat up prepared foods in seconds. If you want to stay home but don't want to cook, one attractive alternative is to purchase delivered or take-out food.

Suzanne's

When she was starting out, Suzanne Reifers didn't consider those market indicators. "Instead of doing market research," says the former speechwriter, "I did research on myself. I lived in this Washington, D.C., neighborhood near Dupont Circle, and there wasn't much there at that time. I wanted a place to buy cheeses and pates." Since Reifers knew *she* would frequent a gourmet take-out shop, she figured other apartment dwellers would, too.

Evidently she was right. The ground-floor take-out shop at Suzanne's, which also includes an upstairs restaurant and a catering operation, contributed $400,000 of her $1.7 million in revenues. "The average ticket is low—around $5—because people pick up two cookies on their way home from work," says the proprietor. "But we do volume." In addition to homemade pastries and salads, Suzanne's boasts some justly renowned specialties: Torta Rustica, a double-crusted quichelike pie stuffed with salmon, cheese, and herbs; and Indian Somosa, "which sounds yucky but is really delicious," according to Suzanne, who adds that the cream cheese-stuffed pastry contains a vegetable puree topped by a yogurt-and-poppy-seed sauce.

Suzanne Reifers opened Suzanne's with "you're going to laugh—$130,000," when she came into a small inheritance. That is incredibly low considering the capital went for a sit-down restaurant as well as the take-out boutique. Reifers says she kept costs down by doing her own massive renovations to turn a dilapidated, turn-of-the-century townhouse that housed a jewelry and watch-repair shop into an attractive restaurant and retail food shop.

A Food Service Bargain

Anything under $200,000 is indeed paltry for a restaurant. However, one major attraction a take-out operation holds for entrepreneurs is its relatively low opening cost. You can open a gourmet carry-home shop for $100,000, compared with a total start-up cost of $500,000 to $1.5 million for a full-service restaurant. With no seating to worry about, you need just half the space of a typical restauran—say 1,000 square feet—to accommodate a take-out operation. A well-stocked display case full of mouth-watering delicacies serves as your best decoration. Kitchen and clean-up facilities are smaller. And if you specialize in just one or two foods, start-up costs are even lower.

A take-out operator also doesn't suffer the crazy hours that a restaurateur puts in. People who want to run a food service operation and still spend time with their families score this advantage high. Depending on your neighborhood, you might open in time to catch residents who buy a croissant and royal Dutch chocolate coffee on their way to work. But you surely dish out the last yellowtail tuna by 7:00 or 8:00 P.M., when the restaurant next door still has hours to go before taps.

Take-out counters need an abundance of help, because customers consider convenience of supreme importance and don't relish waiting in long lines. But you can pinpoint the heavy traffic crunches fairly easily: when workers stream home from work, or, if you're in a commercial area, at lunchtime. So part-timers can make up the bulk of your staff.

Not Who You Are but Where you Are

Where you hang your take-out sign is probably even more important than what you serve, unless, of course, your customers expect delivery. If 75 per cent of your gross comes from deliveries, opt for the lower-rent district. Suzanne's tacks on a $10 delivery charge, which admittedly is pretty steep for customers who spend just $8.99 to stock a picnic basket. But her intent is to accommodate those few customers who really want deliveries and encourage most people to stop by the shop.

Today, however, say "delivery" and most consumers still think pizza. That reputation stems in large part from Tom Monaghan, who, in 1961, traded in his Volkswagen for controlling interest in a Ypsilanti, Michigan, pizzeria. Since then his creation, Domino's Pizza, has revolutionized the entire food delivery industry with its promise of hot pizza in 30 minutes. Domino's has grown to more than 6,000 corporate and franchise stores, with worldwide sales of over $3.1 billion.

According to David Smith, a Domino's vice president, "The job of getting the product out in 30 minutes is accomplished in the store, not on the delivery route." A fairly open secret is Domino's insistence on a simple menu, consisting of several varieties of pizza and only one beverage. "That way," continues Smith, "we focus on one concept: delivering our product within 30 minutes. We've got it down to 60 seconds from order to oven, and we're always looking for ways to shave seconds off the process.

But if customers come to you rather than the other way around, look for accessibility. Take-out only works on a well-traveled street in a densely populated area, which rules out most smaller towns altogether. Also, make sure you have the right population within a few blocks of your store. Shoppers won't do you much good, since they need a place to sit in order to eat. On the other hand, a railroad station could be perfect as tired commuters pick up your moo goo gai pan on their way home. "My partner and I spent a lot of money getting a good lease in Georgetown," says Geoff Elliott, who opened Take Me Home in the affluent Washington neighborhood ten years ago. "But our customers didn't match what we wanted to do. Georgetown is populated by tourists [who eat in restaurants rather than order take-out foods] and older residents [who are not from the 18 to 44 age group the NRA says is most likely to order take-out]." Thanks to a busy lunchtime trade from area office workers, the carry-out menu still contributes about 20 per cent of Take Me Home's $375,000 in annual sales. But Elliott survives on the catering service he added when he realized the strategic location mistake he had made.

A Combination platter

Like Geoff Elliott and Suzanne Reifers, many entrepreneurs combine take-out with other types of food service. You can use a kitchen and chefs for dual purposes. Indeed, your kitchen can prepare take-out foods before the restaurant lunch or dinner crowd arrives. Suzanne's operations complement each other. "The retail shop goes gangbusters at Christmas when the restaurant is dead," she says.

Decide what statement you want to make with your food. Ethnic take-out operations like Mexigo in New York City have proven popular, as have fast-food deliverers. But if you're taking the gourmet route, suggests Suzanne Reifers, "you need a well-rounded place. You can't put in just a little bit of this and a little bit of that." In addition to the quiches and broccoli, red pepper, and corn salads she proffers, Reifers sells shelves full of packaged specialty foods, like virgin olive oil.

Reifers discovered another must is pastry. "When I began, I assumed people in these health-conscious days didn't want desserts," she recalls. "So I hired a chef who would spend half her time preparing desserts and half pates. The desserts were so popular we had to hire a full-time pastry chef, assistant pastry chef, and cookie baker." Now 35 per cent of all shop sales are sweets. "I guess when people decide to splurge on calories they'd rather get something really delicious than buy a Heath Bar," says Reifers.

Gourmet take-out is still a city phenomenon, since smaller towns and suburbs lack the numbers to support carry-out services. Most suburbanites settle for supermarket-prepared take-outs and drive-through windows at fast-food chains. However, some operators say the gourmands and closet gourmets could get their shot in the future. Thanks to the success of operations like domino's more and more Americans consider buying somebody else's cooking to eat in their home as an accepted alternative. what's the next carry-out hot spot? "I might consider opening a gourmet take-out in Topeka," says one operator.

31

Wrap Restaurateur

Job description: *A wrap restaurateur owns and operates an eatery offering primarily wraps—typically a tòrtilla or flatbread filled with ingredients such as chicken, shrimp, beef, vegetables, sauce, and so on.*

- *Start-up cost: approximately* Rs. 3 Lacs
- *Breakeven time from initial investment: as little as two years*
- *Future growth potential: high*
- *Nutritious food concept that appeals to health-conscious consumers*
- *Exciting food concept business that allows for flair and creativity*

Wrap me up two wraps to go!"

Even though it's a mouthful, Americans are repeating that phrase, or something very similar, more and more these days. Wraps are sweeping the country, and, along with them, so are wrap restaurants. It's the latest trend in eating that doesn't seem as if it will be "all wrapped up" for many years to come.

Rapping About Wraps

What is a wrap? Strictly speaking, it's a cousin of the burrito and the sandwich, for it shares similarities with both. Basically, a wrap is a tortilla or flatbread filled with a variety of ingredients, such as chicken, beef, fish, and vegetables. Sometimes it also contains a sauce or spread (barbecue sauce, salad dressing, salsa, and so on). The name "wrap" comes from the fact that once all these ingredients are put onto the tortilla, it is folded, or "wrapped," over so that everything remains inside. This makes wraps the king of convenience foods.

The convenience of wraps is one factor that helped spur their popularity. With the ever-busy, ever-mobile lives more and more Americans lead, wraps are the perfect solution for eating on the run: Just grab a couple while on the road and eat them with one hand while holding onto the steering wheel with the other.

Another factor driving the wrap revolution is they're more nutritious than fast food. As people seek healthier but yet still convenient ways of eating, wraps have become more popular.

Of course, none of this would matter if wraps tasted like boiled tarpaper, but fortunately that's not the case. The ingredients inside these tasty treats are limited only by the imagination of the maker. Fish, chicken, beef, seasonings, lettuce, onions, tomatoes, peppers, and bacon are just some of the ingredients found inside wraps.

It is believed wraps originated in California in the mid-1990s and have gradually spread eastward across the United States. Today many cities have wrap restaurants; some have even brought in top-notch chefs to add their own unique flair to the menu. At California-based World Wrapps, such menu selections as Mango Snapper and Caribbean Jerk Pork helped redefine the wrap and move it to a higher culinary level.

Several national restaurant chains have examined the wrap trend and pronounced it viable enough to get in on the action. KFC Corp. added flatbread-wrapped sandwiches called Chicken Twisters to its menu. TGI Friday's introduced rolled sandwiches called Wrappers in its restaurants, while Au Bon Pain added Wraps to their menu. The fact that these national chains adopted wraps is the clearest indication yet that wraps have gone mainstream in a major way.

Wrappin' At The Capital

Sometimes entrepreneurs just jump into a new field with both feet, with little more than hope and a good idea. Rick D'Alessandro, however, knew exactly what he was doing when he and his brother Ed opened Capital Wrapps in Bethesda, 'Maryland, in 1996. Not only did Rick have two decades of experience in the full-service restaurant business, but he was also well aware of wraps long before they became one of America's favorite foods.

D'Alessandro knew restaurants in the Hispanic section of San Francisco had long sold Mexican-style food wrapped up in tortillas. He decided to bring that concept East, where his family lived. At the same time, wraps were just starting to emerge on the West Coast, and D'Alessandro realized the wrap concept could be applied to a large variety of foods besides Mexican.

"I said to my brother, 'This is a phenomenon. We should consider doing this here [in the East],' " he says.

D'Alessandro and his brother devised the entire wrap men for their store. Thanks to experience, D'Alessandro knew what ingredients would taste good together, while not straying too far from the wrap concept.

Without advertising, Capital Wrapps opened in the winter of 1996, and the restaurant was immediately flooded with so much business that the two could barely keep up with the demand. Word of mouth helped keep business at a fever pitch, and favorable stories in such newspapers as the *Washington Post* and the *Wall Street Journal* continued to send a steady stream of customers through its doors.

Capital Wrapps has 1,600 square feet with 50 seats inside the restaurant and 17 on the patio. Prices range between $5.50 and $6.25, and 25 different wraps are available in small and large sizes. The restaurant also offers salads and smoothies to drink. (By offering smoothies, Capital Wrapps is mirroring a trend of other wrap restaurants around the country that combine smoothies and wraps because of the nutritional value of both. See page 118 for information on juice/smoothie bars.) Capital Wrapps also "unwraps their wraps" and puts the entire thing in a bowl.

D'Alessandro credits the quality of the food at Capital Wrapps with the eatery's success. "I can't tell you how many people come long distances to our place, simply for the quality," he says.

Wrap ' EM Up

Like any food service business, start-up costs are high for a wrap restaurant. Anticipate spending between $250,000 and $300,000 initially to get a 2,000-square-foot restaurant with seating off the ground. This includes acquiring a location, equipment (for both food preparation and business), ingredients, and staffing. During busy times, it takes at least five people to staff a restaurant.

Additional costs come from marketing. (Not everyone can be as fortunate as Capital Wrapps and do a landmark business without spending money on advertising.) If $300,000 sounds like an awful lot of cold hard cash, try finding existing space that once accommodated a restaurant. This will be less expensive than acquiring a brand-new location or refurbishing one that didn't have a restaurant in it initially. As D'Alessandro advises, the location that you choose is a critical factor in whether your restaurant sinks or swims.

"It all depends [success] on the environment that you're going into. That's the key," he says.

As far as recouping your start-up costs, the food service business is more difficult to figure out than most because of the many variables that impact profits: consumer acceptance, cost of ingredients, rental cost, staffing costs, and so on. However, D'Alessandro, who has been a restaurant industry consultant, estimates that on annual sales of $600,000 to $700,000, an owner can realize profits of approximately 20 per cent. Thus, it can take a few years to recoup your initial investment. (Again, making a profit in the food service industry sometimes is an uncertain proposition. For example, some wrap restaurants had sales in the seven-figure range yet lost money due to management inexperience.)

As far as location, since wraps are still a relatively unknown food, it's best to find a spot where people are amenable to trying new things as well as where a commuting lifestyle is prevalent.

Do Wraps Have Legs?

As with all food business trends, the main question about wraps is if the concept has "the legs" to go the distance and become an established part of the American diet, or if they're just a fad that will fade away.

"I don't think that wraps are going to go away," says D'Alessandro. He also added his feeling that a wrap restaurant needs to have other items on the menu in order to survive.

Because wraps do offer many positive benefits, such as portability, nutritional value, taste, and the ability to combine numerous ingredients together to have a different taste experience each visit, they seem to have the potential to become a permanent staple in the American menu.

32

Adult Day Services Provider

Job Description: *An adult day services provider helps seniors with their daily needs, including nursing care, transportation, meals, social activities, eating, and bathing.*

- *Start-up cost: high (depending on location, facility, and services offered)*
- *Future growth potential: high*
- *Staffing: variable (depending on facility and type of service)*

Born of a need to provide seniors with health, social and support services, the [adult day services] industry is gaining momentum, fueled by longer life spans and an older population," *stated Entrepreneur Magazine,* naming it one of 1998's "hottest" businesses.

Although the industry is growing rapidly, many people are completely unaware of its existence. In fact, *Entrepreneur* called it "one of the best-kept secrets around." However, with the growing number of aging baby boomers, adult day services are destined not to remain unknown for much longer.

Day Trippers

Although some date the emergence of the industry to the early 1970s, in reality it started in the late 1940s. That's when psychiatric day hospitals began adult day services to assist patients following their release from mental health facilities.

Gradually the idea spread. In 1978 the Health Care Financing Administration of the U.S. Department of Health and Human Services published a directory listing nearly 300 adult daycare centers in the country. In 1979 the National Institute on Adult Daycare (NIAD) was organized as a unit of The National Council on the Aging, Inc. In 1995 NIAD became the National Adult Day Services Association (NADSA).

Care With Dignity

Some people may confuse adult day services with assisted living facilities. The difference, according to NADSA director Mary Brugger Murphy, is that assisted living provides 24-hour care, if necessary, while adult day services cover a preset number of hours.

"Adult day programs are typically six, eight, ten hours per day," she says.

Murphy feels that this type of care for older Americans is catching on because it simply makes sense. "It's such a very logical way of serving increasing numbers of very frail, very old people. As the population shifts, and more people live longer and become more frail, we have to find better ways to serve them."

Logic is indeed one component that drives this industry. Instead of sending a healthcare professional to the home of a stroke patient, for instance, it makes more sense to take that person to an adult day service center where the professional can work with that person and others at the same time. This also provides clients with much-needed social interaction.

As Shaune Shields, executive director of the Greater Seacoast Adult Day Services Center in Portsmouth, New Hampshire, points out, adult day services are designed to help seniors who don't need 24-hour care while maintaining their dignity and independence.

"The goal is to keep people living in their homes as long as possible," she says.

As is typical in most programs, Greater Seacoast does a nursing assessment of patients when they first enter the program, to see what services they need to provide. This is done in conjunction with information obtained from physicians detailing patients' physical status. Although there is no profile of a "typical" adult day services patient, Seacoast is focusing on the frail elderly and those with Alzheimer's disease. Why? Because that's what the community needs.

Community Research Critical

There are an estimated 4,000 adult day service centers operating in the United States. However, as knowledge of the industry spreads, demand for these centers continues to grow. Mary Brugger Murphy says that anyone interested in getting into the field should start by surveying the local community.

"Human services are not really a build-it-and-they-will-come phenomenon," she says. "You really have to know the community. You have to do a good market analysis of the community and find out what's there, what the competition is, and how many people need to be served."

Murphy warns that the analysis must be thorough. While a freestanding adult day services facility may not exist in a community, prompting someone to believe that the way is clear to open one, an existing nursing home or hospital may already offer those same services. Approximately one-third of the adult day service centers in the United States are freestanding facilities; the remainder are folded in with a hospital or other healthcare provider.

If you're interested in getting into this field and believe you see an opportunity, your next step should be to contact the NADSA. Adult day service regulations differ from state to state; NADSA can direct you to the agency in your state that oversees the industry. The association also has a set of voluntary standards and guidelines that it urges anyone getting into the field to follow. Outside of these, there are no uniform national standards governing either the operation of centers or the qualifications of staff members.

"A very useful contact is with the state association of adult day providers," Murphy says. "In Ohio, for example, the state association provides a two-day training course in how to start an adult day program. This is a very good way of determining if this makes sense for you."

Fees for adult day services vary, depending on the region of the country and the range of services provided. Daily fees range between a few dollars all the way to $185, depending on the services provided and reimbursement levels (where applicable). greater Seacoast charges a flat rate of $6.50 per hour, with a minimum of $39 per day and a maximum of $45.

even at that rate, however, Greater Seacoast is losing money on each patient. The primary reason is that government reimbursement to adult day services facilities is extremely low, because the whole concept is so new that traditional government medical payment plans do not recognize its existence.

"Adult day services is the new kid on the block," says Shaune Shields. The major source of funding for adult day services is private pay. However, some programs accept people who are Medicaid eligible.

Another consideration before opening a facility is transportation. Although those seniors who can drive use their own cars to get to the facility, many can't and suffer from conditions (such as Alzheimer's) that rule out public transportation. Thus many centers, such as Greater Seacoast, hire vans to pick up patients at their homes. However, this is often another moneylosing situation. Greater Seacoast, for instance, charges riders just 25 cents per ride but is billed for van use at a rate of $25 per hour.

As far as what services to offer, it depends on what exists in the local community. The "average" adult day center offers a wide range of services, including: transportation, social services, meals, nursing care, personal care, counseling, therapeutic activities, and rehabilitation therapies. It is recommended that you focus on providing services that aren't readily available in your area.

Murphy says, "If there's a community where there already is a very strong network of sophisticated and accessible healthcare services, but people with Alzheimer's who are relatively healthy have nowhere to go, then that becomes your target population, at least to start with."

NADSA has defined three different categories of services to use as a general guideline: core (a client needs socialization, some supervision, supportive service, and minimal assistance with activities of daily living); enhanced (a client needs moderate assistance); and intensive (a client needs maximum assistance).

Early in 1999, NADSA unveiled an accreditation program for adult day service centers. Developed through collaboration with CARF, the Rehabilitation Accreditation Commission, the program sets national standards by which the activities at centers are monitored and rated.

Services offered also dictate staffing needs. For example, your staffing needs will be much different if you're going to serve a mobile population as compared to one that is severely impaired.

Another cost consideration is the actual building itself. To build one entirely from scratch costs in the hundreds of thousands of dollars. However, sometimes renovating an existing facility is no bargain, either. Greater Seacoast spent approximately $900,000 to totally overhaul a building that had been built in the 1950s.

"You have to be in this business because it's a mission for you," says Shields, speaking about some of the financial pitfalls. "You have to do it from the heart."

Active Growth

Active Services Corporation exemplifies a successful adult day services company. By mid-1999, after just four years in existence, the Birmingham, Alabama-based company was operating 36 adult day health centers and had become an industry leader.

Active Services was founded by Kenneth W. Oliver in 1995, a veteran with more than 20 years in the healthcare industry. Oliver started the company when he realized that patients often had needs that were not met by visiting facilities that offered just one type of service. Friends or family usually had to ferry the patient around to other facilities to receive the re-quired treatments. At the same time, Oliver's elderly parents became ill and required almost continuous access to the health-care system. As the child who lived the closest to them, it fell to Oliver to help his parents get the services they required, and he was again reminded of how difficult it was to coordinate everything. Thus was born the idea of creating a company that offered a wide range of services.

"Basically, we created a platform of service that is a comprehensive point of care," says Oliver. "A person recovering from a stroke or cardiac problems who is experiencing difficulties with the activities of daily living can be brought into a congregate setting and have 10 or 11 hours of interaction with other people, while also receiving [necessary] care."

Because of ignorance about adult day services, Oliver says that "the biggest challenge" that Active Services faces whenever it goes into a community is to get the word out about itself and its services. The company advertises and also tries to get the local media to do stories on the company and its services. It also develops a list of 20 to 30 key sources (physician offices, advocacy groups, discharge managers at hospitals, and so on) and contacts them to explain their programs and services.

"It's ongoing," Oliver says of the public relations effort. "We continue doing that, even after we've opened."

In terms of a payment schedule, Active Services normally uses a per-diem system based on the level of care required. The less-intense level of care costs between $45 and $50 per day, while the most extensive care costs approximately $65.

The Future Is Now

Adult day services is an industry that's just coming into its own. As with assisted living, demographics—such as the projection that the number of people over 65 is going to double in the next two decades—favor continued growth.

"I think the field is wide open," says Oliver. "It's estimated that today, we're meeting 30 to *40* per cent of the need in the country. This need will at least double in the next twenty years. [This industry] has an extremely bright future."

"I think it will expand. It's so logical that it can't help but take off," Murphy adds.

33

Aerobics/Exercise Instructor

Job Description: *An aerobics/exercise instructor teaches fitness through the use of aerobics and other exercise routines.*

- *Start-up cost as low as Rs. 25000*
- *Potential first-year earnings: Rs. 1 Lac*
- *Breakeven time from initial investment: one month to three years*
- *No staffing required*

Karen Shaffer taught French by day, but her passion was the Jazzercize exercise classes she took several times a week. Deciding to combine her love of dance exercise with her love of teaching, she bought a Jazzercize franchise. "I began by teaching at an adult school, then rented church facilities," she recalls.

Like many aerobics students who make the leap to instructor, Karen Shaffer got hooked. "Each routine is a performance and I ham it up. I teach people to make the most of themselves." She points to a svelte woman who was once overweight. "Before class she talked about her new boyfriend. The students give such positive feedback."

A Way Of Life

Although the national obsession with exercise has already begun to level off, Karen decided a steady core of exercisers would always want to flex and stretch and move to the music. So she and another franchisee went into partnership; instead of continuing to scrounge around for subpar Y and firehouse facilities to rent for their classes, they plowed $60,000 into opening their own Jazzercize salon in a Pennington, New Jersey, shopping center. (Shaffer talks with near reverence about the custom floor they now possess.) Today, except for minimal salaries, they still pour every dime into making the business work, but Shaffer foresees a steady 5 percent growth every year; and she never contemplates returning to the less strenuous drills she once led conjugating French verbs in a classroom.

According to studies by the Sporting Goods Manufacturers of America, women 18 to 34 do aerobics more often than any other group. But these Generation X'ers are not bumping and grinding to those old Jane Fonda videos that were hot in the 1970s. Instead, they sweat and strain to videos put out by MTV and the New York-based Crunch fitness gyms; these are videos with an in-your-face attitude, complete with heaps of sarcasm and funky music. This "new" style of aerobics has become so popular that it's even gotten a name: GenXercise. True, the double-digit numbers of those who discovered aerobics each year in the 1970s may never again occur, but aerobics isn't losing adherents, either. The difference now: Aerobics entrepreneurs can no longer be mere instructors. Today it takes marketing acumen to keep those revenues in shape.

Breaking In

IDEA estimates that most of the aerobics industry's instructors work part time. If you wonder whether you can make a living doing sit-ups and jumping jacks, why not hold on to your current job and moonlight?

Three avenues lead to exercise instruction:

- Independent contracts. Many instructors freelance at health clubs or studios that pay by the hour. You don't need to worry about marketing since somebody else rounds up students. Bare-bones start-up capital covers leotards and Reeboks, and possibly some tapes and a portable stereo if your club doesn't provide them. If you go the independent route, be sure to carry liability insurance if your employer doesn't.
- Satellite classes. Following Karen Shaffer's entry strategy, many instructors lease community facilities, such as a recreation center or school gymnasium. You probably can hold initial costs—for rent, tapes and a stereo system, clothing, and insurance—below $2,500. If you join a franchise, tack on another $500 or so. (Jazzercize, for example, sells fran-chisees videotapes with its routines and provides training and the use of its name. In return, the franchise takes 30 per cent of revenues, after expenses.) Operating with a floating home base, as Karen explains, has its drawbacks—when basketball season begins for a school, or when the church expands Wednesday bingo to Thursdays the landlord grabs back the site. After scrambling to find a new place, invariably you lose members who won't travel with you.

- Opening a studio. One estimate is that converting a 2,400-square-foot empty shell into an aerobics studio would cost $32,600 to $60,200, depending on how much you spend for a ceiling, floor, lights, sprinkler, mirrors, air conditioner, professional sound system, and fans. This figure assumes a studio hosting 30 classes weekly could attract a total attendance of 600. If you charge a fairly typical $3.50 per head and pay instructors $10 an hour, you'll net around $88,000 per year. From that, deduct overhead, advertising, and debt service.

Diversify

Of course, you can offer other moneymakers beyond those 30 classes. "It's imperative to add things other than aerobic classes to survive," advises Barbara Fisher, who runs Bodies by Fisher in a Victorian brownstone in the Back Bay section of Boston. "You can only offer classes at the times when lots of people want to take them. During the other times, offer individual consultation, rent the space to dance groups, or offer skin care or nutritional counseling." And don't forget clothing and food and drink concessions.

Many studios expand their repertoires beyond challenging workouts. Lead classes for special groups such as pregnant or overweight women or even children. You also can offer less stressful exercises, such as low-impact aerobics or, if you have access to a pool, aquatic routines.

The biggest untapped market is spelled M-E-N. The National Sporting Goods Association has estimated that men make up less than 15 per cent of aerobics' participants, a stat ambitious entrepreneurs regard as an opportunity. (Even though the Gen X videos are designed to appeal to men as much as women.) And some observers see hopeful signs. Kathie Davis of IDEA notes that some high school football teams now emulate the pros by including aerobics in their conditioning. Could be players will continue aerobics after their football glory days are gone. Davis suggests aerobics instructors make slight changes to erase the effeminate stigma, such as offering a sports conditioning class—basically aerobics with dance references deleted from routines. Instead of incorporating graceful flourishes into the routine, clench those fists.

Get Out There And Sell

"Try to tap all markets," Barbara Fisher advises. Many corporations pay dues as an employee benefit, so why not call on area employers and leave a notice on their bulletin boards? Once you book your own facilities to capacity, add outreach programs. Some schools that have cut back on physical education classes hire instructors to lead after-school aerobics in the gym as an extracurricular activity. Ask the recreation director of a senior citizen condo whether residents might like aquatic aerobic instruction in the pool. Barbara sends instructors to hotels and corporations for on-site aerobics and goes through the convention bureau to find meeting organizers. "Propose health breaks instead of coffee breaks. Corporations provide yogurt and juice instead of coffee and donuts, and you lead 15 minutes of stretching and breathing to break up the seminars. Low-impact aerobics won't leave them sweating."

While many aerobics instructors build a loyal following of students who stay with them for years, count on constantly replenishing your exercisers. As many as 6 million of those 23 million aerobics participants are debutantes, and a similar number of exercisers drop out each year. To replace the transients, budget for advertising: newspapers, direct mail and handout flyers, and even radio and TV in some markets. Studios can of-fer open houses and guest passes, while freelance instructors can demonstrate at the local country fair. You can even offer a membership as a prize in a charity-related fund raiser.

34

Ambulatory Care Center Provider

Job Description: *An ambulatory care center provider treats medical patients on a walk-in basis, usually without an appointment.*

- *Start-up cost as low as Rs. 7.50 Lacs*
- *Potential first-year earnings: Rs. 5 Lacs*
- *Breakeven time from initial investment: one to two years*

The healthcare industry is changing faster than you can say "freestanding emergency medical centers." On one hand, modern medicine is increasingly able to cure all manner of deadly diseases, allowing us to live longer and healthier lives. On the other hand, we're paying for it. According to a story in *Time magazine*, Americans spend $733 billion a year on medical care, which is nearly twice what they spent just seven years ago.

As insurance companies and Medicare throw up their hands with cries of "We're not going to take it any more," premiums increase and payments to patients fizzle. in response, the medical establishment is scurrying for ways to provide quality healthcare at more affordable rates. Instead of prescribing lengthy hospital stays, physicians recommend home healthcare. Instead of treating heart disease when an attack necessitates surgery, employers are signing on for preventive care with health maintenance organizations.

Doc-In-The-Box

In addition to home healthcare, observers report a trend toward ambulatory care centers—patients walk in without an appointment at any hour of the day or night. Because private walk-in centers operate without a hospital emergency room's high overhead, they can charge a small percentage of what a hospital might charge for the same procedure. For example, Jerry Hermanson, president of North Federal Management Group, says the four

Minor Emergicenters that his group operates in Pompano Beach and Deerfield, Florida, charge $125 for administering to an arm injury that requires suturing and X rays. "A hospital in my area would charge $225 for the same procedure," says Hermanson, a hospital administrator before he opened the first Emergicenter.

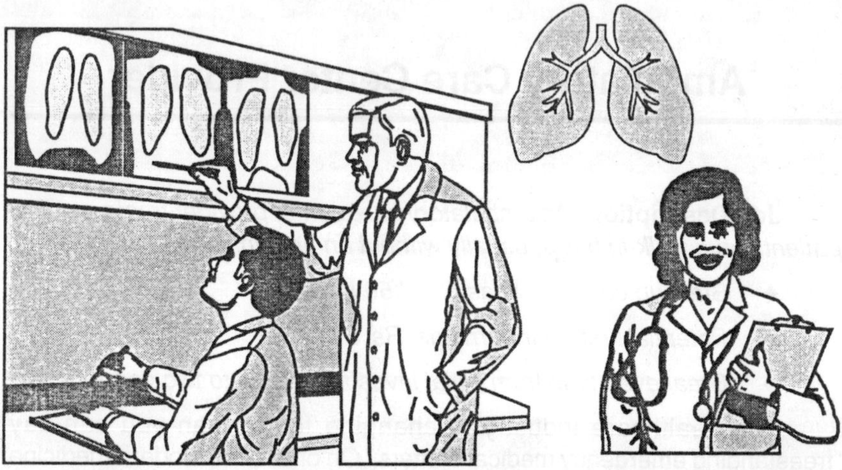

Lured by less costly bills and shorter waits for treatment, patients turn to ambulatory centers in increasing numbers. With every treatment, they learn to trust the care they receive at the centers the media used to call "doc-in-the-boxes." The public's heightened awareness, along with increased visits, result in more centers opening to fulfill the demand. According to an article in *Compensation and Benefits Review,* "ambulatory care ... is growing rapidly ... due to managed care incentives." The article also stated that experts believed this growth would continue.

Whatever Ails You

The complexion of the centers is changing. The early clinics treated almost exclusively non-life-threatening emergencies such as sore throats or sprained ankles, as reflected in such trade names as Minor Emergency Center or Urgent Care. In the future, many operators expect that primary-care facilities will provide the biggest boost to the new business. These facilities treat patients for all kinds of illnesses on an ongoing basis, just as general practitioners have always done. A separate trend is toward centers that specialize in such areas as birthing, X rays, and ophthalmology.

You can build a freestanding clinic for about twice the cost of setting up a general practitioner's office (which doesn't require a laboratory or X-ray equipment). While the initial cost is higher, you'll turn profits far faster: Seeing patients in volume means higher revenues. If you rent real estate and lease medical equipment, you can fund an emergency center that operates 80 hours a week for as little as $250,000. That assumes you're doing some advertising and paying only for two doctors, two nurses, two receptionists, and two X-ray technicians for the year or so before breakeven. If you buy your own building and equipment, or staff a larger center, plan on needing more capital. Some of the larger medical equipment companies can provide a list of equipment, pharmaceuticals, and incidentals you need to get started.

You can afford to pay your staff salaries similar to what they would make working in a hospital or doctor's office. Doctors, for the most part, are young and see working in a center as a way to increase their experience.

The medical community splits in about a dozen different directions on whether they like the walk-in centers. "Local primary-care physicians see us as direct competition," says Jerry Hermanson, who consults for hospitals and individuals wanting to set up ambulatory care centers. "Since we refer patients to specialists, the specialists don't object." Hospitals, already feeling the revenue pinch as insurance providers insist on shorter stays and fewer tests, recognize that the emergency centers are stealing their emergency room clientele. Their reaction: If you can't beat 'em, join 'em. Nearly 50 per cent of hospitals set up their own freestanding centers, says the National Association for Ambulatory Care. The hospitals operate a center either as a hospital adjunct or as a joint venture in partnership with an entrepreneur.

Marry A Doctor

As often as not, the opening partner isn't even a doctor. In fact, some centers are backed entirely with non-M.D. dollars, although, says consultant Arthur E. Auer of Auer & Associates, "I find centers don't work unless a physician has a billfold on the line. If you work with a partner who has medical expertise, the centers can represent good business opportunities."

They sure can. Once you break even on annual revenues of a half-million or so, you probably can keep 20 per cent ($100,000) as pretax profits. Since you commit to low-cost, quality care in order to beat out hospitals, the key to profitability involves volume. Jerry Hermanson says a center needs to treat 30 patients a day at $50 each to break even. That would represent annual revenues in the $525,000 range. An even busier facility with two doctors on board at all times could bring in double or more the annual revenues.

A revolving door waiting room is just as important to the patient as to the medical center. After all, most patients don't worry too much about whether you are cheaper than the competition; they expect their insurance carrier to reimburse the cost of the visit. But who wants to wait all Saturday afternoon in a hospital to get that nasty burn treated when they'd rather return to the barbecue? "We look at a 20-minute turnaround from the time the patients walk in the door until they leave," says Hermanson. "It may take another five minutes if they need a test, or ten minutes for an X ray. But if the visit takes longer than that, it's time to open another center."

Which is just what Hermanson did. When the first Minor Emergicenter grew too busy in Pompano Beach, he and his three partners opened another one five miles away in Deerfield, Florida. Hermanson wanted the second clinic near enough to benefit from shared advertising but distant enough to avoid overtaxing the patient base.

Where You Want To Be

Location is as important to a walk-in clinic as it is to a retail store. In addition to considering what clinics are nearby, check out other medical competition, such as hospitals and primary-care physicians. Competition isn't always bad. If the emergency room in the only hospital in a five-mile radius is overburdened, your center may catch the overflow just by proximity. A dense population is important, but it should be the right kind of population. For example, Jerry Hermanson warns against locating in a retirement area. "The over-65 population has already established a relationship with a doctor, so they are low utilizers of emergency centers."

Hermanson also looks for a good industrial and residential mix, since Minor Emergicenter's employers refer 15 per cent of its patients. "We have an active marketing campaign to get work-related patients," he explains. "We provide a group rate for preemployment physicals, for example." While his company doesn't discount worker's compensation treatments, businesses often refer employees for minor injuries because the centers are convenient and swift. In a similar fashion, Minor Emergicenters also contact schools and camps to suggest students stop by for required physicals.

You might also lean toward a location that allows bold signs. If you're too discreet, patients who have passed your clinic a thousand times may not recall you exist as they drive the other direction to take care of that earache.

Health Fairs

Increasing chunks of health providers' budgets are going for advertising. Even hospitals dole out great gobs of money to bring in "customers" nowadays, and your walk-in service has to compete. Although Jerry Hermanson advertises in the Yellow Pages, the newspaper, and through direct mail, he says the best returns come through community involvement, such as participating in chambers of commerce health fairs.

Minor Emergicenters enjoy about 55 per cent repeat business, meaning more than half of its patients have visited the centers before. That's a fairly high statistic, considering most consumers see walk-in clinics as emergency facilities. But Hermanson says the staff physicians court the repeat business. "We make a point of following up visits with next-day phone calls" to see how an infection is healing, he explains. In the minds of entrepreneurs who are opening the ambulatory clinics at an increasing rate, patients are quickly accepting walk-in service as an alternative for ongoing care as well as emergency treatments.

35

Diet Clinic Provider

Job Description: *A diet clinic provider helps clients to lose weight through diet and eating strategies.*

- *Start-up cost as low as Rs. 5 Lacs*
- *Potential first-year revenues: Rs. 2.50 Lacs*
- *Breakeven time from initial investment: several years*
- *Excellent opportunity for people with physical disabilities*
- *No staffing required*

Behind every successful weight-loss clinic is a former fat person. After years of unsuccessful dieting, the typical entrepreneur found the secret formula to losing 50 pounds ... 75 pounds ... 100 pounds.... Once the dieter loses all that excess weight, the natural thing to do is to found a diet company or buy a franchise. In fact, knowing that previously overweight individuals understand the rules and can best empathize with their clientele, both Diet Center Inc., Rexburg, Idaho, and Fortune Life Center, Charlottesville, Virginia, sell franchises only to individuals who have completed their programs.

Sybil Ferguson, who founded Diet Center based on a strategy that helped her lop off 58 pounds, offers some clues as to why about 70 million Americans are overweight: "Ten years ago, the average man burned 3,500 calories a day; he now burns only 2,800 calories. Women ten years ago burned 2,400 calories daily; today they burn only 1,800. Based on these figures alone, a person could gain up to five pounds a month if his or her eating habits are basically the same as they were ten years ago."

"I Think I Can, I Think I Can"

While some diet clinics combine exercise with nutritional advice and others sell diet supplements, the majority stress behavior modification using individual diet counselors. The theory: "If you change your eating habits, you can become thin." Once they've provided hints on how to eat for health, the centers back up that message with loads of positive reinforcement and subtle peer pressure that comes with scheduled weigh-ins.

"We stress 'Breakthrough Thinking,'" explains Jeannie Geurink, who was a client with 100 pounds to lose and then a franchisee before she bought the Slender Center parent company in Madison, Wisconsin. A 256-page manual and individual counseling sessions lead Slender Center clients through FRIA, an acronym that stands for Focus (on how to change your eating behavior), Relaxation (you can't change your behavior if you're uptight), Imagery (imagining that you are thin motivates you to carry through), and Affirmation (think positive, you can do it!).

Diet Clinic Provider

The dilemma weight-loss centers face is snaring clients who have heard it all before. The typical customer, a woman under age 50, has been through numerous self-help diets in the past. None worked in the long haul, otherwise she wouldn't be 25 to 35 pounds too heavy, which is about average among Slender Center clients. Now you must convince her that your solution really will help her. "Our message tells people not to feel guilty about those times they tried and failed to lose weight," says Geurink. "Don't feel guilty about asking for help. Then we offer a written guarantee that, as long as dieters make no deletions, additions, or substitutions to our diet, they can lose two to three pounds per week."

Plan on spending as much as 25 per cent of gross on advertising and marketing when you're first establishing a reputation. Advertise in newspapers and the Yellow Pages, and possibly ra-dio and TV in markets where rates are low or where you can share expenses with other centers. Once you are better known in the community you can downscale your ad budget to 7 to 10 percent of gross, since most clients come through referrals from skinny customers.

Missionary work helps, too. Set up booths in health fairs or ask the local radio or TV talk show host if you might do a spot on nutrition. Also, more corporations are investigating "wellness programs." You can offer a corporate discount to attract employees.

Find Us If You Can

One reason you have to advertise so heavily involves location. Many diet clinics look for an easily accessible—but not terribly visible—site. This advice could change in the future if the heavy crowd becomes less inhibited about walking through the doors of a diet clinic. But many clients today "don't want to meet their neighbors when they go into a diet clinic," says Jeannie Geurink. "They have a fear of failure until they're about 20 pounds down." Geurink recommends a professional office setting near, but not in, a mall. "Even a back entrance or upstairs is okay," she says. Of course, the benefit of choosing a secondary rather than a prime location involves start-up costs. Depending on what backup materials you offer, even franchisees likely can hold initial capital in the $20,000 ballpark.

Your staff-to-client ratio depends on your market and the approach you take. Slender Centers usually begin with just the entrepreneur and a part-time counselor to handle the 30 to 75 clients that a start-up clinic might schedule per week. The weigh-ins, which range from twice a week to daily, usually last about 15 minutes, during which time the counselor discusses FRIA with the client in conjunction with the particular weight loss and problems encountered. Slender Center's fees differ from location to location. But in the Madison company-owned center, a ten-week program with daily weigh-ins costs around $600. Each client receives four weeks of stabilization counseling after the weight loss is achieved and six months of maintenance supervision at no extra charge.

What type of person makes a good counselor? If you're joining one of at least 15 franchise organizations, you can pick up a knowledge of nutrition and the basics of a particular program from them. Solo entrepreneurs can take nutrition courses at community colleges. Beyond that, "it helps to be outgoing," says Barbara Davies, who runs the Diet Center of Hunterdon in

Flemington, New Jersey. Barbara admits she was introverted un-til she lost 100 pounds in nine months with Diet Center before buying her franchise. "After losing all that weight, I really like myself—and others like me, too," she says. "That gives a person confidence."

Diet clinics have no fear that they'll run out of clients. Despite the growing emphasis on health, more Americans are overweight than ever before. Particularly as the millions of baby boomers age, pounds increasingly become a problem. "I can see acceptance growing every year since I first started," observes Jeannie Geurink. "People still have reservations about joining a weight-loss program, but that reluctance is declining. She also believes that the future trend will be for someone to automatically join a weight-loss center anytime they need to lose five pounds."

36

Medical Transcriptionist

Job Description : *Using a computer and transcription machine, a medical transcriptionist transcribes the medical records (letters, histories, physicals, progress reports, and chart notes) dictated by a healthcare professional.*

- *Low start-up cost*
- *Breakeven time from initial investment: rapid (one year)*
- *Future growth potential: high*
- *Ideal home-based business*
- *No staffing required*

Get me a medical transcriptionist stat!"

Okay, may be it's not exactly what the doctors on *ER* say, but it's not too far removed from what thousands of real-life physicians, nurses, and other healthcare professionals *are* saying today and every day. Faced with growing demands on their time, but still required to document all aspects of a patient's history, harried physicians are turning to medical transcriptionists for assistance. They are the unsung heroes of the healthcare industry, producing reams of legible, accurate medical documentation that physicians and others increasingly rely on. This dependence has made medical transcription a burgeoning industry—and, quite possibly, your ticket to establishing a satisfying and rewarding business.

Take Two CCs Of Typing And Call Me In The Morning

In 1986 Linda Jackie, a pianist and music teacher, purchased a word processing company in Montvale, New Jersey, called A Personal Touch. Although her instincts were good, her timing was bad. At the same time, personal computers became widely available, and suddenly all those customers who used A Personal Touch for typing their documents decided to do it themselves with their own PC. Jackie had to find something else for both her and her company to do—and fast.

Noticing repeated classified ads in the newspapers for medical transcriptionists, Jackle set her sights in that direction. At the time, there were no courses available to learn how to become a medical transcriptionist; you either knew how to type and understood the unique language of the medical profession, or you didn't.

Jackle had the typing skills but lacked the medical knowledge. However, with true entrepreneurial elan, she got her first job in the field by claiming to have five years' experience.

"She [the client] sent me a jiffy bag full of microtapes."Jackle laughs. "After I stopped crying, I bought a bunch of books and learned how to do it."

Getting her first job helped Jackie establish her business in the medical transcription field. Next she approached her family physician, told him that she was doing medical transcription, and was soon working for him as well. The company's biggest break came in 1990, when it successfully bid on a contract to do medical transcription for a local hospital. From this point the company grew steadily.

"A lot of it [growth] was by word of mouth," says Jackle. "Word of mouth happens. Doctors talk to other doctors; they go to the administrator of a hospital and say 'Who do you use [for transcriptions]?' The majority of our calls come in from one doctor who happens to know another doctor who we work for."

Depending primarily on word of mouth, A Personal Touch steadily expanded its customer roster. Today the business services approximately 30 clients, including several hospitals and multipractice medical groups.

Jackie estimates her company produces around 7,000 pages of medical transcription a month. She employs numerous medical transcriptionists, all of whom are independent contractors working from their homes.

A Burgeoning Field

During the past five years, Linda Jackle estimates her business experienced tremendous growth. Although some of it reflects the company's excellent reputation and high-quality documentation it produces, part of her success is attributable to the explosive growth experienced by the entire medical transcription industry.

One reason it experienced an upswing is that more doctors are utilizing transcriptionists. Insurance companies now demand clearly typed medical records to avoid deciphering a doctor's chicken-scratch handwriting. Hospitals and physicians in their own practice are discovering it's better to outsource their medical transcription rather than paying in-house staff to do it and worrying about staffing changes, illness, and time pressures. The advent of managed care and its voracious appetite for written documentation also has helped increase the need for medical transcription.

As a result, the medical transcription field is scrambling to find enough qualified workers to fill an ever-growing need. According to the American Hospital Association and the American Association of Medical Transcription, there is a significant shortage of medical transcriptionists in *all* settings, not just hospitals.

A Transcription A Day Keeps Bringing In The Pay

If you decide that typing and medical lingo are the perfect combination for success, there are a couple of ways to start a business in the medical transcription profession.

Before you take the plunge, however, you must be skilled at the keyboard and understand the often-arcane language of medicine. You also must be organized, dedicated, and able to work under pressure; doctors frequently wait until the last minute to dictate their material and then need it in a frantic rush—sometimes as little as two hours.

If you decide to set up your own medical transcription company, you'll naturally need a computer. It's not necessary to buy the most powerful, top-of-the-line model, because you're going to use it exclusively for word processing. Most transcriptionists use an IBM-compatible machine, with either WordPerfect or Microsoft Word. You'll also need a top-quality printer.

Along with a computer, you're going to need a transcription machine. Similar to a tape recorder, it has a foot pedal to adjust its speed so the typist can keep both hands on the keyboard. The machine plays the dictation tapes, which are generally micro- or standard size. Quite often it's possible to purchase used transcription machines through newspaper ads. Since you don't need an outside office or employees, your total start-up cost for this venture is around $5,000—all of it on equipment.

Some transcriptionists and transcription services have moved away from tapes and use digital "call-in" systems. Doctors dial into the system via telephone, dictate their notes, then hang up. The transcriptionist then accesses the dictation from the system. These call-in machines, while the latest in dictation technology, are extremely expensive, costing approximately $100,000 new. A preferred method is leasing (which is what Jackle does); a typical lease costs around $2,000 per month. With this method, you also need a special $1,200 telephone for accessing the dictation system.

Another possible expense is taking the certification program offered by the American Association for Medical Transcription, which costs $300.

Even with a leased digital call-in system and special telephone, start-up costs still shouldn't exceed $10,000. It's possible to see a return on your initial costs with either method in as little as one year's time.

Earnings vary in this business. If you get paid by the line, the fee is typically 10 to 12 cents per line. (The average number of lines per pages is 45.) if you get paid by the page, the fee ranges anywhere from $1 to $2.35 per page in dense metropolitan areas such as New York or Los Angeles. In Less-populated regions, the per-page rate is lower.

Eventually you can earn a good living running a medical transcription business, but Jackle warns that it's going to take time to build up your clientele and your cash flow.

"This is not the kind of business that you open up and immediately start making a ton of money," she said. "You can get there, but it's going to take a lot of hard work. If you do your homework you're going to make money—you're just not going to be rich overnight."

The Prognosis

While medical transcription appears to have a bright future, the one dark cloud on the horizon is the possible emergence of voice-recognition computers. Individuals in the field worry the industry could witness a severe impact if doctors can sit down and dictate their notes into a computer that will then "type" them.

However, problems with voice-recognition technology make this only a theoretical threat at this time. In addition, the attraction of medical transcription for physicians is they dictate into their telephone or a hand-held tape recorder, almost anywhere, such as their car or while in the elevator. Actually sitting down in front of a computer to dictate notes might take more time than most physicians have. Still, Jackle has a word of caution for future transcriptionists.

"If you're going to do this, get very good at what you do," she says. "With the advent of voice recognition, the mediocre tran-scriptionists will lose their jobs. We'll only need the ones who are really good, who can understand the doctors, have a good eye and good ear for grammar, and can proofread to make sure things are right."

If that last sentence describes you, then maybe it's time to scrub up and prepare to "operate" your own medical transcription business.

37

Carpet Cleaner

Job Description: *A carpet cleaner shampoos and cleans carpets for homes and businesses.*

- *Start-up cost as low as Rs. 3 Lacs (if leasing cleaning equipment)*
- *Potential first-year earnings: Rs. 10 Lacs*
- *Breakeven time from initial investment: extremely rapid (one month to one year)*
- *Ideal home-based business*
- *No staffing required*

When Bobbie Carter calls to estimate the fee for Carter's Carpet & Upholstery Cleaning Service, she has no guarantee she'll get the job. But she puts her equipment in her minivan just in case. Nine times out of ten, the customer can't resist Carter's enthusiasm : She's sure her cleaning method beats anybody else's in the small town of Franklinton, Louisiana. She clinches the sale by pulling out before-and-after photographs illustrating the miracles she performs. The pitch ends with Carter suggesting she start with just one room. If all goes well, she ends by cleaning carpets throughout the house.

Party Lines

Carpet cleaners say the domino effect doesn't stop with doing multiple rooms in the same house. Joe Wasson, proprietor of Hoosier Carpet Care in Rushville, Indiana, figures "one job well done equals three other jobs because word-of-mouth advertising works so well in this business." Bobbie Carter furnishes an example: "One day I was doing an estimate that led to cleaning the woman's carpeting. The mother-in-law was visiting and had me come to her house after I finished. From there, I did such a great job they asked me to do the carpeting at the jewelry store the daughter owns."

Carter solicits goodwill by leaving a thank-you note with every job and calling back the next day to make sure the customer remains pleased with the job. "I always mention my work is guaranteed and if you have a problem I'll come back."

Recommendations come only if you do a superb job, of course. So make sure you buy equipment capable of results. Joe Wasson stresses the importance of walking through a home with the customer before attempting any cleaning. "Let them know which spots won't come out, and they won't be disappointed," he suggests.

Even though word of mouth is the strongest business builder in this or any other industry, carpet cleaners say you drum up business any way you can, and different methods of securing clients work best for different entrepreneurs. One Colorado cleaner did his first carpet at the bank that loaned him the money to buy his equipment.

Carpet cleaners are split on the value of advertising, although most do some advertising. Bobbie Carter says her best inquiries come from simple three-line ads in the newspaper's classified section. "The ad costs just $26 a week, so one job pays for the ad and that job usually leads to others," she calculates. Carter's vivacity makes her a natural salesperson, and she uses her personal contacts to develop customer leads.

In contrast, Joe Wasson's more subdued personality means he relies more on advertising to pull in customers. Recently Wasson allotted fully 35 per cent of his gross—which amounted to $40,000—to advertise anywhere and everywhere. "I use radio, newspaper, leave coupons door to door. I donate my services to raise money for charity."

Wasson also pens a newsletter that he sends to customers every three to four months. "I tell what type of vacuum works best and how to take out certain stains by yourself. Getting my name to the customer periodically reinforces repeat business," he explains. He estimates that "60 per cent of customers whose carpets I cleaned a year ago have already called me back to do them again."

Households are just one type of home for carpets. The more ambitious carpet cleaning services send letters and make cold calls on businesses. Commercial accounts offer several advantages. Carpets in an office complex are often much bigger jobs than a single house. Also, restaurants or retail establishments need their carpets cleaned often, and you may land a contract that promises repeat business in exchange for a slight discount. Finally, says Bobbie Carter, "The people who work in a business often hire you once they see what a great job you did on the business's carpet."

How You Charge

Just as carpet cleaners differ in how they approach advertising, they also support two schools of thought on pricing. You can price either by the room or by the square foot. Joe Wasson says he switched from square-foot pricing to room rates to simplify matters. "I was charging about 12 cents a square foot. But I found I often had to make two trips: one to estimate a job and a second trip to do the job itself," he explains. "It was just too time-consuming." So he switched to a flat rate of $17 a room, which he says works out to around 9 cents a square foot. "I can offer the customer a better price and still make more money because I don't waste time," he says. Also, room rates make advertising more effective because many people have no idea how many square feet their rooms contain.

Bobbie Carter disagrees vehemently with Joe's room-rate reasoning, however. She says most people hire her on the spot so she doesn't waste many trips by estimates. Besides, "Is it a 9-by-12-foot room, or 12-by-24?" she asks. "People get mad if you quote them one price then try to charge more if their rooms are too big." Instead, she charges 15 cents a square foot when she doesn't move furniture and 22 cents when she does. "I only weigh 77 pounds," says Carter, who has to hire somebody to move the furniture if customers want rugs cleaned under the bed or behind the chest.

One attraction carpet cleaning offers is the relatively low entry cost. Since you work out of your home, you basically need equipment and a way to transport it. Usually the family car suffices in the beginning, so your budget will cover heavy-duty equipment, which can run several thousand dollars. "I arranged for a loan divided into 48 monthly payments of $107 each for $4,100 worth of equipment," says Carter. "But business was good enough in the first eight weeks that I made 16 payments and still put some money in the bank."

In addition to equipment, you also need industrial-grade supplies. Of course, you can buy supplies as you go, paying for the road eventually. them from cash flow. Carter used an income tax refund to stock up on $600 worth of cleaning fluids in order to get a bulk discount from the Von Schrader Co., of Racine, Wisconsin, which manufactures her equipment and supplies.

Von Schrader, which provides carpet cleaners who use its equipment with such backup materials as advertising and a tollfree number to answer any questions about carpet cleaning, says entrepreneurs average $30 an hour. Many carpet cleaners begin part time, moonlighting on weekends or evenings until they build enough reputation to quit a day job. Therefore, if you clean carpets part time—say 10 hours a week—you could expect to add $15,600 to your income, minus the cost of equipment and advertising. Full-timers who clean carpets 40 hours a week can gross $62,400. Of course, that kind of hustle leaves little time for such necessities as marketing and travel to and from each job.

Piggy-Back

No law says you have to stop with carpet cleaning. Upholstery cleaning is one natural piggy-back service that offers better profit margins even than carpets. "I see carpet cleaning as a way to get in the door," says Joe Wasson, who also cleans upholstery, cars, and full houses.

Another way to increase income is to add employees. Wasson recently invested $3,000 in a second set of equipment and hired an employee who has a car. "I make 10 to 20 per cent on the jobs someone else does, and still pay them a good salary," he says.

Adds Bobbie Carter: "I expect to have six to eight trucks on the road eventually."

38

Drycleaner

Job Description: *A drycleaner uses non-water-based methods to launder clothes that are* not suited *for conventional* cleaning *methods.*

- *Start-up* cost as *low as Rs. 3 Lacs*
- *Potential first-year earnings:Rs. 2.50 Lacs*
- *Breakeven* time *from* initial *investment: several years*

The drycleaning business mirrors the mood of the country. In the late 1960s and early 1970s, as America donned miniskirts and cut-off jeans, and as demonstrators took on political issues, drycleaning shriveled. People were not concerned with their appearance. Also, technology brought us polyester, the miracle synthetic that never sees the inside of a drycleaning plant.

Now, however, influenced by the "Dress for Success" ethic, Americans again long for creases in their trousers and blouses of real silk to offset their three-piece suits.

What's to keep the pendulum from swinging away from drycleaners? Simple demographics. Explains Marvel Zuercher, who runs The Habit Cleaners in Berne, Indiana: "Working mothers don't have time to iron even cotton clothes that you can wash." But isn't drycleaning expensive, compared with throwing the sweaters on the gentle cycle? What happens when the country isn't feeling quite so flush? Several franchises hedge by specializing in discount cleaning. For example, Clean'n'Press Franchise Inc., of Phoenix, Arizona, cleans any garment for 99 cents. But even traditional cleaners don't worry much about economic slumps. "No business is depression proof, but this comes close," says Ken Faig, director of education for the International Fabricate Institute (IFI). "In bad times, people don't buy clothes and have to keep the old ones in good shape."

Do It Your Way

That bigger picture of drycleaning may have been in the back of Marvel Zuercher's mind when she bought The Habit, but really she wanted a job. "I had been a librarian and teacher when I quit to have a baby," she recalls. "When my son went to kindergarten, I wanted to go back, but jobs weren't available. This business came up for sale, so I grabbed it."

Zuercher, with her sunny disposition and combative attitude toward such indignities as cooking grease on wool slacks, has a personality right on target for a drycleaning entrepreneur. "I'd always had some mechanical ability and an interest in selling, which fits in real well with what I do. I just about majored in home economics in college."

Running a drycleaner, she says, is almost an extension of the home: "I can keep my son near me. Brian has a corner of the office where he studies. Summers are slower, so I spend more time at home." True, drycleaners keep long hours, but the three trusted employees Zuercher inherited when she bought The Habit pinch-hit when she wants an afternoon off, and she shuts down entirely between Christmas and New Year's and during a slow week in August.

If you don't know anything about drycleaning, don't despair. Franchises welcome newcomers with open arms. For independents, the IFI hosts a three-week intensive course, and regional trade groups sponsor seminars. For example, the Neighborhood Cleaners Association, headquartered in New York City, spreads its 80-hour curriculum over 10 weeks.

Ambiance

There's no rule that drycleaning establishments have to be stark cubbyholes in rundown shopping centers. When The Habit's lease expired, Marvel Zuercher bought an 84-year-old carriage house. Her designer not only turned it into a modern drycleaning plant, he also added such touches as flower boxes and French doors that open onto a drive-under balcony. The brown-and-white barnlike structure reflects the Swiss character of the little Indiana town (population, 3,500). An *American Drycleaner* article praising the 1,800-square-foot structure, which won "Top Ten" honors in the magazine's Plant Design contest, noted its practical advantages: "Promoted subliminally are good looks, cleanliness, and the fact that people feel better when they know they look their best."

Modern equipment, which recycles the fumes and vapors, allows entrepreneurs to locate small drycleaners in previously unlikely settings, such as shopping centers. The *American Drycleaner* magazine, which estimates a typical plant at 2,000 square feet, tracks a trend to units less than half that size that require just one or two operators. Of course, you still need easy access to a parking lot because customers won't cotton to carrying their dirty laundry through a busy mall.

Such an environment costs extra, but you could lease and equip a modest location for *$96,000* to *$135,000.* If you decide to launder shirts as well, budget another $20,000 to *$25,000* for additional equipment. For operators who wish to have the expertise of a franchise outfit behind them, a few thousand dollars will give them an affiliation with a group such as Miami-based Dryclean-U.S.A., or One Hour Martinizing, which is headquartered in Cincinnati. To buy an existing business, figure on spending about one year's projected gross revenues.

The IFI says an average plant grosses *$191,666* a year. Without taking a salary, figure a pretax profit of *30* per cent, or $57,500—if you're average. Cash flow is good, since customers pay (in cash) when the work is done. You may have to bill if you line up large-volume jobs, such as cleaning uniform rentals, but your revenues will increase, as well. Also, decide whether your particular community will support facilities to launder shirts or dryclean furs. If you're unsure in the beginning, you can always subcontract that add-on business with another professional.

How To Pull Them In

Drycleaners don't budget much for advertising, unless they intend to lure customers from a competitor. But savvy operators increase business through education. Marvel Zuercher gives tours through her plant to civic and high school groups. "They see how we can clean better than they could at home," she explains. You could also give visiting lectures on topics such as "How to Care for Your Clothes."

Zuercher says the most important marketing tool is to let customers know you care about their clothes. She often jots notes on The Habit stationery explaining how customers might treat similar stains in the future. Or she just tells them when they come to pick up their clothes. "We educate customers so they'll be happier with their investment in clothes," explains the former English teacher. "For example, don't rub a silk tie when you get something on it—just blot it to absorb the moisture. Then take it to your cleaner." She also tells customers when they can wash garments just as well at home. "If they trust me to give them the right information, I may lose a particular sale, but I gain a customer."

39

Home Decorating Retailer

Job Description: *A home decorating retailer* sells paint, wall*paper, curtains, flooring, and other materials used to decorate a home.*

- Start-up cost as *low* as Rs. *10 Lacs*
- *Potential first-year* earnings: *Rs. 15 Lacs*
- *Breakeven* time *from* initial investment: *several years*

When Bill Elliot decided to begin laying the ground-work for his new life, he quits his job as a cable TV installer and went to work for the Benjamin Moore paint company. His friend and soon-to-be-partner Steve Huggins, a schoolteacher, had worked summers in a paint store. After a year, they had completed enough on-the-job education to open Upstate Color Center. Since the paint line they wanted to carry was already assigned in their hometown, they moved 185 miles to an untapped territory in Easley, South Carolina.

Upstate Color is one of almost a thousand home decorating centers that open each year. According to the National Decorating Products Association (NDPA), the industry rings up annual sales of $12.75 billion. Is now a good time to be in the business? "We've barely scratched the surface," says Bill Elliot.

Customers Coming And Going

Decorating centers draw customers from two sources: homeowners and the building trade. During strong building cycles, you can sell contractors items such as paint and linoleum, and offer homeowners curtains or blinds for their new windows. When high interest rates slow home building, many individuals remodel their old abodes. "Existing housing—most of it over 20 years old—is prime for new exterior and interior design," says a recent issue of *Decorating Retailer.* "And the new residents of these houses ... are profiled as vitally interested in fashionable home decorating."

The industry association says it takes about $100,000 to open a 2,500-square-foot home decorating store that expects to do at least $350,000 in annual sales by the end of its second year. Smaller stores, of course, cost less, as do shops specializing in one or two product lines, such as paint and wallcover-ings. But here's what the NDPA says the average store (which counts 38 per cent of its business in paint, 24 per cent in wallcoverings, 12 per cent in sundries such as drop cloths and paint brushes, 9 per cent in floor coverings, 12 per cent in window treatments, and 5 per cent in "other," such as picture framing, bath boutique items, and art supplies) should set aside:

- $15,000 for fixtures (you might shop for used shelving in good shape)
- $45,000 for inventory (some dealers offer "buy now, pay later" plans)
- $90,000 to *$120,000* for operating expenses during the first two years
- $30,000 to $60,000 for accounts receivable if you anticipate dealing with contractors or others who don't pay as they go

Home Decorating Retailer

Like most other retailing enterprises, a home decorating store takes several years to hit full stride. But the NDPA finds the typical dealer has *1*.8 stores and *$932,000* in yearly sales. You need the volume, because pretax profits average *$21,830.*

The Supplier Connection

While you carry hundreds of different items, you can get them from just a handful of suppliers. Bill Elliot uses just five for the 1,600-square-foot Upstate Color Center: one paint company, two brush manufacturers, and two sundry distributors.

Choose suppliers with care, because manufacturers can be particularly helpful when starting in the home decorating business. Some paint suppliers offer free dealer training courses and help with site selection. A few even help track down financing. However, experience can come only by working in a decorating center. *Decorating Retailer* advises, "If you have a difficult time finding an opening for yourself as a temporary and eager but ignorant deco center employee, contact major paint or wallcovering manufacturers and perhaps they can find a spot for you among the stores they supply."

Some suppliers also advise on store layouts. If you shoot for a homeowner customer base, you may want a pretty shop with model windows showing off the latest in woven verticals and a plethora of in-store displays. If your business comes from builders who buy in bulk, you might opt for a filled-to-the-rafters image. "Some people have a small display area and keep the majority of their paints in a back storeroom," says Bill Elliot, who estimates a 50-50 split between customers and contractors at Upstate Color. "We feel if a customer sees hundreds of gallons of paint, it *reaffirms* we're in the business."

Not Much Walk-In Trade

In areas where rents are high, many successful operators settle for an accessible, but not necessarily prime, location. "We're a block off the main artery," says Elliot. "If you have good products and good service, customers will find you."

Because home decorating products are not an impulse buy—and because profit margins are generally on the skinny side—many entrepreneurs restrict their conventional advertising to a Yellow Pages ad and sporadic eighth-of-a-page ads in the neighborhood pennysaver. If you advertise, be sure to inquire about co-op ad allowances from manufacturers. With their help, advertising may not be as expensive as you think.

Inexpensive marketing works well in the home decorating area. If you have a van, paint it with a bright logo for all the world to see. When the van isn't delivering valances and floor tiles, park where it's visible from a main drag. Contact area builders regularly to remind them you offer discounts for bulk buying. Bill Elliot also calls on local industry periodically. "They paint every year or two and we give discounts for large volume," he says.

40

Kitchen And Bath Designer

Job Description : *A kitchen and bathroom designer custom-plans and installs kitchens and bathrooms in homes.*

- *Start-up cost as low as Rs. 5 Lacs*
- *Potential first-year earnings: Rs. 8-10 Lacs*
- *Breakeven time from initial investment: two to five years*

You rarely see a bathroom without a Jacuzzi any more," says Ann Patterson, who launched City Design in West Des Moines, Iowa, alongwith her husband, Rick Martinez. "Sometimes you see one Jacuzzi for the parents and another for the kids. I did one $40,000 bath that we turned into a sunroom with skylights and curved glass walls. It had a sunken Jacuzzi, of course. And a fireplace."

Out Of The Water Closet

A fireplace in the *bathroom?* And not in Beverly Hills, but in *Iowa?* Needless to say, Americans have brought their bathrooms out of the water closet. And as for kitchens, well, we're putting in labor-saving devices such as microwave ovens meant to get us out of the kitchen. Then we turn our kitchens into entertainment and creativity centers by stocking them with televisions and range-tops that grill. If you want to do your Julia Child number, you can prepare anything from shish kebab to sashimi with professional-quality equipment. But 30-foot-long kitchens aren't just for cooking.

"Something's happened to the way we view kitchens and bathrooms," agrees Russell Platek, a certified kitchen designer and director of education for the National Kitchen & Bath Association (NKBA). As business booms for kitchen and bath designers, more people are setting up shop. "Last year alone our association membership grew by 15 per cent," he says.

You can enter the kitchen and bath business as a retailer, designer, installer, or all three. After Ronald Robinson had managed someone else's store for 15 years, he and his wife, Ida, set up Top Notch Kitchen & Bath Boutique in Mount Vernon, Illinois, primarily as a showcase of kitchen and bath equipment. "We do some installing, but an installation takes Ronnie three days to complete," says Ida. "That cuts into the time Ronnie has to sell on the floor." Product sales command a higher profit margin than design or installation because sales is less labor intensive. You can realize as much as 30 per cent of revenues as profit. As a result, Top Notch typically designs a kitchen or bath, measures and orders the equipment, and lets someone else worry about installation.

Using another approach, City Design relies as much on design and installation as product. You might have to drop profit margins by as much as 5 per cent to pay for the time it takes to install a kitchen or bath, but your overall fees can be higher because you charge for construction as well as products. Another source of income comes through designer fees: homeowners, architects, or contractors ask you to draw the plan but not to build it. On sales of $5 million, a large shop with several designers in a metropolitan area could see profits of $1.25 million.

Off (But Not Too Far Off) The Beaten Track

In either case, you must get the customer through your door. Instead of a slot in a high-rent mall, look for visibility with the kinds of customers you need to attract. City Design is one street away from the antiques district, an area with stores and restaurants where "people in the income bracket we serve go to play and shop," says Ann Patterson. These potential customers have seen City Design but don't drop in to browse because it's not on the main drag. "I cannot afford walk-in traffic," says Ann. "I figure to pay for my overhead, I need to average sales of $40 an hour. If I spend half of every day chatting with people who are not interested in buying, I can't pay that overhead."

Even though your average customer buys only once or twice from your shop, their purchase is a big one. Ann Patterson's kitchens average $15,000, and her typical baths cost $5,000. In a major urban area, the averages can be even higher. To make sure the people who put in a custom bath buy from you, it pays to advertise. Francis Jones, executive director of the NKBA, believes in marketing that encourages people to dream up their ideal rooms in the first place. "Our competitors do not come from our industry," he says. "They come from the auto, vacation, and investment industries," other businesses geared to high-income dreamers who eventually carry out their fantasies.

The NKBAs Russ Platek suggests that a mature design firm spend 3 to 5 per cent of its gross on advertising and a brand-new firm allot up to 15 per cent to get the name out. In addition to advertising in such places as symphony and theater brochures, City Design rides its manufacturer's cooperative plan to advertise on television. Ann Patterson also keeps close ties with architects who refer clients to her since few architects tackle her two specialties.

A Whiff Of Possibilities

Because each design is customized to fit a particular home's configuration and a particular homeowner's taste, "we see a product that's not even conceptualized until we do the work," says Patterson. Therefore, your showroom permits a customer to sense the possibilities of a truly interesting kitchen or bath. The NKBA says a minimum-size showroom would need 1,200 square feet, although Top Notch utilizes 6,800 square feet to accommodate its five lines. With just two manufacturers, City Design operates with under 2,000 square feet. Neither store warehouses items. Instead, both avoid high inventory costs by waiting for a customer down payment before placing an order.

A couple of tips on the showroom designs: If you plan to design and install, look for higher-end merchandise and ask for exclusive rights in your area from the manufacturer. "When you have to pay for design time out of the cabinet margins, there's no room for bidding wars," says Ann Patterson. Also, before putting in a sample room, ask the vendor how long till obsolescence: You can only hope for two years before models change. Stocking new appliances every year is common as manufacturers constantly update, but you can sell the floor samples. Cabinets are a different story since they must be custom fitted to exact measurements.

Professionals

Salespeople need to be experienced estimators. Most customers have no earthly idea what converting their dreary linoleum scullery into a cheerful dream kitchen will cost. There's no need to give firm figures at this stage, but you must be able to estimate based on the size and age of a customer's kitchen, the appliances needed, and the cabinetry he or she likes. Even in new houses, Top Notch will estimate off a blueprint, "but we won't order until we can measure a job," says Ida Robinson. "Contractors have a way of moving a wall a couple of inches, and that's enough to destroy the measurements."

Before going the extra steps of measuring and designing a kitchen, Ann Patterson asks for a $250 to $500 retainer, although she applies that fee to the final cost if customers buy cabinets from her. "I figure for every hour I spend with the client, it takes two to three hours of pricing, paperwork, and drawing," she explains.

To arrive at a close appraisal, the installer accompanies Patterson to estimate his time as well as the time for such sub-contractors as electricians and plumbers. After the installer determines labor and equipment charges, the customer receives a standard NKBA contract that outlines down to each electrical outlet what City Design will do.

City Design asks for 25 per cent of its fee when the contract is signed, 50 per cent more when construction begins, 15 per cent when the kitchen is in working order, and sets aside the last 10 per cent for contingencies. "Maybe a special-order tile didn't come in, or one cabinet came in damaged," Patterson explains. "By asking for our fee in stages, the client can't hold more than 10 per cent if something goes wrong.

No licenses are required to either install or design kitchens and baths. But you'll need some training. Auburn University in Auburn, Alabama, offers a bachelor's degree in the kitchen and bath field, which includes a minor in business administration. If you're not interested in a four-year program and already have a carpentry, engineering, or art background, check out the NKBAs home study and regional traveling courses for both designers and installers. The association even offers a certification in kitchen design.

41

Maid Service

Job Description : A *maid service cleans private residences.*

- Start-up cost as low as Rs. 20,000
- *Potential first-year earnings: Rs. 50,000*
- *Breakeven time from initial investment: extremely rapid (one week to several months)*
- *Ideal home-based business*
- *No staffing required (initially)*

With over 45 million working women in this country, is there any wonder that maid services are booming?

If you don't mind housework, there's lots to be said for running a cleaning service. "Getting started was so simple," admits Ruby Burgis, who left a personnel management position at Aetna Insurance to launch Personal Home Care in the Atlanta suburb of Norcross, Georgia. Her entry vehicle was an ad in the Gwinett County newspaper's classified section, which landed her "a tremendous response. There's such a need for domestic help," says Burgis.

And the potential? Solo practitioners can't shoot too high, probably no more than \$20,000 to \$30,000 a year. But add a few employees and let their brooms do the sweeping. If you spend your time managing others and rounding up jobs, you can keep 40 to 50 per cent of the take yourself—as profits. The only overhead you need worry about is advertising to collect both employees and clients, relatively simple bookkeeping, a few supplies, and insurance.

There are three aspects to running a maid service. In reverse order of importance,consider :

Next To Godliness

Cleaning

"Just because you know how to clean house doesn't mean you know a thing about the housecleaning business," warns a Chicago entrepreneur. "You have to know so much about managing—managing people, managing your time." The importance of delivering a clean house to clients can't be overemphasized, but polishing a house to a shine is the easy part. If you're diligent and pay attention to detail, you can accomplish almost any housekeeping chore.

The key to the cleaning business is organization. To clean efficiently, set and stick to a cleaning routine. Ruby Burgis devised a training program for her maids that begins with a session in her office. There each maid receives a manual Burgis wrote that walks them through the basics of dusting, vacuuming, glass polishing, and bathroom and kitchen scrubbing. Then she

accompanies them on their first job to teach by example. Admitting "I hate housecleaning," Burgis cleans right along with employees on their first house or two to show them her own methods. She provides a checklist for clients who want such extras as laundry or window washing, and tacks on extra charges.

Most operators swear by the team system. Two to four maids visit the same houses every week, so they become familiar with the customers' needs. The team divides the chores, rotating tasks among the members from house to house to reduce monotony. Ruby Burgis disagrees with the buddy system, however. "I want people to have their own personal housekeeper who would be in the house for several hours." A good maid can develop a following.

You can either furnish equipment and supplies or ask to use the customer's. Stocking your own cleaning arsenal ensures you have the best ammunition to clean with, and, except for a vacuum, which can cost several hundred dollars, supplies are inexpensive. However, an urban service that relies on public transportation might request that customers provide the equipment so maids won't have to drag mops on buses.

Generating Leads

Finding Clientele

You don't need 60-second spots on prime-time television; inexpensive advertising works just fine in the maid business. You can target specific audiences with flyers stuffed in mailboxes or mailed via zip code. Leave your number on the supermarket bulletin board. One-inch ads in the classified sections of neighborhood or pennysaver newspapers often provide the best leads. If you provide company cars, mark them with your telephone number and logo.

Maids, while no longer only for the rich, aren't for the lower-income brackets either. Target advertising to professional neighborhoods whose households earn $40,000 or more. Families need more help than do singles.

Follow up those leads promptly and at the customer's convenience, You may need to visit people on evenings or weekends to accommodate working people. Some entrepreneurs guess the price for the first visit in order to avoid the nuisance of an estimate trip, but "How can you quote standard fees when a three-bedroom, two-bath house can be 1,800 square feet or 4,000?" asks Ruby Burgis. Also, touring the house with the customer allows you to sell extras like carpet cleaning.

To price a job, have in mind an hourly fee per employee and guess how long a cleaning will take. Households with children or pets or collections of knickknacks require more time than homes of professional couples who like sleek, modern furniture and who travel constantly on business. Also, you can offer lower prices for weekly cleanings than monthly marathons, since the house had a thorough scrubbing just the week before.

Carry liability insurance to pay for any breakage. The larger maid services also are bonded to cover theft. Although she spends about $150 a month to blanket six employees with both kinds of insurance, Burgis says customers rarely ask whether she's covered. "You need the liability, but smaller services can usually just give references in lieu of getting bonded," she says.

While the bulk of your revenues will come from steady residential clients, you can also discover other sources of dirt to clean. For instance, unless you are very busy, don't turn down one-time cleanings for people who are preparing for the holidays; you can charge more for one-shot deals, and they sometimes blossom into regular arrangements once clients see how their houses sparkle. Be creative in your advertising. One service suggests gift certificates as presents for new mothers. Burgis does some offices for entrepreneurs whose houses she cleans; but she warns that heavy janitorial work requires contracts and a complicated bidding procedure. Also, network with people who have lots of houses to clean, such as real estate agents who might recommend you to clean houses before or after a sale. Or check with apartment contractors who need postconstruction cleaning.

The Maids

Employees-Getting Them and Keeping Them

Don't underestimate the frustrations here. Getting good, reliable people is tough, and you must constantly refill your employee ranks since turnover is notoriously high in this industry. Ruby Burgis uses the same newspaper to advertise for employees and attract customers. In addition, she asks workers to recommend friends who might want jobs. She also lets the state employment service know when she needs maids.

If you think hiring employees is tough, getting them to stay committed for a long time is tougher. "When a maid doesn't show up, I take the job," Burgis says with a groan. "In a pinch, I've used friends, boyfriends—whoever can help me out." Turnover is a fact of the cleaning entrepreneur's life. But some tricks of the trade make life a little easier.

First, make employees realize their importance. Some franchises issue uniforms to create a professional team spirit.

Second, don't be greedy. Remember, the housekeepers do the hard work, so pay them well. You can outpay most jobs that hire unskilled labor by offering a respectable $10 an hour and still keep an equal amount to cover overhead and profits. Since your maids likely subcontract as independent operators, you don't pay for benefits such as health insurance. Hint: Properly trained employees complete jobs more efficiently, which allows them to squeeze more houses into their cleaning schedule. Since you pay by the job, they make more money and therefore stay on board longer.

Third, offer flexibility. The maids with families particularly like part-time work. If you need more employees to work Friday afternoons, pay them a bonus.

The Matchmaker Approach

Ruby Burgis, who started Personal Home Care as a typical maid service, changed her focus to deal with the constant employee turnover issue. Now, instead of taking responsibility herself for maids who clean clients' homes, she matches maids and households. It works this way: After an individual answers her ad, Burgis trains the maid in specific houses that contract with her for services. After a two- or three-week training stint, during which time the maid gets a salary, the maid buys the rights to clean that house as well as others that Burgis lines up. If a home-owner decides within 14 days that the housekeeper is not up to par, Burgis finds a replacement. "A contract is based on the amount of monthly income it will bring," she explains. "If it's a weekly house that pays $50 for each cleaning, I charge $200 for that contract. If thge maid does fivee houses a week, the fee would be $1,000."

As a result of the new approach, Burgis still has to attract maids to train and customers to clean for, but she doesn't worry about a maid quitting after six weeks.

Meanwhile, burgis points out a side benefit of her business. Since she hates housework, she knows exactly whom to call when she wants her *own* house cleaned.

42

Water Conditioning Dealer

Job Description : *A water conditioning dealer sells products and systems, primarily to households, that remove contaminants from commercial water supplies.*

- *Start-up cost as low as* Rs. 50,000
- *Potential first-year earnings:* Rs. 75000
- *Breakeven time from initial investment: one year*
- *High growth potential*

American drinking water has been called a political time bomb. According to the 1997 National Water Quality Survey, one out of five Americans is dissatisfied with the quality of the household water supply. Even more revealing is that one out of three people surveyed believes that the water is not as safe as it should be.

Okay, Americans voice outrage that the H_2O flowing so freely from our taps may be poisoning us. But are we doing anything about it? According to the Water Quality Association's latest figures, the answer is a resounding "yes." The 1997 National Water Quality Survey found that 32 per cent of those queried currently use a home water treatment device other than bottled water, as compared to 27 per cent just two years earlier. But industry observers say we ain't seen nothing yet. RainSoft Water Conditioning Co., which franchises from Elk Grove Village, Illinois, estimates that less than 10 per cent of the market for home water treatment devices has been sated. That, say dealers, gives them a huge market as the country becomes more and more aware of the problem. More than nine out of ten households remain to respond to their promises of pure water. "Not every home is a potential sale," says Harold Posey, who operates Posey Fresh Water from Houston. "But nearly every home is."

It's A large Neighborhood

To show how much faith he has in the growth of his industry, Harold Posey invites competitors to move in next door, saying there's more than enough business to go around. Posey has installed at least 7,000 water treatment units in Houston since he began and insists his own market remains less than 10 per cent tapped. With reported sales of $3.5 million, he says he does better than 15 per cent pretax profits.

Harold Posey knew he was on to a good thing when he first discovered the water conditioning industry as a vice president at ITT Financial in Denver a decade ago. He was a banker back then, and, "when customers applied for financing, I would get a finance statement on their business. I reviewed finances for water conditioning companies each year and started noticing how fast these dealers were accumulating wealth. I began to compare them with other industries. The more I looked, the more intrigued I became."

Unable to withstand the lure any longer, Posey bought a RainSoft franchise in Houston, where he had once lived. "I remembered how bad the water was—and how dynamic the city." Those two elements convinced him to invest $50,000 to set up shop, which primarily involved marketing.

Even today, Posey budgets 12 per cent of gross for advertising and lead development, on top of what he spends on the sales staff's salaries. He builds sales through two approaches: telemarketing to generate leads, followed by direct door-to-door sales to nail down those leads. He turns a battery of six full-time and six part-time telephone operators loose to cold-call potential customers, such as upper-income households or businesses such as restaurants or drycleaners that need especially good water. Only after an operator gets a nibble does the 18-person sales force go into action. "That approach keeps the salespeople in front of qualified buyers," says Posey. "I don't send them to a house on stilts with chickens in the front yard because they won't buy the systems." An average Posey Fresh Water sale hovers around $2,500, which includes a system to soften the water, a drinking-water unit under the kitchen sink, and installation.

Unlike most products, you must customize each water treatment package to a particular client's needs. That means you have to test each tap, since additives differ by water district and household. But thanks to training available from vendors and the Water Quality Association, you don't have to be a chemical engineer to test the water or a mechanical genius to install the units.

You target two basic customers with water treatment equipment: residential and commercial. Most sales so far involve units to soften water and make it taste better. More expensive units can remove contaminants in drinking water, as well. "Most water supplied by municipalities in this country is potable—meaning safe," says Harold Posey. "But it's not palat-able-meaning it tastes *baaad.*"

Whether you approach a residential or a commercial customer, and whether that customer is interested in water treatment or water conditioning, you have three basic ways to make money:

- Sales
- Leases
- Service

Water Conditioning Dealer

Sales

To maximize your cash flow, try to sell products outright. Particularly in the early days, a rush of cash from a $750 reverse-osmosis unit feels real good going into the pocket. If you work it right, you don't even have to pay for the inventory until a customer places an order. If you sport a healthy credit rating, many dealers waive their fees as long as you stock equipment in a bonded warehouse. Of course, once it leaves the warehouse on its way to a customer, you'll have to cover the cost of the item.

Large industrial companies and businesses generally prefer to buy equipment rather than rent it. Buyers, they reason, claim depreciation as an expense and spend less in the long haul. In addition to contacting hotels and hospitals directly, you can call on contractors and engineers putting up new sites.

Businesses are particularly good customers for a couple of reasons. Sometimes fees top $100,000 on a single, large installation. One system to purify water for a hospital's kidney dialysis machine costs about $30,000, and a hospital usually buys more than one unit. Also, a business lead often means repeat business. A contractor who likes your water in a fast food operation might ask you to outfit a white-tablecloth restaurant as well.

Leases

"Renting is like prostitution: You sell it and still own it," Harold Posey says with a grin. It looks like this: You front the $400 to $500 equipment costs and charge customers $20 a month to use your unit. Within two years you've collected your entire investment. And, since those $20 payments come in indefinitely, everything else is gravy. "Leasing is going to be my retirement," says Posey, who hopes to increase his lease business from 10 per cent of sales to 30 per cent in the next year or two.

Homeowners in particular like leasing since the $20 monthly fees don't sting the way a $700 purchase does. Now that operators are selling more water treatment systems to middle-income Americans instead of just the wealthy, observers predict that leasing represents the wave of the future.

Service

One more way to build residual income involves service contracts. One out of every five Posey Fresh Water customers spends $10.50 a month on a preventive maintenance contract. Once a month, Posey's service department delivers salt, which is used to clean the units filters, right to the customer's door Posey Fresh Water also dispatches technicians to fix anything that might go wrong.

Posey warns start-ups not to promise service until they have the volume to support technicians. He also warns that maintenance headaches throb until entrepreneurs learn proper installation. Once you pass through the learning curve, though, service calls likely will diminish. "I have a lot fewer problems today than I did in the beginning, even though I have 7,000 accounts out there now," says Posey.

Water softening units have, until recently, been the staple of the industry. Now dealers sense an increasing willingness to invest in drinking water systems as well. That's good news for treatment companies, which can make bigger sales by offering both options.

43

Auto Detailer

Job Description : *An auto detailer completely and meticulously cleans the interior and exterior of a car, including such typically ignored parts as the engine.*

- *Start-up cost as low as Rs. 1 Lac*
- *Potential first-year earnings: Rs. 5 Lacs*
- *Breakeven time from initial investment: rapid (six months to one year)*
- *Excellent home-based business*
- *No staffing required*

During slack times when Peg Mosey sold Fords in Fort Wayne, Indiana, she wandered into the cleanup area to watch the staff polishing and vacuuming cars before putting them in the showroom. "I used to spend two to three hours a week cleaning my own car and I thought, if you use professional products, this is not hard work. It's just time-consuming."

One summer Peg borrowed $5,000, using a certificate of deposit as collateral. She paid $400 for supplies, and bought a buffer and a wet-dry vac. Then she plopped down rent money for the building that was to house her new auto detailing business. With what was left over, Peg bought signs for her own spotlessly clean five-year-old Grand Prix that displayed her phone number and address. Voila! Car Tender was in business.

The Old Jalopies Never Looked So Good

According to the Automotive Vehicle Manufacturing Association (AVMA), the typical passenger car on the road today is 7.5 years old, up from 5.5 years in 1970. That's the oldest average since the Korean War. People hang on to their cars because new ones are so expensive these days. According to the National Vehicle Leasing Association, leasing now accounts for more than 30 per cent of the average 15 million plus vehicles sold in the United States each year. And, whether new or old, the cars are being better taken care of. According to the International Carwash Association, today there are 22,000 car washes in operation, each serving an average of 71,000 cars per year.

But it costs hundreds of thousands of dollars to build a conveyor or brush carwash plant, and it can take years to recover your investment. Entrepreneurs like Peg Mosey have found an inexpensive way to enter the auto appearance field and are cleaning up. Instead of counting on high volume to bring in the bucks, they charge handsomely for doing an extraordinary cleaning job, one car at a time, by hand. Called detailing, the work they do would make a dress sergeant proud. "I shampoo seats, do the dash with Q-Tips, the chrome with steel wool," Mosey rattles off. "I completely dress the engine, treat all the rubber." Her 29-step process takes up to five hours per car and runs $125.

It's tricky, but you can also ride into the business by way of the executive parking lot. Some detailers outfit vans with the equipment they need and round up BMW and Caddy owners as they leave their cars on the way to board meetings. To set up a mobile shop, you need access to running water and permission from the municipality as well as the company whose lot you camp out in.

If you don't want to go it alone, you have the option of franchising. Boca Raton, Florida-based Tidy Car figures a new franchisee needs $75,000 to $85,000 to open its average 1,500- to 2,000-square-foot shops. That capital covers the $20,000 Tidy Car licensing fee and $15,000 for a store-opening media blitz as well as equipment, inventory, leasehold improvements, and payments on a courtesy van to shuffle customers in and out. Since Tidy Car gives you four weeks of training, you don't need to know the first detail about detailing before signing on. The parent company also teaches you related skills, such as how to install sunroofs.

From Volkswagens To Jags

independent detailers cater to several groups: luxury car owners and corporations, car dealers, or limousine operators to whom image is everything. peg Mosey has rubbed sparkles onto everything from a 67 Corvette show car where she spent days removing every last speck of dust from the engine (the owner won top points in the cleanliness category), to a 23-foot travel trailer. "That was like cleaning someone's apartment. It took six hours."

Mosey recommends passenger cars go through the complete treatment twice a year and offers discounts to regular customers, such as the Mercedes owner who has her wash his car once a month. But "car dealers are my cushion," because they provide steadier work than the individual owners of Porsches and BMWs. Mosey spends a little less time detailing a dealer's used car but charges just $65. "They can usually get a couple of hundred dollars more at auction for repossessions if the cars are really clean," says Mosey.

In addition to the luxury and car-dealer market, Tidy Car considers all of the 201 million vehicles on the road its potential customers. To entice such volume, it charges a little less than most independents and advertises a lot more heavily. Its franchise material also notes this: "There are many nonretail ar-eas where significant revenues can be generated, such as insurance companies (i.e., flood-damaged interiors), commercial fleet accounts, institutional and government accounts, body shops, car rental companies, and new-car dealers who may purchase Tidy Car services at wholesale prices for resale to new-car buyers as part of their option package."

Gary Goranson, then a regional sales manager for Magnavox of Canada, began Tidy Car 15 years ago. He originally sold his car-polishing and detailing services from a van parked on the street. Tidy Car's more than 400 locations still offer those services, along with such extras as window tinting, rustproofing, and sunroof installations. Goranson's theory: Once you get customers in the door, why stop with just cleaning their cars?

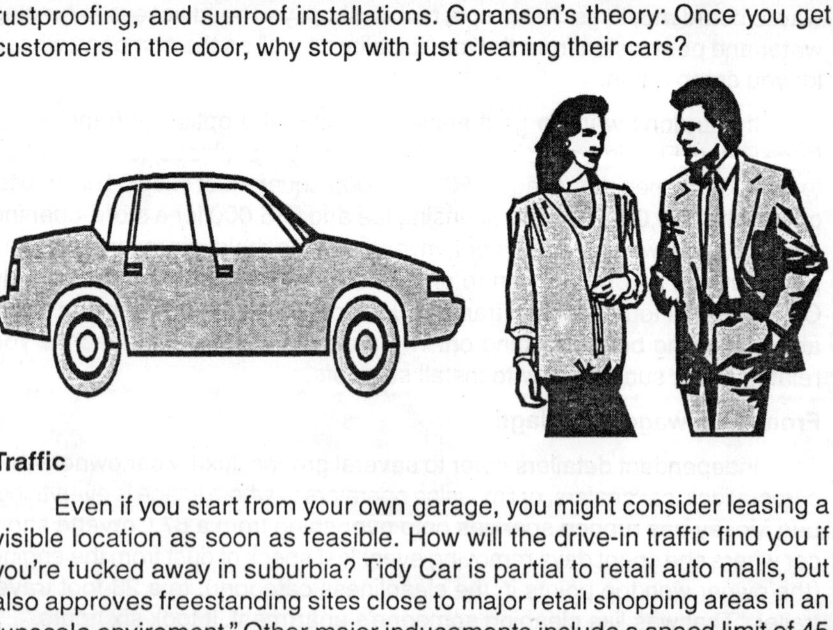

Traffic

Even if you start from your own garage, you might consider leasing a visible location as soon as feasible. How will the drive-in traffic find you if you're tucked away in suburbia? Tidy Car is partial to retail auto malls, but also approves freestanding sites close to major retail shopping areas in an "upscale enviroment." Other major inducements include a speed limit of 45 mph or less (so drivers have time to see the prominent sign as they pass) and a daily traffic count of 20,000 vehicles.

Although it buys the old saw about location, location, location being the three most crucial aspects of success, Tidy Car says "the next three factors, in order of importance, are advertising, advertising, and advertising." Marketing is even more important if you can't afford a prime Main Street address. Peg Mosey uses flyers, newspapers, magazines, and TV, and gave away a detailing job as a promotion in a radio station tie-in. Tidy Car insists new franchisees set aside $15,000 for a splashy opening ad campaign and follow that up by budgeting 5 to 10 per cent of revenues for advertising on a regular basis. Don't be afraid to call car dealers and other potential corporate clients and offer them package rates. The worst they can say is "No thanks."

In her first year in business, Peg Mosey hired an employee to buff the cars and still netted $15,000. She is bullish on the future, noting "the consumer market hasn't been tapped." While the government won't let Tidy Car talk about profitability since each franchisee differs, a spokesperson allows this: "Most of the [older] dealers are remodeling and building new Tidy Car buildings-and buying new cars and boats for their families."

44

Beauty Saloon Provider

Job Description : *A beauty saloon provider performs various services to enhance personal appearance, including haircuts, makeovers, pedicures, and manicures.*

- *Start-up cost as low as Rs. 50.000*
- *Potential first-year earnings: Rs. 2 Lacs*
- *Breakeven time from initial investment: several months to several years*
- *No staffing required (initially)*

I remember a woman who had horrible eyebrows." Erika Zimmerman, proprietor of Erika's Hair-Um, Inc., in the Chicago suburb of Darien, shudders. "The arch made her look so stern, so I asked if she found it easy to make friends. She was distant with me, too, but she admitted she'd always had a hard time with people.

"Well, I told her there was nothing wrong with her face," continues Zimmerman, lacing positive reinforcement along with recommendations that she reshape the woman's eye-brows. "I said her face was classic, but her eyebrows gave her a domineering look. You know, that woman was so grateful! She said, 'I've had to go through my whole life without someone pointing out what a simple change in appearance could mean!' "

One-Stop Beauty Shopping

Observers suspect beauty shops of the future will fall into two camps: franchises that offer low-cost haircuts and deal in volume; and full-service salons like Erika Zimmerman's that provide, along with cuts and perms and coloring, such specialties as eyebrow arching, skin care, manicures, body massages, and even fitness facilities. According to Business Information

Services, the average salon pulls about 31 per cent of its gross from haircuts, 17 per cent from perms, and 30 per cent from hair coloring. That leaves *22* per cent from other areas, including nail care, retail sales, and skin care. (In addition, many of the country's *150,000* hair-care salons that do not offer additional services themselves rent space to concessionaires.)

But the dependence on hair care alone appears to be changing. For example, *Modern Salon* says 54 per cent of those salons that offered manicures increased their nail-care business during a one-year period. Of course, you can still start with just hair care and grow. But you should have a good idea of which path you want to pursue, since growth will depend on one of two approaches: Either you must pull in lots of customers for hair care, or you can sell more services to fewer customers. Your pricing, your advertising, your equipment purchases, even whether you choose to start as an independent or a franchise may all depend on which star you shoot for.

More evidence that "full service" is replacing strictly haircutting comes from the 1999 Job Demand Survey conducted by the National Accrediting Commission of Cosmetology Arts and Sciences (NACCAS). The survey found that 70 per cent of salon owners classified their salon as a full-service shop, while just 13 per cent considered it as a haircutting salon.

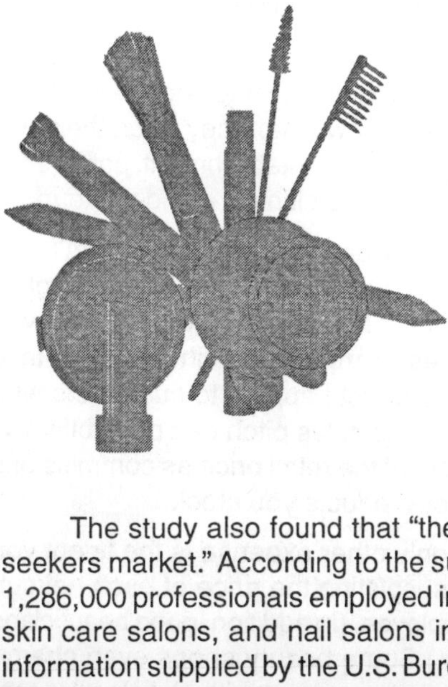

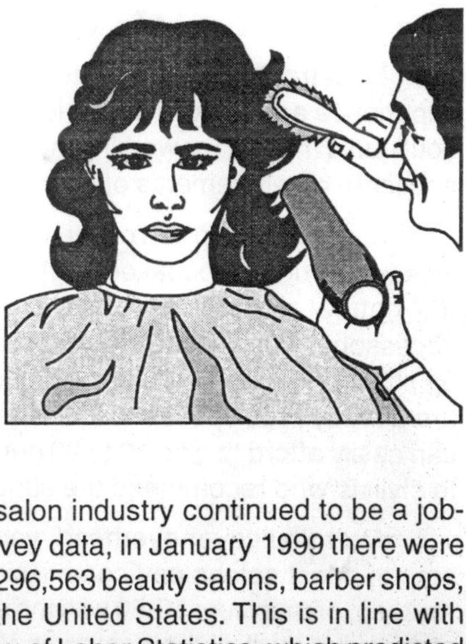

The study also found that "the salon industry continued to be a job-seekers market." According to the survey data, in January 1999 there were 1,286,000 professionals employed in 296,563 beauty salons, barber shops, skin care salons, and nail salons in the United States. This is in line with information supplied by the U.S. Bureau of Labor Statistics, which predicted that "employment of barbers and cosmetologists is expected to grow about as fast as average for all occupations through the year 2006. Increasing population, incomes, and demand for cosmetology services will stimulate job growth."

Erika Zimmerman gambled on the supermarket over the fastfood approach when she spent $100,000 to create Erika's Hair-Um in a former residential site, In addition to equipment purchases for six hair stations and a skin-care and steam-and-massage room, the cash went for visual effects. Zimmerman gutted the house, knocking out the attic to create a cathedral ceiling and skylights. She also landscaped the outside with pine and apple trees. The entrepreneur felt that establishing a special ambiance would alert customers that she was more than the traditional beauty parlor. "When I opened, there was no such thing as a total-concept salon under one roof," Zimmerman says. "Still, many beauticians haven't visualized the upgrading of the industry." Has the gamble worked? Evidently. Zimmerman estimates half of her $157,000 gross comes from skin and nail care.

Where The Cash Comes From

Your first expense goes not for your own beauty boutique but for your training. Although all states require cosmetologist to be licensed, the qualifications necessary to obtain a license vary. Generally, a person must have graduated from a state-licensed barber or cosmetology school, pass a physical examination, and be at least 16 years old. Public and private schools offer last 6 to 12 months. An apprenticeship program can last from 1 to 2 years.

Most freshman beauticians sign on with an existing shop both to gain experience and to build clientele who will follow when they open their own boutique. While you're working in someone else's establishment, polish skills and learn other elements of your trade, such as skin care and makeup.

A well-run shop can cover rent, utilities, and miscellaneous costs (such as advertising and bookkeeping) through retail sales. Many salons neglect the natural add-on business of selling shampoo, makeup, and even accessories such as jewelry and scarves. Margins are high, the items take up little space, and carefully selected products appeal to customers who are already predisposed to look stylish. The sales pitch can be subtle. You can easily afford to give 10 to 20 per cent of the retail price as commissions to stylists who recommend the superior products you stock.

After you cover overhead, your only other expense is the talent you employ. Most salons pay commissions, splitting the price of each haircut, makeup, or manicure 50-50 with the employee. (In addition, good beauticians often pull a third of their salary in tips.) Some beauty shops even charge stylists for supplies. Another approach is to contract with stylists who rent space from you and charge their own rates.

Depending on your salary arrangements with employees—and whether you count your own paycheck as an expense—expect to keep between one-third and one-half of the fees you collect as profits.

Selling Beauty

Beauty salons typically advertise in newspapers and the Yellow Pages or hand out flyers announcing specials. But letting the services sell themselves is your most effective marketing tool. You can do this in three ways:

- Make each element of your boutique visible. "A customer having her hair permed will see another who's having a body massage and realize how relaxing that looks," observes Erika Zimmerman. "It's contagious. She asks for a massage, too." Ask stylists to recommend manicures while they're coloring a client's hair; throw in a bonus to the employee who generates the most nail business of the month.
- Build steady clientele. For example, instead of selling a facial here and there, package treatments. Zimmerman offers a five-treatment skin-care special for $155 and points out to customers that, if paid for separately, it's a $260 value.

Also, you can call on groups such as nursing homes and offer to do their hair at a discount during slow morning hours. And don't neglect your contacts. Zimmerman sells gift certificates to a plastic surgeon and a cosmetic dentist. "When they're finished with patients, they send them to us for a complimentary treatment," she explains.

- Involve your customers as salespeople. Some promotions are apparent to the customer. You can give away a free manicure with every three friends the customer brings in. Your other marketing partnership with a customer is less conspicuous—but more effective than any advertising you'll ever buy. Namely, get your customers to recommend your establishment. Hair-Urn's skin-care business boomed when Zimmerman packaged treatments not only because of the perceived value, but also because results are much more obvious with weekly skin care than with sporadic treatments. Customers sign on for repeat packages and act as walking billboards. Their friends remark on the glow, and clients recommend Zimmerman.

Knowing the value of word of mouth, Zimmerman and her five stylists take pains to teach clients how to care for their new hairdos or show them how to perform at-home skin-care techniques. The longer customers look good, the longer their friends will ask for recommendations.

45

Vocational School Operator

Job Description : *A vocational school operator teaches job skills and prepares students for a host of occupations.*

- *Start-up cost as low as Rs. 8-10 Lacs*
- *Potential first-year earnings: Rs. 10 Lacs*
- *Breakeven time from initial investment: six months to several years*

Donald Beardsworth likes to say the secretarial students he attracts at the International Business College in El Paso, Texas, and its six Southwestern branches "qualify for everything but the IRS." About 80 per cent pay for 100 per cent of their tuition through government loans and grants; many students are on welfare and some lack high school diplomas. A few have college degrees but can't find a job. "My philosophy is to give them six to nine months of training, period. If they don't have a high school diploma, we give them a GED [general education diploma] prep course and take them to the testing center so they get their equivalent. We get them off the welfare rolls and onto the tax rolls."

Educating The Public Privately

Like Don Beardsworth, most presidents of vocational and trade schools are pragmatic sorts. But you don't have to scratch too deep under that tough exterior to find caring educators who provide the computer-repair or truck-driving education a public school doesn't. Proprietary schools supply about one-half of the postsecondary vocational education in this country, according to the Association of Independent Colleges and Schools, an accrediting body. As high schools move further to basics (reading, writing, and arithmetic), their curriculums have even less room for typing, bookkeeping, auto repair, or electronics.

The market for vocational school graduates remains strong. According to the Career College Association's *Private Career College Fact Book 1998-99,* the 725 member institutions that belong to the group educate more than a quarter of a million students annually for employment in more than 150 occupations.

Workers' desire for a fast education is tantamount to a hunger: the recognition being, to put food on the table, the breadwinner needs to acquire new skills. Displaced assembly-line workers learn to repair robots. Former steelworkers learn to retrieve information from databases.

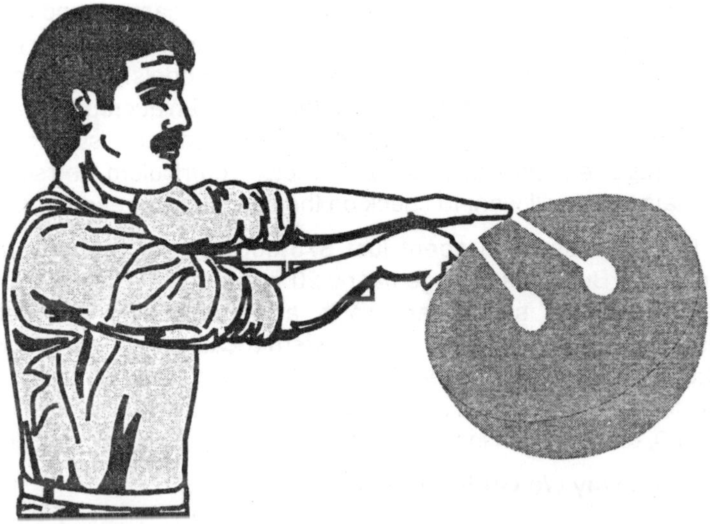

To Start Or Buy

Despite the need for private-sector education, starting a school isn't easy when you factor in paying rent, recruiting teachers and students, buying equipment, and winning accreditation. (The exception may be small cosmetology schools that take just a handful of students at a time. Start-up costs are minimal, and the school receives income from cutting customers' hair as well as from tuition. The drawback? Cosmetology schools operate in a highly competitive field.)

For the most part, "It's easier to start by purchasing a school,' says Joseph Thompson, president of Antonelli Institute of Photography and Art, a Plymouth Meeting, Pennsylvania, school that offers two-year associate degrees in photography, art, and interior design. He explains that the accrediting groups will not consider a school until two to three years after start-up. And even then a school must prove it is financially stable to get a stamp of approval. Why is accreditation so critical? "Students cannot get government funding unless the school is accredited," Thompson explains, noting about 40 per cent of his students receive grants or loans. "And if you attract affluent students whose parents pay the tuition, they look for accreditation to make sure you're giving a good education and getting jobs for the students."

Thompson, a former photo-lab operator, says to check the *Wall Street Journal* ads and business brokers to see what schools are on the block. Costs vary, depending on whether the school has a campus and how much equipment it owns. A school that teaches medical technicians, for example, pays more for teaching tools than a school for models. But, as a rule-of-thumb, expect to spend $1,000 per student to buy an accredited institution. In addition to students, your purchase price also buys such assets as instruments or equipment, a library, instructors, curriculum, and sometimes real estate, so you'll want to check on the conditions of each.

Don Beardsworth spent just $75,000 for the then 75-year-old International Business College nearly 20 years ago. "When I took over, it had 154 students," says Beardsworth, a former banker who worked in admissions departments for two mid-western vocational schools. "Now we've got 1,900 students and seven locations. I wouldn't take $3 million for the school today." Recently the school made 8 per cent pretax profits, or about $480,000, on $6 million in tuition revenues.

This Is The Way We Go To School

Because you offer fast education, those students you inherit when you purchase a school won't be with you for long. Don Beardsworth starts new classes every three weeks and must replace his entire student body every six to nine months. Therefore, advertising and recruiting are crucial. "The main school has 600 students and 5 admission specialists," he explains. "They go to high schools to give demonstrations and explain financial aid. They invite students to come for aptitude tests." (About 5 to 7 per cent don't pass.)

Schools with high class turnover usually budget 10 per cent or more of revenues for advertising: newspapers, radio, direct mail, even TV. Afternoon television soap operas could be renamed "trade school traumas" considering all the vocational-school advertising breaks.

Above all, recruiters sell students a new life after school—a new job and a new career. "You'll be out of business real fast if you don't place your graduates," warns Beardsworth. International Business School has at least one job developer on each campus who constantly calls on employers to line up interviews. Placement is why people pay $10,000 for a two-year education at Antonelli instead of about $4,000 at a community college, adds Joe Thompson. "We tell students we teach more, faster. We use the latest techniques. Our graduates go out and start their own photography studios or get good jobs."

To keep that competitive edge, a school needs two things good instructors and up-to-date equipment. Trade schools generally offer instructors and administrators at least competitive salaries and benefits. Since trade schools are more involved with recruiting and placement than their public sector cousins, you may need one administrator for every instructor on board.

Keeping Current

Look at your market frequently to see what changes are taking place, and change your curriculum accordingly. For example, many southern California schools give business courses in Asian languages. All executive or medical secretaries who graduate from International Business College can operate word processors and input data. An adequate response to the business environment requires having the latest teaching equipment. You don't have to buy it, however, since many manufacturers offer lease packages. Don Beardsworth says he spends about $150,000 to outfit each new 50-student branch school. As long as you keep the same curriculum and student-teacher ratio, branches automatically receive accreditation if the parent school has passed muster.

What about the future of trade and technical schools? Proprietary schools receive much of their tuition indirectly through government funds to students, and no one knows from year to year what Washington has in mind for students. But increasingly, older Americans are switching careers after their first choice fails them in some way. More and more, they look to private education to help them make that switch.

46

Wedding Consultant

Job Description : *A wedding consultant helps a bride and groom plan either all or any part of their wedding.*

- *Start-up cost as low as Rs. 25,000*
- *Potential f first-year earnings: Rs. 1 Lac*
- *Breakeven time from initial investment: rapid (one year)*
- *Future growth potential: high*
- *Excellent home-based business*
- *No staffing required*

It's a sad but accurate commentary on modern life that everybody's busy nowadays. Between work, business trips, shopping, meeting friends, managing schedules, and the 1,001 other details that people deal with every day, life often seems to fly by in a blur.

With all that going on, who's got time to plan a wedding and deal with florists, caterers, dressmakers, musicians, printer, limousine drivers, photographers, and everyone else involved with making wedding magic? The answer is the wedding consultant.

For nothing more than a moderate fee, a wedding consultant will make all those problems go away for the prospective bride and groom. While the future Mr. and Mrs. count down toward the Big Day, a wedding consultant tackles the seemingly insurmountable mountain of detail that needs to be resolved before that day arrives. While the wedding consultant is down in the trenches, dealing with fussy florists and jaded caterers, the happy couple float blissfully above the fray.

Is it any wonder that more and more brides-and grooms-to be are clamoring for the services of qualified wedding consultants ... and that the wedding consultant field is booming as a result?

"People e-mail me through our website [all the time, saying]: 'I want to become a wedding consultant. How do I do that?'" says Rosanne Falduti, executive director of the National Association of Wedding Professionals, Inc. The association receives several calls a month inquiring about becoming a wedding consultant or planner.

Although it may seem as if the wedding consultant profession is relatively new, actually it has been around for some time. Its roots are in the field of event planning; once you've planned a major trade show and figured out the logistics of where and how to get a gigantic arch made out of 10,000 balloons, it's not too great a stretch to organize a beautiful wedding.

However, the field has become more prominent in recent years, due to several factors. One of these is the increasingly frantic pace of life. Many people can't even cook for themselves at the end of the day, let alone tackle a strategic nightmare like planning a wedding.

"Life has gotten so hectic," Falduti says. "People just want someone to come in and take over."

But even more critical to the burgeoning popularity of wedding consultants is the removal of mothers from the equation. Years ago, when the majority of women stayed at home, planning their daughter's wedding was the ultimate event in the life of many mothers.

Today, however, the typical mother-of-the-bride is more apt to be working or pursuing her own dreams and ambitions. With a mother's schedule often just as chaotic as her daughter's, it's easy to see why the client rosters of wedding planners are growing.

Flexibility Is Key

A wedding planner must be versatile. He or she must be prepared to do whatever the client wants, from planning the entire wedding to just organizing a small part, such as the flowers or the photography. Wedding consultant Sue Totterdal offers several options to prospective clients.

"I have three packages," says Totterdale. The first is similar to a consultation, in which, for $45 per hour, she sits down with the client and points the way toward getting the proper vendors.

The second and most popular package is more inclusive. For $600, Totterdale recommends vendors, makes certain that everything is running on schedule, and ensures that the ceremony rehearsal, the rehearsal dinner, the reception, and other events all go smoothly.

The third package is the most inclusive and the most expensive. Totterdale handles every detail of the wedding, leaving the bride and groom little to do but show up on time and exchange their "I dos." She prices this service similar to a gratuity, charging 18 per cent of the total cost of the affair. With the cost of an average wedding between $20,000 and $25,000, the fee generated by this third package can be substantial—particularly if the happy couple adds a tip, as often happens.

Location, Location, Location

However, a word of caution before you run out and get your 'wedding consultant" business cards printed: Not every part of the country is fertile territory for this type of business.

"Using a wedding planner is a demographic thing," Rosanne Falduti pointed out. "If the area can afford it, then they'll use it more than the areas that can't afford it."

Where you're located also affects the prices that you can charge. Totterdale says that if she lived in a more populous area, such as Miami, she could raise her rates to be comparable to what others in the area charge.

"You have to keep it [your rates] competitive," she says. "I found out that if you charge by the hour, or charge a per centage [of the total wedding], nobody will hire you. They want to have a fixed cost."

Cool Under Pressure

What qualities make a good wedding consultant? One of the most important qualifications is having a good, solid background in the hospitality industry, so that you can handle the logistical arrangements that a wedding requires. There are so many aspects to planning a wedding that a novice can't hope to know them all—and that's exactly what clients will be counting on you to provide.

Hospitality industry experience also gives you familiarity with vendors, and knowing which are reliable and which aren't is critical to the success of both your job performance and the wedding itself. Vendors are just as eager to please wedding consultants as they are the bride and groom, because they know that reputation is everything in the wedding business.

"They [the vendors] know that if they don't show up on time, if they're not ready on time, then I'll never use them again," Totterdale says.

A wedding consultant also has to be fast on her feet and be able to adapt to any situation without panicking or disturbing the ceremony that's going on around her. In a pinch, Totterdale has fashioned a bride's throw-away bouquet from individual flowers and a piece of ribbon when the florist forgot to provide one and also cooked nonstop for several days when a brides mother forgot to get a caterer.

It goes without saying that a wedding consultant has to be a detail-oriented, organized person. You also have to be an even tempered, "people person," someone who can get along with the diverse personalities of brides, grooms, mothers, mothers-in-law, vendors, clergy, and a hundred other people.

Networking Is Key

Networking skills are essential to succeeding as a wedding consultant. Business associates give you referrals and vice versa. Having a strong network within your local wedding industry can make or break your business. Just ask Sue Totterdale.

Before starting her own event planning/wedding consultant business, Totterdale and Co., in 1995, Totterdale was the executive catering director for a major hotel in her area. When the hotel expanded its activities into weddings, Totterdale gained both the experience and the contacts that helped her business thrive when she went out on her own.

By her own account, Totterdale has done over 800 weddings. Currently she handles about two dozen weddings per year, although she admits that if she pushed, her reputation is such that she certainly could take on more clients.

"This is a wonderful home-based business," Totterdale says. Although some consultants who combine weddings with other services, such as event planning, have an office, many others, like Totterdale, operate out of their home.

What makes the wedding consultant business even better is that it requires little in the way of special equipment, so start-up costs are low. A good computer is necessary, one with a color monitor, color printer, and powerful-enough modem to hasten Internet access and downloads (for all those color pictures of flower arrangements and cakes that the bride saw in some magazine). To facilitate customer communication, an e-mail account, cellular phone, and fax machine are also necessary.

Subscriptions to the major bridal magazines are also important to a wedding consultant, since brides-to-be read these publications and reference items they see in them. Additional start-up monies should be allocated for brochures, business cards, and other marketing expenses. Registering for and attending bridal trade shows is another necessary expense, because it gets your name out and your face known, and keeps you in touch with trends and new vendors.

So if you've got a hankering to get folks hitched, the wedding consultant business may be right up your "aisle-way."

47

Real Estate Agent

Job Description : *A real estate agent sells homes, commercial establishments, and other types of structures.*

- *Start-up cost as low as Rs. 35000*
- *Potential first-year earnings: Rs. 3 Lacs*
- *Breakeven time from initial investment: six months to one year*
- *No staffing require*

When you bought that colonial last year, one of two thoughts undoubtedly crossed your mind. Either "I'm sure glad that's over!" or "That was an exciting experience.... It might be interesting to be a real estate agent."

You're not alone in wanting to enter an industry so tied to the American dream of owning one's own home. The National Association of Realtors counts approximately 1 million real estate agents. These agents have their hands more than full, thanks to a robust economy and low interest rates that have fueled the housing market to explosive new levels. In June 1998, according to the federal government, sales of new homes climbed 3.8 per cent to a record 935,000-unit annual rate. This was the fastest pace since record keeping began in 1963, said the Commerce Department. While observers expect sale of commercial properties to suffer during the next few years because of tax law changes, real estate agents expect home sales to remain strong. Regardless of what interest rates do, we still see a strong demand for housing," says Elizabeth Duncan, director of media relations at the National Association Realtors, "Households are still being formed and they need a place to live."

A Two - Year Runway

Because real estate is a regulated industry, the entry path is well marked Although exact requirements differ depending on the state where you practice, you must to follow three steps to open your own brokerage firm:

- Licensng. Community colleges and universities offer evening or night courses to prepare you or several weeks or months to take your state's test, which leads to a license.
- Apprenticeship. After you get a license, you sign on as a salesperson with an established broker for two years or so, a step most states require. During your training, you learn what the schools don't even attempt to teach you, so choose your mentor carefully. Not only should you look for an agency with abundant

listings so you can make a livining while you learn the ropes, you also should ask about benefits such as in-house training programs. "Most agents are independent contractors who set their own hours and are their own bosses—under a broker's guidance,'" explains John Major, a Coeur d'Alene, Idaho, broker. Agents get paid on commission, so put aside some money for groceries, rent, and so on to tide you over until your first sale. While commissions differ depending on the sale price of the house and the amount of advertising the client requests, residential commissions average 6 per cent.
- Brokerage. Many agents never take this step, but if you want your own office, you'll probably be ready to become a real estate broker after a couple of years of apprenticeship. The state licensing board looks at your performance record—the number of listings

you've handled and the sales you've closed—and may set requirements for continuing education. Now you can hang your own shingle and hire other sales agents if you wish. You can opt for a simple, one-person office or a computerized, multiperson franchise. (Currently about 18 per cent of all agencies are franchised.)

If you want to offer elaborate enticements to bring in buyers, such as Video listings and limousine tours, factor those costs into the start-up budget. You also may want to set aside money to design a website and advertise your own agency, as well as the houses you sell. Many brokers routinely distribute newsletters or flyers to homes in their territory in hopes of someday picking up the sale when the owners decide to move.

People make fortunes by building large real estate brokerages. But according to the Department of Labor's 1998 *Occupational Outlook Handbook,* the average salary of a full-time real estate agent was $31,500 in 1996. The middle 50 per cent of agents earned between $20,500 and $49,700. The top 10 per cent earned more than $75,400, and the lowest 10 per cent earned less than $12,600.

Technology is also affecting the real estate profession, particularly in the area of start-up costs. Whereas the cost of opening a one-person agency might have been as little as $1,000 a decade ago, today's beginner is likely to spend about $4,000. Why? Because besides the usual office equipment, experts advocate that first-timers get a digital camera, computer, cell phone, e-mail account, and website, as well.

According to those who generate salaries way above the norm, the best brokers have three things going for them : product knowledge, a willingness to hustle, and an inborn sales ability.

Know Your Business

Product knowledge boils down to understanding your market, the particular ranch or split-level you represent, and, perhaps most important, the financing climate.

The albatross hanging around the neck of every real estate agent is interest rates. Even when money is plentiful and consumers can borrow at reasonable rates, today's real estate agent must understand the thousand-and-one financing techniques available. Those who don't risk attracting home buyers who can't find the money to buy a home. But if you're savvy, you may be able to steer buyers into financing packages that will let them buy even in difficult times. For example, you might explain the benefits of seller financing to a couple who could afford to accept monthly installments on the sale of their home.

"Agents don't just talk the financial lingo but actually act as a go-between between the lender and buyer," says Elizabeth Duncan. "The agent has to understand the implications of a mortgage. Would a couple be better off with a 15-year mortgage that they can pay off faster with a lower interest rate? Or would lower pays over 30 years be better?" Bone up on current financing by talking with area bankers and even take courses if necessary. Most large franchisors provide continuing classes in financing techniques.

"A smart real estate agent may not know every financial structure available," admits John Major, "but knows where to look to find financing." He says good agents in his small Idaho town keep in touch with up to ten lending institutions. "I've seen agents fail because they make only one phone call to a banker who won't lend to the customer. Then they just give up without calling more banks. There are lots of reasons why banks won't loan money, so you have to know everything about the bank and about your client." For example, some banks shy away from commercial loans, and the client may want to turn that quaint Victorian into a restaurant. Or possibly the client forgot to tell you he is unemployed, so meeting the monthly mortgage may be iffy.

Lenders will jump at the opportunity to talk with you, either in their offices or in yours. "After all," says Major, "the bank is in the business of lending money." A chat every six months suffices in stable periods, but you'll have to gauge the current financing climate.

Hustling

Next comes a willingness to devote time and energy to your practice. Not only must you unload your current listings in the least time possible, but you also must line up a steady stream of new clients. You must be visible: An attractive office on Main Street will draw more buyers and sellers than a dilapidated back-alley storefront. Check with the local government to see the ratio of realty offices to houses before setting your sights on than others. a particular site.

Once you're established, don't wait for clients to sniff you out. Call and write area homeowners to offer free appraisals. Send postcards to everyone within a six-block radius when you get a listing. Even if they're not in the market to sell this month, that family with the Cape Cod may remember you when the They all nee time comes.

Empathy

Finally, those who succeed in the real estate business display a natural affinity for buyers and sellers. If you have sold cars or insurance or dresses, you have a leg up in the real estate business. Although a home is the biggest purchase most consumers ever make, "sales is sales," insists John Major.

In addition to uncertainties about the flow of credit, a few other outside forces rock the real estate business from time to time, so an even disposition and a supply of Rolaids make life easier. Notably, even in the best of times, the industry is seasonal. "We do a tremendous business in the spring and summer when everything's beautiful," says Major. "But we only sell to skiers in the winter."

The best agents make the most of drawbacks, planning winter vacations or using slack times to take—or give—courses in various real estate activities. For example, some states require a different license to sell industrial or commercial property as a major part of your business.

While anyone in realty decries the notoriously cyclical nature of housing, Major insists the business isn't much worse than others. "Housing fluctuates to the economic pitch of the nation. When everything else is down, so is housing. But there's always a market, even in economic downturns.

"Consider the supply-demand factor," he continues. "There will never be any more land created than what we have now. But everyday, more babies are born. New families are created. They all need housing."

48

Children's Clothing Boutique Retailer

Job Description : *A children's clothing boutique retailer stocks unique, high-end clothes for kids.*

- *Start-up cost as low as Rs. 5 Lacs*
- *Potential first-year earnings: Rs. 10 Lacs*
- *Breakeven time from initial investment: several years*

Today's upscale children's retail market is a shopkeeper's fantasy come true. As discounters clothe the masses and department stores scrape margins on midprice points, children's boutiques flourish by offering $150 Giorgio Armani blazers in size toddler 2 or $650 Krizia sequined "cocktail" dresses for the under-six set. And 200 per cent markups on $900 christening gowns can cloak a lot of mistakes.

Demographers and social scientists say the American baby boom generation is bringing up its own babies with panache. With mother working, modern parents possess the money (and perhaps the guilt) to buy their kids the best, including the best clothes. Two sets of statistics suggest that the population of children is growig ad that an increasing number of parents can afford to cloth their darigs with the help of Ralph Lauren and Liz Claiborne:

- The increasing preteen population. The Census Bureau counts 44.7 million children under age 13. Whether the birth rate continues to climb or not, existing kids need a fresh closetful of clothes every year to grow into. In response, the children's clothing market has been growing faster than a five-year-old grows out of his or her jeans. According to Reuters Business Report, in 1998 children's clothing sales earned $30.1 billion, a jump of 3.8 per cent over 1997 and an 11.5 per cent increase over 1996.

- Affluence. The IRS tells us that 14 million households (16 per cent of the U.S. population) have incomes of $50,000 or more. In addition, the government counted 10,800 individuals with annual incomes of $1 million or more.

Kiddie Cachet

"I cater to—I hate to say it—yuppies," admits Dorothy McNish, who named her Little Rock, Arkansas, boutique after granddaughter Elecia Michelle. "People want top quality for their children—something everyone else doesn't have. These women waited longer to have children. They've been in the workforce and have money to spend. They don't think twice about spending on their children. When they see what they want, they buy it."

Indeed. Dorothy does carry a line of Philippine smocked dresses in the $32 retail ballpark. But bestsellers include $80 to $350 French and Italian matching sets and "little dresses" for up to $800. Three years after start-up, Elecia Michelle was grossing nearly $20,000 a month and Dorothy was close enough to profitability to taste it.

Doris Cerutti, the grande dame among pricey children's clothing shopkeepers, allows that Cerutti's "used to be practically alone. Now there must be 20 children's shops in a 20-block radius." But for Cerutti, on the upper-crust, Upper East Side of Manhattan, competition has been healthy as business has continued to grow. In her case, a shop on every corner merely legitimizes the trend; parents accept a $120 price tag on a pint-size Burberry raincoat without blinking. Meanwhile, numerous affluent areas still lack a glitzy kids boutique, forcing moms (and grandmoms) to make semiannual pilgrimages to Madison Avenue or Rodeo Drive.

Discounting the hordes of wealthy, middle-age matrons who decide it would be "fun" to open a "sweet little shop," one consultant claims some successful shopkeepers live better than heads of large department store chains. "If you're an astute merchant and religious about working, retailers can live like barons," he insists.

Image : You Are What You Wear

Because you must locate in affluent areas to be near your clientele, rent may be on the high side. Your most expensive element in start-up, however, will be inventory. A very small boutique can go easy on the decor and squeeze in for $60,000 or so. But opening a bigger store with adequate stock in an urban highrent district may cost $250,000 or more.

If you want to operate an exclusive children's clothing store, you must look the part. The most important aspect of image is simply the merchandise on the floor. "Make a statement with your clothing," insists Doris Cerutti. If you intend to sell top-of-the-line clothing, "don't reach out for the masses," echoes Dorothy McNish, who worked in ladies' and children's stores before opening her own boutique. That's not to say you shouldn't stock basics like overalls and jeans, but make them unique since no boutique can compete with K-Mart on prices. "We're not a museum," says Maggie Chafen, who carries $24 Esprit short sets as well as $300 Joan Calabrese dresses at her Dottie Doolittle boutique. "San Francisco residents are not kings and queens. Real people don't send their children to school in $200 dresses, but they want one for parties."

Like other apparel retailers, children's merchants spend a lot of time scouting out new merchandise. Chafen, who opened Dottie Doolittle fresh out of business school, estimates she spends $150,000 annually to stock her 2,000-square-foot store by shopping Europe twice a year as well as New York. Dorothy McNish not only filled her store but also decorated it on a $62,000 shoestring. Acknowledging it's vital to keep a full stock, she and her husband, Bill, "do" New York markets four times a year, and Dallas, home of another major merchandise mart, once. They hit the local boutiques as well as the apparel shows to see what competitors sell.

Doris Cerutti advises new shops to "get attached" to a buying office. For a stiff fee, these professional clothing buyers, most located in New York, will help determine the number of items you need in each size, the amount of inventory—all manner of things.

Vendors also court the boutiques, making client rounds once a season. McNish credits designers with providing helpful hints and putting her on the track of other sources of merchandise. It won't hurt to ask for exclusive rights to a line within your trading zone. You might even get them.

Image : We've Got The Look

The other component of image is the shop's decor. Rugs and mirrors create enough of a look for some retailers, but exclusive boutiques need a one-of-a-kind look that would impress an interior designer. Dorothy McNish has thought out the 1,200 square feet of Elecia Michelle, complete with "pale *gray* carpeting and pale, pale, pale pink walls," in minute detail. Take just the window display, for example: "We're in an old bank building with windows from the roof to the ground. A banister identifies the display area and keeps children out of the window. We lay merchandise on an easel and a white bench. Stuffed animals sway on a little swing when the air conditioner blows. I always keep ferns or fresh flowers or decorated baskets in the windows."

However, remember that children (and their parents) are your customers and strive for a comfortable, safe setting. "I hire people who like kids," says Maggie Chafen. "I don't want a tense atmosphere." You surely want toys for the kids to play with and to strive for subtle childproofing: Hang rather than fold merchandise for easier maintenance; dangle those charming mobiles high from the ceiling where kids can see but not touch them.

We Do It All For You

Upscale clothing stores for all sizes exude an almost snobbish pride in their service. Create a personal relationship with customers through such touches as alterations, gift wrapping, delivery, and maybe even special ordering. "In department stores you find your clothes and bring it to one of *14* cash registers,' says Doris Cerutti. "We're the opposite. We have one register and 14 salespeople. Our customers feel it's important to have someone help outfit their child in 13 minutes so they can get back to their apartment or country house." Steady Cerutti customers buy from their own salesperson, who is familiar with their children's sizes and tastes.

Even smaller shops like Elecia Michelle, which Dorothy McNish runs with just two saleswomen, see one-on-one attention as crucial. "When we get a shipment, we call a customer to say we have such-and-such. 'Would you like to come in?' Then we put that merchandise aside. People spend *$600* to $1,000a trip. I couldn't survive without the call list."

Doris Cerutti goes one step further: Her sales *staff* delivers samples for customers who like to shop at home.

The question remains: Will today's affluent moms and dads abandon upscale children's boutiques and designer clothes from Betsey Johnson in favor of JCPenney and Oshkosh? The editor of *Kids Fashion* doubts children's clothing will ever be the same: "Women learned to dress when manufacturers first began mass production of clothes. Men caught on in the 'S0s when they got beyond black suits and white shirts. The only thing left was kids—and Europe has been way ahead of us for nears.

"Whether the boom will cotiue, no oe kows," he says. "But the tred is here to stay."

49

Florist

Job Description : *A florist sells flowers and houseplants, creates floral arrangements, and offers a variety of other products and services relating to flowers and plants.*

- *Start-up cost as low as Rs. 1 Lac*
- *Potential first-year earnings: Rs 20,000 per month*
- *Breakeven time from initial investment: several years*

When a florist thinks of heaven, Holland comes to mind. "You imagine bicyclists carrying a loaf of bread and a bunch of flowers," says Marcia Schaaf proprietor of Schaaf Floral in Minneapolis.

In fantasizing what could be, consider that the average European spends $50 on flowers every year, compared to just $20 spent in the United States. But there is hope: The Society of American Florists (SAF) reports that posies are much more popular than they used to be. The total retail sales of floral items has surged to $15 billion.

Season by season—or rather petal by petal—Americans are developing a love of flowers. Tradition continues to dictate floral displays at holidays and such festive and somber events as weddings, proms, and funerals. But the real sales increase comes from Americans' increasing fondness for occasional arrangements gracing dining room tables for no particular reason at all. Citing the ad campaign launched by the Society of American Florists, Drew Gruenburg, SAF director of communications, says Americans today are more likely to "Give Flowers to Someone Special: Yourself."

Artists Beware

While the future of the flower business does sound rosy, florists average yearly revenues of around $209,182. Of course, some florists can tap larger markets. C. S. Cosentino's single, super-market-size shop, Cosentino's Florists, in Auburn, New York, brings in more than $500,000 annually. Ken

Royer's Flowers Inc., with 11 units throughout Pennsylvania Dutch country, generates $6 million in annual revenue. "The margins are there," says Royer. "All you have to do is get enough volume."

C. S. Cosentino, who also consults, warns would-be florists that "if you're an artiste—if you love flowers—stay away. If you're a businessperson who enjoys flowers, you have a chance." You must first and foremost recognize that you're in a business to make money, not flower arrangements. Strive for volume through advertising and location and trim costs through business savvy.

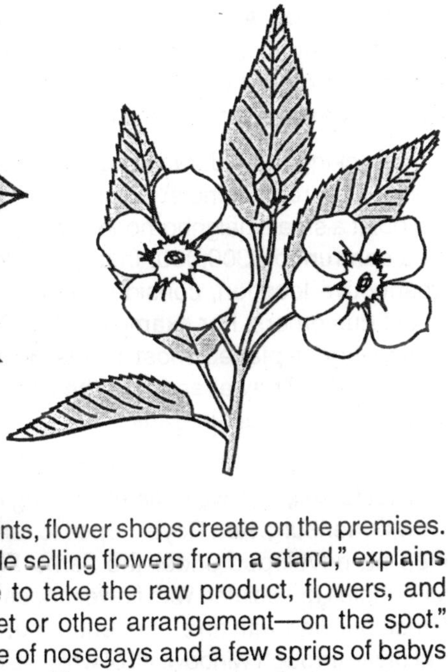

Unlike other retail establishments, flower shops create on the premises. "Flower shops are not Eliza Doolittle selling flowers from a stand," explains an FTD spokesperson. "You have to take the raw product, flowers, and manufacture a product—a bouquet or other arrangement—on the spot." Thanks to the florist's skill, a couple of nosegays and a few sprigs of babys breath become a special anniversary gift.

Because of such variables as labor talent and product perishability, it's hard to control markup. Ken Royer's solution to the problem is an assembly-line approach that has earned him the moniker "the McDonald's of the Flower Industry." During holiday periods, Royer employs 40 people to create designs in a central location. He posts a "menu" of arrangements at each store and then advertises specific items such as a Daisy & Mini (carnation) Basket. This way he cuts labor costs, saves money by buying in volume, and passes the savings on to his customers by selling many flowers with price tags well below the usual $18 to $20 minimums set by competitors. For example, Royers chain sold 1,400 Candlelight Centerpieces for $12.50

each during one Christmas season. While a single store can't match his volume, it can adopt a modified version of Royer's assembly line. Offer fewer arrangements, but promote those so you sell baskets and baskets of each item.

Shaking Out The Cobwebs

Until recently, the traditional florist aimed at reducing over head rather than building business. Take advertising. While the 3.5 per cent of sales that Ken Royer devotes to direct mail, newspapers, and cable TV isn't overly generous by other retail standards, it's about 2.5 per cent more than most florists set aside. And florists generally ignored the rule of thumb that location holds the key to success. In fact, since customers traditionally ordered most items over the phone for delivery to a hospital, the practice was to pick the least expensive site available.

Bucking the old traditions, modern florists are trading up to the high-profile, high-rent districts, which is pushing the cost of entry higher. You still can outfit a small, neighborhood shop for $50,000, but really elaborate urban sites can run to $300,000. In addition to scouting out the clientele in your prospective location, consider the other businesses in the area that will attract customers. For example, C. S. Cosentino reports that a successful Florida florist placed most of his 30 shops within a quarter mile of a McDonald's. "They already did the site selection for him," he explains. That florist basks in walk-in traffic.

The industry also is polishing its interiors. "The florist has a beautiful product to sell, and we're finally putting it where the public can see it," says Drew Gruenburg. Ken Royer hopes to rent franchisees a $225,000 prototype shop he developed under the name Flower Link. Compared to the dark cubbyholes associated with flower shops of the past, this store is astounding: a brick building with an atrium entrance, exposed wood ceiling, mezzanine, and drive-through window, all of which is splashed throughout with the colors of hundreds of flowers, of course.

The flower industry offers more start-up help than most small-business fields. Consultants, colleges, and trade schools offer both design and business courses, and numerous publications publicize the latest industry developments. FTD and Telefloral, the two largest wire services, offer management as well as creative advice through hundreds of seminars. (Wire services aid shops in fulfilling the 15 per cent of business that comes from out-of-towners. The customer simply contacts a local florist, who calls the head office of the wire service he or she subscribes to. The wire service relays the order to a member in the distant town, and a clearinghouse settles accounts between the parties once a month.)

The Basics Of Juggling

Entrepreneurs point to five different areas in which you need to develop skills to successfully run a flower shop.

1. Selection and care of your product. "Trial and error is expensive when you deal with perishables," warns C. S. Cosentino "You must know how to handle flowers—how to cut them underwater, which preservatives to store them in, a myriad of things." If you're big enough, you can order flowers directly from importers, local greenhouses, and growers in the California and Colorado "flowerbaskets." However, most small- and medium-size firms secure their lilacs and birds-ot-paradise through wholesalers.

2. Flower arrangement. Although both art and science combine to create a centerpiece, ironically, design skills may be the easiest to learn. Scores of community colleges and even some four-year colleges offer courses.

3. Customer relations. While all retailers deal with customers florists encounter people at such emotional times as weddings and funerals. You must react sympathetically to a bereaved relative one moment and hold the demanding hands of a parent of the bride the next.

4. Delivery. In the beginning, you can sign on with a delivery pool or hire a part-timer with a station wagon. However, costs mount as volume grows. Marcia Schaaf, who owns five delivery vehicles, also subscribes to a pool whose driver drops orders outside her normal zone for a fee.

5. Collections. Some florists honor just the major credit cards, but those with house cards say the paperwork and cost of collection is worth the trouble to build a loyal clientele. "We mailed out 15,000 of our own cards when we opened our last store," says Ken Royer. "It's an invitation to buy in the store."

Schaaf says 70 per cent of her credit purchases are on her own card. Because in-house cardholders represent a sort of inner circle of ready-made buyers, many florists direct advertising pieces to them. A computer that spews out address labels allows Schaaf to send out periodic circulars to her 4,000 or so card-holders.

The Competition

New variations of the flower shop are appearing all around: supermarkets, stands at the entrances to subways, and mall-based kiosks. Besides the 27,341 retail florist shops in the United States, the Society of American Florists estimates that there are 23,000 supermarkets with floral departments and 10,857 retail nurseries and lawn and garden supply stores that also sell the beautiful buds. Instead of cutting into the floral pie, however, these retailers create consumer awareness of flowers for every-day and might even signal a need for a good florist shop in an area.

Despite the notion in the industry that competition is healthy, C. S. Cosentino recommends that new florists specialize. He points to a florist who advertises to the 8,000 to 10,000 offices in Syracuse, New York. A bevy of weekly customers builds volume quickly. Marcia Schaaf likewise developed a "good corporate base" in Minneapolis and traces her best leads to her community involvement. Since she is on the board of the city's chamber of commerce, all the businesses know her.

Another lucrative specialty is parties. Approaching caterers to discuss your strengths doesn't hurt, although Schaaf says a little reputation goes a long way in the party game. "Consider each wedding you decorate a showcase for your talents; do something unique that caterers will remember the next time they recommend a flower shop."

Like other retailers, florists work long hours and weekends. Nevertheless, says C. S. Cosentino, "because what we do is a craft, the hours don't seem as long."

50

Professional Women's Clothing Retailer

Job Description : *A professional women's clothing retailer sells female attire for the workplace and other formal occasions.*

- *Start-up cost as low as Rs. 5 Lacs*
- *Potential earnings: Rs. 5 Lacs*
- *Breakeven time from initial investment: two to five years*

The story of Just Grand, a clothing store for professional women located on Grand Street in St. Paul, started out well, just grand. Then its partners hit a too-fast expansion period that put them on speaking terms with Chapter 11. But the moral to the story—hang on and learn by one's mistakes—makes for a happy ending. "We can't expand now because we have so much debt to service from our previous attempt," says partner Marilyn McNutt. "But once we pay that off, we will grow. We know now where to avoid mistakes, and we also know from the success of the remaining store that the concept is valid. We'll do lots better next time around."

McNutt and her three partners can hardly he blamed for pursuing their concept so enthusiastically. Looking at the changing role of women, it seemed they couldn't lose. The U.S. Census Bureau reports 36 million American women work full time outside the home. Increasing numbers of these women abandoned the "pink ghetto" of low-paid clerical jobs to enter the executive ranks. And the one piece of advice every business woman's magazine shouts to this day is: Use your newfound income to dress the part.

Just Grand opened intending to dress the executive woman with panache, "The professional woman doesn't want navy blue suits with white shirts and red ties," says McNutt, who taught sales marketing before joining Just Grand. "She wants to look good without being too traditional. She wants something classy that she can wear for three or four years without tiring of it."

Home Sweet Home

After four years, based on the reception working women gave to the pilot store, the partners decided to grow. Within nine months, *they* opened seven stores. The next year, only the original remained. "You always hear about the importance of location," says Marilyn McNutt. "But unless you experience a bad site, you can't believe how important location really is."

The concept of an executive clothing store for females has one drawback: Department store buyers also want to dress the professional woman. Recognizing that competition, you've got to locate smack dab in the middle of lots of professional women; know your merchandise and present it in a way that makes boutique shopping convenient, and offer superior service.

Just Grand's most serious expansion mistake involve locations. The entrepreneurs spent a lot of money getting what they thought were good locations in expensive shopping malls, But they found that not just *any* foot traffic will do. Shopping malls in the suburbs may be great for a cruise-wear shop, and might stock some executive wear if the demographics are mixed, but malls that draw primarily from middle-class neighborhoods may not attract enough women who need $75 silk blouses. You may be better off in the financial district of at least a midsize town, but check your customer base carefully McNutt recommends camping out in a location before committing to a professional woman's boutique. Study the type of shopper and ask the landlord to produce demographic information, including the type of households and income levels in the area.

Malls are okay if your customer can get in and out easily and enough executives frequent the area. It may be a stereotype, but the traditional female executive isn't a shopper. She wants to get in, buy her wardrobe, and get out. So don't settle for a middle-of-the-mall spot that means she has to park six blocks away. This convenience is one of your prime draws over depart went stores.

Paying for the location that will make a professional womens clothing store work admittedly will make a dent in your purse Your merchandise doesn't come cheaply, either. Plan on a start up ante of at least $200,000. And like other clothing stores, margins are tight. The only way to get rich in retail clothing is to build a reputation or open several stores. While they are still paying off their debt service, Marilyn McNutt and her partners squeeze salaries in the $20,000 range and haven't declared a profit. But if your debt load is less, partners might figure on a $30,000 to $40,000 salary and profits of $6,000 to $25,000, depending on the size of your store. A solo owner might bump up the salary, although another salesperson will have to come aboard.

Your Merchandis

Just as your customer hasn't the patience to discover a shop hidden in a less-than-prime location, she doesn't want to wade through racks of clothes to find a hidden treasure. Your clothing should portray an image. Display clothing already accessorized with a suede belt and pearls. Don't be mysterious. Know exactly what appeals to your customer and don't stock lots of superfluous items in an attempt to be all things to all people. After all, that's what department stores are for.

Just Grand has fine-tuned its merchandise mix since those early days. Separates (blouses, skirts, and jackets) make up 60 per cent of the shop's sales, dresses account for 15 per cent of the business, and the rest goes to accessories. "Our customer doesn't really buy suits," says McNutt. "She wants the flexibility to mix and match, and she'd rather buy a skirt and jacket that go with other pieces of her wardrobe." Also, "our customer is

older [typically in the 26 to 46 age bracket] than shoppers in a junior's department. She is not necessarily the same size on the top as the bottom, so separates make more sense," adds McNutt. Instead of sizes 6 and 8, Just Grand inventories more 8 to 12.

Any specialty store makes a mistake when it tries to compete with department stores, which can better absorb price markdowns. So the 1,800-square-foot just Grand attempts to carry different items from its competitors. "If a vendor tells me I'll love a particular dress because Dayton-Hudson just bought a slew of them, I say 'Thanks, but no thanks,'" says McNutt. Just Grand also doesn't stock 15 of the same blue worsoted different sizes. "We are a neighborhood store," she points . gut, meaning vice presidents don't fancy meeting their outfit in the eelevator on the way to work.

Make Your Statement

A specialty boutique spells its trump card: s-e-r- v-i-e "Lost of people have a nice selection, but we're known for helping the customer decide what's right for her," says Marilyn McNutt. The ratio of sales help to customers is higher than a department store's because of the personal attention each customer requires. "You need a lot of sales help to mix and match the seperation rates we stock. We don't let customers get out of the store without suggesting they might want a particular scarf for that new outfit." Not only do such suggestions build profitable add-on sales, they also prove to customers that someone pays attention to their needs.

In addition, Just Grand offers free wardrobe counseling by appointment. Partner Kadie DeMay outfits about 30 customers every season. When you realize each may spend $1,000 to $1,500 per wardarobe—each season—you'll understand why this is a profitable service worth the bother. DeMay keeps a file on what each client bought last season and encourages them all to bring items from home for her to accessorize.

You also should consider offering alterations. This doesn't have to be a hassle. just Grand pins hems and other minor alterations in-house and sends the garments for quickie alterations to a tailor. "We offer the service for free," says McNutt. "After all, men's stores don't charge for tailoring, so why should we?"

McNutt says Just Grand won't make the mistake of haphazard expansion again. But she does see a chain of women's professional clothing stores in her future. her reasoning: "We have a wonderful product. The concept works."

51

Rubber Stamp Designer

Job Description : *A rubber stamp designer creates stamps, craft projects, and scrapbooks that have intricate, whimsical, decorative, or humorous designs on them and are used for self-expression and just plain enjoyment.*

- *Start-up cost: approximately Rs. 25000*
- *Potential first-year earnings: Rs. 1 Lac*
- *Future growth potential: high*
- *No staffing required*
- *Artistic business that allows for freedom of expression*

Do you wish you were in a more creative business? Are you frequently struck by flights of whimsy: Do you add a little flair to the letters when you sign your name? Are you perpetually doodling little cartoons of smiling suns, friendly flowers, and adorable angels? Do you enjoy arts and crafts?

If the answer to any or all of these questions is "yes," then you might be ready to make your mark in the rubber stamp business, which the *Dallas Morning News* called "one of the fastest-growing crafts in the United States and Europe."

Stamp Me Five

If all you know about rubber stamps is that your kids used to stamp them all over everything (paper, the walls, clothing, and your outgoing mail), it's time to wake up and smell the ink. Today the rubber stamp industry—yes, *industry—is* hotter than a volcano.

Nowadays it's not kids but adults who express themselves with rubber stamps. Devotees use them to create their own greeting cards, gift wrap, bookmarks, stationery, and a variety of other paper-based items. Serious stampers use them for everything from handmade door knockers and pillows to ceramic tiles, blinds, wall borders, and scrapbooks (sometimes called memory albums). The uses of rubber stamps are limited only by your imagination.

Rubber stamping is so hot there are trade shows, conventions, publications, and Internet sites all dedicated to the art of rubber stamping. There hobbyists can sell and swap stamps, trade ideas on usage, and tell people how much enjoyment they get from stamping.

Choosing A Method

There are two basic methods for starting a rubber stamp business. The first is to limit your business strictly to designing (that is, drawing) the stamps and use outside vendors for the actual production. The second is to do both the design and production yourself.

The advantage of the first method is simplicity. You can't Making find an easier and quicker way to start a business than one that requires just pencil, paper, and imagination. However, the disadvantage is the expense of using outside vendors. The benefit to an eng of the second method is that you can control many aspects of sign in a design and production, thus eliminating unexpected (and costly) vendor delays and mistakes. The bad news is that this method means high start-up costs and requires a significant amount of workspace.

Susan Brown, owner of Wood Cellar Graphics in Coleridge, Nebraska, operates a rubber stamping business for which she performs most of the work herself. She began her business in 1986, as a part-time venture. A printer at her workplace asked if she was interested in making business-related rubber stamps at her home.Always a creative person, she soon realized that she might also be able to make her own artistic rubber stamps to sell.

She began slowly, attending craft shows and placing small classified ads in country lifestyle magazines to sell stamps, meet customers, and build her business. After a few years, demand for her stamps had become so great that she went into business full time.

Although at one point she had a store and several employees, Brown scaled her operation back to a home-based business. During a typical week she receives orders for between 500 and 600 stamps. This figure is almost double the number she received just three years ago—an indication of how rapidly the keeps the rubber stamp industry is growing.

Making Stamps

Making rubber stamps is a complicated process that requires multiple steps and specialized equipment. For example, Brown starts by designing the stamp. She then sends the artwork out to an engraver, who makes a special plate that contains the design in a raised image. (Engraving is a highly specialized skill and the only part of the entire production process that Brown does not perform herself.)

Once the engraved plate is returned, a special molding material is put onto it. Then the plate is inserted into a machine called a Vulcanizer. It has a hydraulic jack and two heating element plates, one on top and the other on the bottom. The Vulcanizer pushes the engraved image into molding material. The mold is then covered with rubber. The Vulcanizer plates heat to approximately 350 degrees, and the hydraulic jack presses them together to vulcanize the rubber and attach it to the mold.

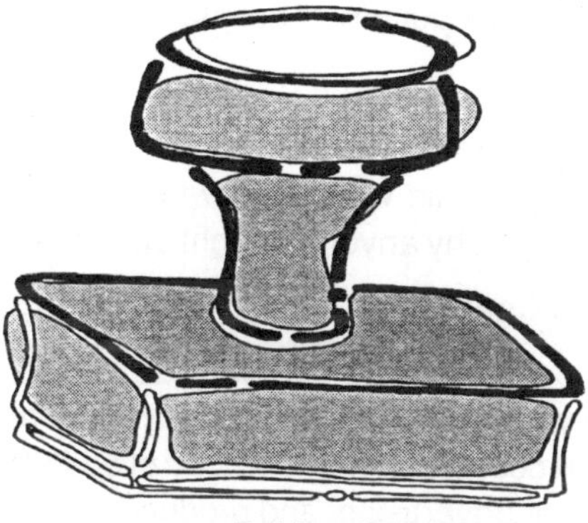

Rubber Stamps

After the stamps are made, they are mounted on wood. For this Brown buys white maple at a cost of $2.50 per board foot. (She usually buys 500 board feet of wood at atime.) Her partner Ken Krei uses an electric saw to cut the wood to the proper size.

Vulcanizers come in different sizes. A new, large machine like Brown has, which can make between 20 and 30 stamps at a time, costs approximately $1,800. Specialized rubber used to make the stamps costs $150 for a 50-pound roll. However, thousands of stamps can be made from one 50-pound roll. This keeps the cost of making individual stamps low.

Stamps are priced according to size. The stamps at Wood Cellar Graphics range from $4 for a ¼" ×1¼" stamp to $12 for a 5" × 6" stamp. Stamp design spans a plethora of interesting and unusual images, from simple yet elegant pictures of birds and animals, to beautifully detailed flowers, to extraordinarily intricate illustrations of desert sunsets and a Christmas tree.

Studying The Stamp Market

One critical factor in operating a rubber stamp business is to study the stamp market with an eagle eye. Tastes change quickly; a design that is hot today may be just a fading memory next month. The trick is to learn which designs have staying power, such as angels, and which have the longevity of pet rocks. Susan Brown constantly analyzes the market, a task that has been made easier by the Internet.

Along with studying the market comes planning. While its nice to catch the popularity wave, there's no reason why you cant generate one yourself. Try to determine what stampers like, and, if possible, develop some signature designs that combine perennial themes with individual expression. Brown attributes the continuing popularity of her stamps to their whimsical, country flavor.

Above all, be patient. Making quality rubber stamps takes practice.

"The first [stamps] I did were just awful." Brown laughs. "They were pretty horrible. I wonder why anyone bought any!"

Stamping Out High Costs

Starting your own rubber stamp business can be costly, particularly if you venture out on your own. The special equipment and materials needed to begin probably will cost in the neighborhood of $5,000. Set aside additional money for a computer, advertising, and producing a catalog, and total start-up costs could be $10,000 or more.

There are ways, however, to reduce that amount. One is to sell stamps at craft shows and similar venues instead of spending heavily on advertising; the cost of vendor registration usually is far less than taking out ads. However, if you feel that you must advertise, consider taking out small ads in magazines devoted specifically to the rubber stamp industry rather than in higher-profile magazines, where ad rates tend to also be high. The downside, however, is that since every ad in specialized rubber stamp publications touts a company selling rubber stamps, it's easy for your message to get lost. To publicize her business, Susan Brown turned to that most modern of marketing tools, the Internet. She built her own web page with a program she purchased and is pleased with the customer response.

Another way to cut costs is to buy a used Vulcanizer, which can cost as little as a few hundred dollars. With the variety of Vulcanizers available, even buying a smaller one will help keep costs low. However, the trade-off is that a smaller machine can make far fewer stamps than a larger model.

Although start-up costs for a turnkey rubber stamp business like Brown's can be high, you can potentially earn around $30,000 per year. At that rate, the breakeven time on an initial investment of $10,000 could come within a few months. However, due to competition and a crowded marketplace, your business is likely to grow gradually. Thus it will take longer to recoup your initial costs.

Stamping : Fad or Future-Oriented

With an industry such as rubber stamping, which is based on want rather than need, there is always the danger that the boom could go bust overnight, similar to the dramatic contraction suffered by the baseball collectibles industry in the mid-1990s, Susan Brown, however, doesn't see that happening.

"I think that the attraction of rubber stamps is that people can create something with them, like a work of ark," she says "Even if you can't draw a straight line, you can create something with rubber stamps. Because of that, I think that the industry is going to continue to grow. People keep coming up with new things to do with them, and a lot of people are just getting involved in it."

So if all this sounds good to you, then maybe you can stamp your way to success—in the rubber stamp business.

52

Telemarketer

Job Description: *A telemarketer sells items exclusively over the telephone by calling people at home.*

- *Start-up cost as low as Rs. 35000*
- *Potential first-year earnings: Rs. 2 Lacs*
- *Breakeven time from initial investment: six months to two years*
- *Ideal home-based business*
- *Excellent opportunity for people with physical disabilities*
- *No staffing required*

The whole world talks about productivity, but business hasn't done much to make selling more productive," observes Lee Van Vechten, publisher of the *Van Vechten Report,* a newsletter for managers of corporate telemarketing groups. As you might guess, Van Vechten offers a solution to the high cost of selling: telemarketing. If you make sales calls—or at least weed out prospects—over the phone rather than via an interstate highway, costs tumble. "McGraw-Hill said that field selling cost about $260 per presentation," says Van Vechten. "The average cost of a business-to-business telemarketing presentation is about $18."

Who Does It?

Telemarketers sell stationery to businesses or carpet cleaning to consumers. Operators make an appointment for a salesperson to call in person or ask, for example, what you like or dislike about *Newsweek* magazine. Operators standing by at an 800 telephone number offer fix-it advice on your washing machine or take orders for the genuine cultured pearls advertised on Channel 3. Lee Van Vechten's definition, however, covers just about everything: "Telemarketing is intensive use of the telephone in the business environment."

Telemarketing companies range from in-house, multifloor departments at large corporations (JCPenney employs around 4,000 telemarketing operators answering toll-free numbers) to individuals who make calls part time from the kitchen telephone. With the industry still young, "nobody's developed statistics on its size, partially because we're a moving target, we're growing so fast," says Sandy Pernick, who runs The Direct Response Corporation. However, telemarketing has yet to reach capacity. The industry is still inventing methods of operation. U.S. *News & World Report* predicts that by 2001, 8 million people will make their livelihood through telemarketing. Van Vechten estimates that just over 2 million telemarketing operators are making calls. "Expect geometric growth," he says.

Impressive growth is exactly what has occurred. According to the American Teleservices Association, telephone marketing for business-to-business sales is expected to grow 10.5 percent annually, while for consumer sales the growth rate is anticipated to be 8 percent. In *1997* telephone marketing accounted for *$238.6* billion in business-to-business sales and *$185.9* billion in consumer sales. Nearly 100 million people in the United State (one out of three) buy goods and services over the telephone each year.

No More $250 Start- Ups

Sandy Pernick invested *$250* to launch The Direct Response from her Des Plaines, Illinois, home. She spent $100 for incorporation, printed some letterhead, and put three people on residential phones. Today the company employs *105* and achieves revenues over *$1* million.

Although occasional successes still start from home, the cottage industry is fast turning professional. The good news is the cost of telephone equipment, WATS lines, and long-distance charges are all skidding downward. A well-run company can easily keep 20 percent of revenues as profits. The bad news is corporate customers have been stung once too often by telemarketers who have disappeared overnight without a trace, leaving customers who call the *800* number to follow up on their order with the message: "This service has been disconnected." Pernick, who was a supervisor for another telemarketer before starting The Direct Response, recommends telemarketing only to entrepreneurs with a direct-marketing background. "Businesses look for a professional image, for stability," she says. For you, that means showing clients the permanence that comes with fancy equipment and employees rather than a card table in a basement.

Your First Telemarketing Client : Yourself

Of course, you still can start small by convincing local businesses to use your services. Locate customers the same way you will operate for them: through telemarketing. After you call prospective clients, many will request a brochure, so be sure to have professional-looking literature ready to mail.

Sandy Pernick asks clients for yearlong contracts. "Educate clients to the fact that stopping and starting a program is counter productive," she says. "If a program works, keep it on full time. Consider it part of your marketing plan." Such long-term contracts do wonders for her scheduling. If in January she knows she will have a minimum level of business in July, she can take on new projects so she doesn't have to lay off staff.

Except for the image issue, you can start a service that only makes outbound calls with just a phone or two. Or you can get fancy by buying an automatic dialer that calls each number in sequence and plays back a recorded message. Traditional equipment that also accepts incoming calls is less expensive—but you need more of it since you also need employees. Telemarketing is both an equipment-heavy and people-intensive industry.

"The industry has a personnel turnover rate of 150 to 200 percent," Pernick warns. "Historically that's because we've been part-time employers and attracted transient workers like students." Her solution is to hire only full-time, permanent employees.

Others argue that turnover is so high because telemarketing leads to burnout. It's hard making 100 phone calls a day. Norm Pensky, who runs Adds Telemarketing from South Pasadena, California, counters this problem by switching people to new assignments often and making sure people take coffee breaks.

Before The Phone Rings

Sandy Pernick insists the actual phone call is the least important aspect of a telemarketing campaign. "You have to plan what to say, decide who to say it to, establish what time to call, and afterwards you have to analyze what people said. That requires more than just subjective opinions. You need number-crunching and you'd better be able to produce an automated report."

Most clients have a good handle on what they want from a telemarketer, but it's up to you to execute their plans. Pernick charges a flat fee for a script (often written in conjunction with the client) and training of her personnel (the client gets involved to impart any technical expertise). Then she charges by the "communicator hour." The industry norm ranges anywhere from $35 to $75 per operator per hour, based on how involved the conversations, the area of the country, and the size of the contract.

Some clients provide lists of contacts, while in other cases the telemarketer finds the most appropriate list. A good way to find customers for your clients is to rent names from publications or associations. If you're calling current customers, completion rate of the questionnaire should be fairly high. But when you make cold calls, only 2 percent may be positives. But, adds Lee Van Vechten, "Most of those rejection calls last less than 1.5 minutes, so those 98 calls who don't buy go quickly."

Van Vechten offers some advice to keep from getting the phone slammed in your ear. "If the customer knows your company, identify yourself. But the consuming public doesn't like telemarketers from organizations they don't know. So, instead of saying 'I'm with Hal's Meat Packing,' ease your way in. Say 'Good evening, this is Lee Van Vechten. I'm curious, do you think freezers save you money on groceries?"

Don't be afraid to change your script, but do so early on Pernick does test runs with two to four callers, then makes any alterations. You won't get meaningful statistics if your approach is haphazard throughout the calling period.

The Looming Shadow

While everyone agrees that telemarketing has explosive growth in its future, observers also say government regulations will shape the industry. Bills pending state by state may limit the types of consumers that telemarketers can ring up. Other bills may restrict the hours you can call. Sandy Pernick notes that most legislation is aimed toward outbound consumer telemarketing; that is one reason she restricts her business to inbound consumer calls or business-to-business telemarketing.

But others say government won't be able to stop the momentum. Telemarketing supporters say telephone selling works. In the future, more and more consumers will become comfortable with the concept, and more businesses will adopt telemarketing because it is inexpensive. With that in mind, experts expect telemarketers will work with legislators to create a good climate. Telemarketing may undergo subtle changes, they say, but the concept is here to stay.

53

Trade Show Organizer

Job Description : *A trade show organizer gathers a group of manufacturers* within *the same industry in one venue so* that *they can* hold *demonstrations of new products, network, and pursue other* sales *and marketing strategies.*

- *Start-up* cost as *low as Rs. 5 Lacs*
- Potential earnings:*Rs. 10 Lacs*
- *Breakeven time from* initial investment: *two* to five *years*

David Cheifetz did not want this chapter written. Companies like his Conference Management Corp. of Norwalk, Connecticut, which stages trade shows for industries as diverse as genetic research and fashion accessories, have been "one of the best-kept secrets around," he says. Like other service businesses, trade shows benefit from high cash flow and no inventory. But trade shows possess another advantage: Unlike most manufacturing, retailing, *or* service businesses, trade shows operate with no accounts receivables; all the money comes before you deliver a product. Whether David Cheifetz likes it or not, competition is catching on. Trade shows are proving enormously popular with businesses, which point to the fact that it takes just half the cost to close a sale that began at a trade show ($550) as compared to a typical sales call ($997). According to the Center for Exhibition Industry Research, over 90 percent of businesses say that exhibitions are "extremely useful" sources of purchasing information. Over 80 percent of exhibiting companies use trade shows to achieve their sales objectives. With statistics like these, it's plain that trade shows aren't a secret anymore.

Casbah

Trade shows are little more than elaborations on ancient Middle Eastern bazaar themes: manufacturers displaying wares for browsing buyers. Modern operators refined the trade shows into a 20th-century selling tool aimed at corporate buyers who stock up en masse.

Trade associations and other nonprofit groups once dominated trade show management. Such an environment, says David Cheifetz, provided "remarkable business opportunities for astute businesspeople, since the kinds of people attracted to nonprofit fields are not terribly aggressive promoters." Professional managers, including individual entrepreneurs, publishing groups, and ad agencies, now operate about 60 percent of the country's expos with more than 10,000 square feet of exhibit space—and nobody even knows how many "tabletop" shows are set up in hotel hallways and suites for small events. These professionals either manage a trade group's operation for a fee or own shows outright.

Up - Front Dollars

You can stage a small tabletop show in a hotel for around $10,000. If you can guarantee a hotel enough rooms, sometimes you can negotiate free exhibit space. On a more ambitious tear, a multi-industry extravaganza staged in a major convention center could cost you around $30,000, assuming you handle all the details yourself. If you hire specialists to decorate a show, for example, add anywhere from $500 to $2,000 to your out-of-pocket expenses. A small show might charge $50 for an exhibit table, while the biggies can go for ten times that. Both kinds of shows return profits with margins of 20 to 50 percent.

You can start with little up-front capital because your customers—exhibitors—foot most of the bills. Explains Wendy Rosen, whose Baltimore-based Wendy Rosen Agency Inc. throws two annual wholesale-only trade shows for artisans, "Most businesses don't see the cash until 120 days after they provide service when the wolf's at the door. But a trade show doesn't need up-front cash because exhibitors pay for their space ahead of time." Rosen staged The Buyers Market of American Crafts on a $500 overdraft from her checking account. Some 85 exhibitors took booths in a suite she rented at the New York Hilton Hotel; 500 merchants showed up, eager to buy crafts to sell in their department and specialty stores. Five years later, 900 pottery makers, jewelry crafters, and woodworkers paid for booth space at her shows, as 10,000 attendees went through the gates. Rosen's two shows together bill about $1 million annually.

You don't need venture capital or even large bank loans to get into the business, but you do require time. Since popular convention centers like McCormick Place in Chicago and the Jacob Javitts Center in New York book space at least 13 months before an event (and up to 10 years for very large expositions during popular times of the year), you should start planning your show 18 months to 2 years ahead of its due date.

Steps

You follow five steps to launch a trade show, regardless of whether you invite 200 people or the entire state of Rhode Island:

1. Before making any commitments, test the concept. A telephone and letter canvas asks prospective exhibitors if they would buy booths and attendees if they would travel to such a show. While testing a first-time concept, many operators hold onto their jobs just in case the idea doesn't fly.
2. Assuming that a high percentage of contacts say they'd jump at the chance to be in your show, line up blocks of hotel rooms and convention-center space. Since a significant cut of their action is the tourist dollars conventioneers spend, popular convention centers managed by municipalities often shy away from brand-new shows. You might have to hold your show in a second-tier city until you establish a reputation. Wendy Rosen says one sure way to get space involves planning a show for an unpopular time. "Every convention center in the country wants business between December 24 and January 1. Tell a convention manager if you cut me a good deal or take care of my insurance, I'll bring you a convention that week."
3. Print a brochure explaining the "who, what, when, where, and why" of your event. You can buy mailing lists from trade organizations and publications to supply the names of potential exhibitors. Follow up with sales calls to nail down booth commitments.

Direct mail, telemarketing, and printing costs during these first two steps range anywhere from $2,000 to *$15,000,* which is money you need ahead of time. From here on out, however, exhibitors foot the show bills. David Cheifetz points out that exhibitors are far cheaper to round up than attendees because they represent a smaller universe.

4. As exhibitor fees trickle in, turn your attention to the people who will visit the booths. Create a program. A typical agenda involves lining up speakers, devising seminars, and arranging special dinners and spousal events. Along with a list of exhibitors, use this program as the calling card to draw the gate.
5. Begin a marketing attack with trade journal and regional newspaper ads and mailings to prospective attendees. Pointing out that a small ad in the *Wall Street Journal* can run *$7,500,* Cheifetz admonishes, "Use your money wisely."

Unlike consumer shows, most trade shows do not charge gate fees. Revenues come from what's left over from booth fees and, sometimes, from selling services (such as seminars) to attendees. Additionally, successful shows sometimes sell lists of attendee names.

More Art Than Science

Once you've lined up acceptances from exhibitors and attendees, organize every aspect of the show in minute detail, from when you'll need cleanup crews to the menu at the awards banquet. Running a trade show "is more art than science," insists Russell E. Flagg, whose New York City—based Flagg Management Inc. runs events ranging from French fashion to ultralight aviation. Flagg, who started his own company after working for two large exposition companies, says contingency plans are crucial. Know in advance what to do if the power fails; if the union assembling the booths strikes; if an unexpected snow-storm grounds transportation.

Exhibition managers emphasize that one disorganized or meagerly attended show kills a concept forever. Who will return next year if this show was a disaster? What organization will hire you to manage their one big event if another expo you ran fizzled? The moral of the story: Don't skimp or cut too many corners.

Organization is key to everything. Like a boy scout, a trade show manager has to be prepared.

Hint: If you opt to learn the ropes as an employee of an existing firm, realize that most shows happen just once a year. It pays to join a major organization that puts on dozens of annual expos. The largest operator, Cahner's Exposition Group of Stamford, Connecticut, staged 230 shows worldwide in one year alone.

Parceling Out The Chores

Most large operators choose to mount the entire show, overseeing chores that range from direct mail tests of the concept to providing tablecloths at the convention hall. However, you can buy every type of expertise for a fee. For example, for anywhere from 85 cents to $2 per person, you can hire an organization to sign in registrants, equip them with printed badges, and provide a computerized list of attendees for next year. "A wonderful cadre of professionals will write brochures, oversee the mailing, put on conferences," says Russell Flagg. "They won't work on dreams, though. Instead of costing you $20,000, it might cost you $150,000 to run a show."

Unless you're shooting for a one-shot deal, expect to lose money on that first event (or two). Although a show's budget may eat up only half the revenues garnered f2rom booth sales, you need the profits to start immediate preparation for next year. "Sink every cent into promoting the show," advises Wendy Rosen. "Exploit the momentum you built for next time."

After the industry accepts a show as an expected annual event, promotion becomes much easier—and profits skyrocket, "You don't have to reinvent the wheel each year," says David Cheifetz. "A good show is like a Mercedes. The salesman doesn't have to tell you it's a fine car. But he still has to sell his product."

Bucking The Odds

Trade show managers fall into two groups: professionals who sight opportunities to throw parties, no matter what the field, and insiders in particular industries who organize a group of friends into a trade show. Wendy Rosen, for one, is proof that outsiders can achieve success. Equipped with a publishing and advertising background, she was designing business cards and order forms for artists when she dreamed up a forum where craftspeople could present their silkscreens and brass bracelets to the retail world. Rosen's almost overnight success came through instinct and application of her talents, a sure-fire idea, and perhaps some luck. Most important, her show brought exhibitors tangible results. "When I first began my show six years ago, exhibitors averaged $30,000 to $50,000 in production a year. Now $1 million isn't uncommon and $150,000 is average," she says. Because of ready access to a wholesale market, "Many clients doubled and tripled volume."

Probably any industry large enough to support a large expo already has one, but don't let that stop you. If David Cheifetz sees room for a better-managed show or a second event in a different area of the country, he rises tactfully to the challenge: "We call the association and tell them we'll stay as far away chronologically and geographically as possible. We ask for their endorsement, but we go ahead if we don't get their cooperation".

Rosen suggests getting in on the ground floor with shows in growth industries. And if you can't do it all, do what you can. "Call up the small associations and offer to handle the marketing, direct mail, or advertising for their meetings," she says. "If an industry is building, you can build along with them."

By segmenting large markets into specific niches, Russell Flagg stages shows for such hard-to-reach audiences as New York lawyers hungry for computer software. "Both sides know the show is not for the general public but targeted to their needs, so they come," explains Flagg, whose dozen shows produced revenues of $1.2 million one year.

As travel grows increasingly expensive, observers forecast fewer massive blockbuster shows. Instead, expect greater numbers of smaller shows scattered across the country. Trade Show Bureau executive director Bill Mee points out that expos have already changed from out-of-town stag-club parties to serious business events. "It's expensive to go to shows, expensive to participate. Now you go for the purpose of doing business."

54

Party Planner

Job Description : *A party planner handles all the details for any social affair, including suggesting the theme, hiring caterers, florists, and so on, and obtaining all other necessary elements.*

- *Start-up cost as low as Rs. 1 Lac*
- *Potential first-year earnings: Rs. 5 Lacs*
- *Breakeven time from initial investment: one month to one year*
- *Ideal home-based business*
- *Excellent opportunity for people with physical disabilities.*
- *No staffing required*

Last week we planned a kidnaping," relates party planner Patricia Watson, who runs Magic by PTS Inc. "The 70 Dean Witter executives knew they were going to a party, but they didn't know they'd arrive at a speakeasy (our warehouse) in a fire engine."

When Watson says "Let's plan a party," don't expect Chuckles the Clown and ice cream for a dozen six-year-olds. "We arrange the unusual—that's what makes us Magic." Her $2-million-a-year Dallas-based firm stages a couple hundred" parties a year, primarily for corporate and convention clients. The extravaganzas range from a Chinese New Year in June (complete with a dragon parade and rice-eating contest) to Mardi/Gras costume parties. Magic's warehouse full of props holds a full-size merry-go-round and 15-foot-tall toy soldiers. In addition to local entertainment, Watson has booked Dolly Parton and Tanya Tucker. For show business blasts, she contracts with a Joan Collins or Tom Selleck look-alike. Chow runs the gamut from haute cuisine to barbecue. It seems no true party planner is limited by anything other than imagination—either your own or your client's.

The Whole Megillah

Using her own definition of a party planner as someone "capable of dotting every 'i' and crossing every 't,' " Patty Watson estimates that only about 500 true party planners operate across the country. So, if you're in an area that likes to throw parties, there's probably room for another party planner. Magic started as an offshoot of a tour business Watson ran for conventioneers and their spouses. But before that, she was a mother and teacher, professions that "basically prepare you for the impossible," she says.

What does Watson mean by "the impossible"? Well, "Party planners conceptualize the whole thing," she explains. "We create the props, arrange the location, send invitations, handle the RSVPs, line up caterers, flowers, food, entertainment, and absolutely anything else that's necessary."

Party planners either plan the entire bash, or plan and execute. If you're restricting activities to pure planning, the price of admission to the business involves lining up customers and subcontractors, such as balloon decorators and caterers. Lease props from a rental store, let the caterer provide the serving personnel, and you can also hire freelancers of all sorts: a '50s party might need a cheerleader to lead cheerleading contests, or a part-time actor to host bubble-gum blowing tournaments. Since the client pays the planner who doles out the various fees, be sure to ask for a hefty enough deposit to cover whatever up-front commitments you make for entertainment, decorating, food, and so on.

If you have some expertise and capital, decide whether you want to handle some functions in-house. For example, many planners also cater, plan business meetings for corporate clients, or rent anything from tents to coffeepots. Each additional operation brings in revenues—but also requires expensive equipment and personnel. Most planners accumulate some props, which, if you grow large enough, will need to be stored in a warehouse. Also, you'll need office space.

While you can certainly start from home, some party planners create magical offices with props stashed in every corner. When you reach this stage, invite clients to your premises before planning their parties. The setting will spark all kinds of ideas.

Likewise, as you grow, you'll need vans to transport all those props to party sites. Splash the vans with a logo that you also use on your correspondence, business cards, and the back of such party favors as photographs. While you should fade into the background during the party, you can advertise your presence as you set up.

Party People

To get started, call folks all over town involved in parties. Those same photographers or florists you book for your parties can provide leads on clients. Let hotels know you can either help out their banquet managers on elaborate projects, or work directly with their customers. Call on convention planners and ask if you can assist them—or any of their exhibitors who might want to throw a private party. If you have an idea of which corporations throw the most elaborate to-dos, send them a brochure or call office managers to suggest they throw a Winter Wonderland theme party this Christmas. You'll not only create ski slopes in their corporate dining room, you'll also pick up the key executives in horse-drawn sleighs.

Try to get commitments months in advance so you can plan in a more leisurely fashion and get better prices for your clients. Patty Watson likes to have eight months' notice for $100,000 parties, although Magic has staged parties for hundreds of people in a couple of weeks. "They just cost more, not only because we have to put more people on the arrangements but because you can't buy in quantity and you pay exorbitant freight costs," she explains. "For instance, if we know we're going to need 100 dozen white roses six months ahead of time, we buy a field and get a better deal."

Set your charges by working backward. Determine how much each element—from catering to props—will cost. Then tack on the cost of your own overhead and profits of 20 to 40 percent, depending on what the market and your client allows.

Before booking a $100,000 party—or even a four-figure wedding reception—clients want references and examples of what you do, so you have to build a reputation. Ask influential contacts to stop by before or during the murder mystery to see the Victorian set you created. Offer to help a charity plan its next luau, and take pictures of the affair. You could split the cost of a professionally produced videotape with a bride and groom if they'll let you use an edited version as a sales tool. The expense of planning a party for free and taking photographs or videos of the event will pay off when you land that big account. If you can put aside a few thousand dollars, kick off your own business with a gala.

The Client's Always Right

To create the right mood and get the touches right, ask clients what they hope to accomplish with the party. If you host a new-product kick-off, perhaps strolling fortune tellers might end each palm-reading with visions of the Caribbean vacation that the corporation will award to the top sales team. If you plan a retirement party, ask about the guest of honor's hobbies and interests, and make theme suggestions around those.

Be sure to outline in detail any outrageous ideas. For example, a gorilla serving during the coffee break might enliven the dullest seminar. But a client who hopes to sell financial services to customers intrigued by what they've just heard on the podium might not appreciate the disruption.

A couple of character traits spell disaster for party planners. If you're a rigid "go-by-the-book" sort, forget party planning. Not only will your imagination be challenged before every party, but you'll have to improvise around unexpected glitches during each event. Also, since you deal with a myriad of details and various subcontractors, disorganization is death. Patty Watson sums it up nicely: "if you've ever planned a 50th wedding anniversary, a dinner party for 100 guests, a graduation, a wedding, and an inaugural ball—and if they've all occured on the same day—and they've all occured in the same place—you can do this. You can be party planner."

55

Tour Operator

***Job Description :** A tour operator* plans, *organizes, and* often *leads groups of people on* unusual *and adventurous tours both in* the *United* States *and abroad.*

- *Start-up* cost as *low as Rs. 25000*
- *Potential earnings: Rs 2 Lacs*
- *Breakeven time from* initial investment: *several* months *to one year*
- *Ideal home-based* business
- *No staffing required*

On a brilliant Vermont spring day, John Freidin and a couple of other professors from Middlebury College embarked on a biking weekend. As the sun splashed through the delicate new leaves, making a dappled pattern on the road ahead, Freidin breathed the crisp air and reveled in the exertion of pedaling the Vermont hills. He could practically taste the contrast to his workday life: his sedentary duties as a professor of history and education. His only conscious thoughts concerned the scenery around him, with a slight anticipation of the good meal and pleasant night's sleep at the country inn still hours down the road.

The next moments changed Freidin's life. "In the middle of the first afternoon, I got a flash that people would like to ride like this if they could stay in a cozy inn and get lots of good food." He reasoned that not everyone knew Vermont's country roads as well as he, and would welcome help in plotting routes and booking inns the right distance down those roads. Voila! Vermont Bicycle Touring was born.

Freidin recently sold his Bristol, Vermont-based company for an undisclosed sum but, he says, "a price I was very happy with." Now he's taking time off to consult, sail, and visit family and friends he neglected while he was nurturing his business to annual revenues of $1.6 million. During those years, he was in-deed busy: Vermont Bicycle Touring escorted 5,200 people a year on bike treks throughout Vermont and bordering states. Most clients come from the Northeast megalopolis, hut Freidin's fame has spread throughout the fragmented tour operator network. "Freidin did it right," says a somewhat reverential Will Weber, founder of Journeys International Inc., of Ann Arbor, Michigan, an "adventure tour" outfit that arranges Tibetan treks and East African safaris.

Trial - And - Error Management

By doing it right, Will Weber means managing a tour operation like a business. John Freidin went so far as to write his own 50-page rule book that he distributed to employees. In it he explains what to do in unusual situations, such as when a cyclist fails to bring a check. (Two possibilities: Either call Western Union with the client's credit card to get cash wired directly to Vermont Bicycle for a fee charged to the client; or show the customer how to write a perfectly legal check on a blank piece of paper.)

For the most part, the far-flung tour guide industry has few rules and a seat-of-the-pants management style. Unlike the related travel-agency business, tour operators have no industry associations trade publications to guide them. Each new operator invents what works for the particular tours he or she conceives, which can range from two-hour mule rides in south-western parks to round-the-world sails in schooners. Some plot "mundane" tours like six stops in ten days on a European vacation for schoolteachers. Others take scuba divers to the Great Barrier reef. But all operators devise boilerplate itineraries and orchestrate all the details, from air travel to accommodations. Entrepreneurs either lead expeditions themselves or arrange for guides. Successful tours shoot for 10 percent pretax profits after salary, but the revelation that you can make money doing what outsiders consider a continual vacation can be slow in coming.

All This And money, Too?

Many dabblers lead excursions for the sheer fun of it, or as a way to pay for their own trips. They simply fail to recognize they can make a respectable living from a kayak and therefore don't pursue such business concerns as advertising or employee relations. Many operators are either young with few financial obligations or have other sources of income. Let's see how John Freidin did it.

After the weekend of the fateful "flash," Freidin acted decisively: "I immediately researched my first bike route and ran classified ads in *New York Magazine* and *Saturday Review of Literature.*" From the few inquiries he received, he persuaded three New Yorkers to take a debut trip in early August; approximately 75 cyclists signed up over the rest of the season, which lasts as long as Vermont's stunning fall foliage does. "Fortunately," he says wryly, "I was still drawing a salary and didn't have to make a living." The next year, Vermont Bicycle Touring made a little money, and within three years, "I was making more than I could as a teacher."

The Power Of The Press

What happened to John Freidin is a boon to most entrepreneurs but almost a necessity to success in the travel field: Vermont Bicycle Touring got publicity. One cyclist told a friend about his trip—a friend who happened to be the editor of the *New York Times* travel section. Soon blurbs appeared in travel sections of the *Boston Globe* and other publications. Freidin admits the publicity "fell into my lap," but you can prod notices by sending press releases and invitations to travel writers. Advertising helps, too, especially if you pinpoint publications that appeal to your particular clientele. Will Weber, for example, prefers *Natural History Magazine.*

Who Wants To Go?

Unlike travel agents, who compete for the greatest possible volume of *local* clientele, tour operators see the world as their neighborhood. If you offer helicopter ski tours in British Columbia, for example, you may be better off advertising in *Ski Magazine* than in the Vancouver newspaper. Knowing only a tiny percentage of the locals will ever book from them, Journeys International does not even list in the Ann Arbor phone book. "Our clients are from all over the world—Mexico, Hong Kong, Japan," says Will Weber. "It's the old global village thing." While such a far-flung clientele may be hard to round up in the first place, it represents a more stable base. "If the largest local business should close down, we don't worry that it'll affect our market," says Weber.

Most operators court steady repeat business, whether they lead $300 bike trips or $3,000 adventure tours. "On every trip, at least a couple of people have been with us on previous trips," says Weber. "We really try hard with the final dinner to leave a good impression." The best leads on new vacationers are referrals of satisfied clients. Journeys International asks participants which friends might be interested and adds their names to its mailing list.

Send US $3,000...

Will Weber's complicated operation, with revenues "of more than $1 million," began the year he and his wife started graduate studies after returning from Nepal, where Will had been in the Peace Corps. "There was nothing at the time that was affordable and offered the cross-cultural experience. All the groups stayed in Western hotels. Our idea was to experience the everyday life you can only get if you mix with the culture," explains Will, who later received his Ph.D. in natural resources.

Will and Joan Weber posted announcements on University of Michigan bulletin boards and landed a radio interview. The process took months. "When two grad students suggest people send them a $3,000 check and offer to take care of all the arrangements ... well, you just don't have much credibility,' admits Will. But ten people eventually signed up, which "basically paid our way back to see friends in Nepal." Unless you are prepared to be satisfied with only the free trips and can forsake financial profits, Will recommends "either money for lots of advertising, or patience."

You also need contacts. "I remember trying to get help from the airlines" in booking a group rate, says Will. "Nobody was interested in talking to us until a man from Air India came out in his big car and took us to lunch. He asked why we didn't advertise, and we admitted we had no money. But he liked our enthusiasm and believed we were worth a gamble. So he gave us $50—'Here, take this and run an ad,' just like that." Needless to say, Journeys International booked not only that first trip but many subsequent flights on Air India. When trying to drum up clients or contacts, dress the part and act as professional as your budget permits. Printed brochures, for example, add to your credibility.

Who Will Lead Your Tours?

Once you grow beyond leading all tours yourself, you must find knowledgeable employees who stay around for more than a year. Many operations are seasonal, providing income only during the six-month tourist season or for the half-dozen 16-day safaris a tour group books. If you're the owner, you either stockpile enough profits to see you through the dry months or book counterseasonal tours. But if you're an employee, your options are more limited.

To keep employees aboard, John Freidin created a byzantine bonus system, based on the number of days a tour guide worked and the number of people taking trips. More seasoned operators earned higher salaries, says Freidin, who now consults for others interested in starting tour operations. Many Vermont Bicycle employees hold traditional jobs during the week and lead tours on weekends for the joint motives of additional income and the opportunity to pursue their cycling hobby.

Freidin found local newspaper ads attracted appropriate guides, probably because "the type of person who chooses to live in Vermont likes exercise and the outdoors." In addition, don't neglect your own customers. They've already demonstrated their love of your business by paying money to participate, and the most knowledgeable or athletic may be good employee prospects. Freidin says he got a surprising number of unsolicited inquires "from people who took tours and decide they'd like to work for us."

Familiarity with your territory—whether it's Kenya or Colorado—helps in finding employees. The Webers tapped sherpas they knew in Nepal who arrange local travel and accommodations, in addition to serving as guides. Some operators contract with established guide operations or book part of a tour through travel agencies. But Will maintains that such profit-sharing eats at margins and also crowds you out of the experience you're trying to provide. "How can you recommend a particular guide whom you don't even know?" he asks. Journeys International employs only locals. The practice keeps costs down, even if you pay American wages. And natives bring a wealth of intimate knowledge no outsider can ever attain. A U.S. guide leading Americans leaves vacationers with an American experience, Will argues.

While you should probably understand birdwatching before you lead a group of birdwatchers to the Galapagos Islands, you don't have to live in Bangkok to offer tours in Thailand. Just hire someone who knows the territory. Before Journeys International establishes a new destination, Will visits the country, sometimes taking a tour with an existing company. Such scouting serves two purposes: "You need some personal credibility—the ability to talk to people about your own experiences." Also, visits allow him to shop for the right local employee.

You Can Buy A Boat Or Start With Zip

No average start-up cost exists in tour operations. Will estimates he spends $10,000 to set up a new trip, including $2,000 for promotion and mailings and $2,000 for an on-site visit. His computer helps him write itineraries and sort mailing lists and contacts with airlines and travel agencies through which he writes tickets. Launching windjammer cruises off Maine could be far more expensive; you must buy, rent, or (if you're really handy—and patient) build a seaworthy vessel.

However, many operators start with no capital at all, using deposits from customers to finance early costs and profits from the first trip to buy additional equipment and advertising. Let's assume you are an experienced whitewater expert who leads excursions down the Snake River. Your basic equipment includes a raft, life jackets, and cooking implements. After a couple of springs building a reputation in Idaho, you might put together an expedition to the Rio de la Plata in Argentina. If you are unsure of details, subcontract with an existing operator. You provide the river expertise and, on that first trip at least, let the old hand arrange travel and accommodations. Next time around, pull the entire package together without the partner. Eventually you may establish a local office and employees while you scout out new rivers and new expeditions.

The Agency Connection

Most tour operators are not travel agents, although a growing number of agencies also devise tours. In order to collect airline fees and issue tickets, an agent must meet certain standards of financial responsibility, business experience, and personnel requirements, which may be beyond most tour start-ups. However, you may want to strike up relationships with various travel agents. If you agree to fork over a share of your bookings, agencies will book their customers on your tours. Or you can turn one specific aspect of your tour, such as airfare, over to an agency. Journeys International writes airline tickets through agents, splitting the commissions 50-50. Because it gets a cut of the airfare, the company can hold land costs to about $50 a day.

It's true you will get your share of freebies, although most operators turn down more trips than they take. Will Weber cites as reasons both business demands as the company grows and the desire to spend time at home with wife Joan and five-year-old daughter Robin. However, the whole family came along on a 16-day family excursion one year. The experience was so successful from both business and personal standpoints that Will plans to schedule one or two family outings a year from now on. When the founder of journeys International speaks of family trips, he's not talking about a week at Disneyland. His Family Trek was to Nepal.

Journeys International's local representatives met the ten-person group in Kathmandu. After two days in a small local hotel, the participants took land vehicles 200 kilometers to the Himalayas. "Every night we set up camp after an *easy* walk—three, four, or five hours," recalls Will. They eventually climbed to a comfortable 8,000 feet. The weather was balmy, although snow one night added to the experience. "The villagers had seen Westerners but never Western kids, so they were real curious. Every afternoon we tried to learn Nepali songs and teach them English ones." At dusk, the group moved into tents where they talked about the majestic vistas and hospitality of their new friends, and played games with the children. Nepalese chefs who were part of the expedition prepared five-course dinners. Soon the group went to sleep, anticipating a wake-up call in time to see dawn frame the mountains.

56

Videographer

Job Description : *A videographer documents various events for posterity, such as weddings, bar and bat mitzvahs, and other special occasions.*

- *Start-up cost as low as Rs. 1 Lac*
- *Potential first-year earnings: Rs. 3 Lacs*
- *Breakeven time from initial investment: one month to two years*
- *Ideal home-based business*
- *No staffing required*

ACTION: You pull back from the white lilies to the lilac softness of the bridesmaids. You glance at your sound equipment when Aunt Minerva begins singing "Oh, Promise Me." As you zoom in on the groom's sober handsomeness, you nod to your assistant in the corner to pan the crowd. The camera catches the tears on Granny's cheeks and the giggles from the nephews in the second pew. As the organ sounds the opening chords of the "Wedding March," you direct your video recorder at the rear of the chapel.

ROLL 'EM: You point the camera at Rutherford Beauford Smythe, the richest curmudgeon this town has ever seen. He recites the bit about being of sound mind and body in a straightforward manner, but leans forward with a gleeful gleam in his eyes when he mentions his brother and only living heir. 'Just wanted to let you know, Rodney, that I meant it when I called you a good-for-nothing. You may have bamboozled Mother, but not me. You're not getting a cent of my millions, because I'm leaving it all to the Society for Siamese Cat Research."

Video For Fun And Profit

Video technology has opened opportunities to a new group of professional videographers. Some assignments require highly skilled artistry, such as taping a high school talent contest where baton twirlers and disco dancers perform under rotating lights. Other situations—taping a legal deposition or an interview for a video dating service, for instance—mostly demand a steady hand or a tripod and some bright lights.

The possibilities in video production are limited only by the imagination. In addition to traditional filming forums, such as recording news and entertainment events, videographers now tape consumer specials, such as a bat mitzvah. In the legal realm, states increasingly allow videotaped depositions and "day-in-the-life-of" tapes that show how an injury affects an accident victim's daily routine. Real estate agents show clients videotapes

instead of driving them from house to house. Manufacturers send training videos as part of their product package. Trade associations and universities, job applicants and video dates—everybody sees video as a vehicle to get their point across.

Here's The Rub

Video possibilities may be unlimited, but to turn them into a living wage, you've got to convince buyers they need your service. Videographers may spend as much time educating the public about their services as they do on assignments.

As a videographer operating in the booming video revolution, you've got a choice. Either you can work part time at videotaping, or you can create full-time opportunities by selling as if your livelihood depends on it.

Weekend Work

Especially if you concentrate on the consumer end—taping parties, weddings, or even household possessions for insurance purposes— you can start part time. Most assignments fall on weekends anyway. Professional videographers recommend working with party providers to advertise your services by placing signs or business cards in their shops. For example, bridal shops, florists, printers, and so on are all frequented by couples planning their weddings. If you want to reach people throwing parties or gala affairs, try putting your information at catering halls or gourmet food stores that might cater such events.

You can track down the party givers yourself. Check the society pages of your newspaper for engagement announcements and synagogue records for upcoming bar and bat mitzvahs. Match their names with addresses from the phone book and send them a flyer explaining your services.

You don't need much capital to start because companies rent equipment. As for the advantages of renting, "You're always assured of getting the most up-to-date machines," writes Canape. "You never have to worry about repair and maintenance. You don't have to worry about storing your gear or insuring it."

The disadvantage: Renting can be expensive. When you build enough volume to warrant purchasing equipment, select brands that will be compatible with pieces you plan to add later. In addition to the basics (a camera, player, and color monitor), you may start with lights and sound equipment and a van to lug around all the paraphernalia. If you don't want to spring for editing equipment right away, you can rent editing facilities—or even farm the work out to editors—for $25 to $75 an hour, depending on how fancy you want to get. Outfitting a sophisticated production and editing studio and hiring an assistant or two might push start-up costs to $250,000.

Jumping In With Both Feet

If you decide to enter video production full time, chances are you've studied the technique either in college or with a production company. Some manufacturers provide fairly sophisticated training, as well.

While consumer taping can be lucrative, the anniversary or sweet-16 party you tape is a one-time affair. Likewise, legal taping may offer repeat business from a few clients but probably not enough to pay all the bills in the beginning. So don't specialize in your first year. Instead, start with a variety of assignments from as many avenues as possible. If you keep your sales hat on the same rack with your creative hat, you may come up with video opportunities potential clients haven't thought of before.

There are three ways to make money in this business: charge a lot for single assignments, resell the same tape many times, or cultivate repeat customers. Single windfalls come primarily to those who build massive reputations. Clients include cable netsworks and local television stations that need extra footage. Multiple sales—beyond commercial hits like aerobic tapes—require marketing imagination. For example, Gruenberg Video Group Inc. of New York City sells video yearbooks to high school students. Entrepreneur Paul Gruenberg trains student crews at various schools to tape events during the year. He hires freelance editors to pull visions of proms and pep rallies into a final, $30 product, complete with background music and clips of newsworthy events of the year.

Taping Attorneys

But most videographers look for repeat business: for example, relationships with attorneys. If you pursue the legal market, first bone up on what's acceptable in your state. Some states don't allow video wills. Others restrict what can be taped during a deposition or the manner in which it can be photographed. For example, most courts prefer a stationary camera to zooms and fade-outs.

To tap the legal market, mail an introductory letter to lawyers whose names you've rented from a local bar association or chosen from the Yellow Pages. You can advertise in local legal journals, although Jerry Fried, president of Ace Audio Visual Co. in Woodside, New York, warns that telemarketing or direct mail can be expensive. "I feel our service is need-based. When the customer needs the service, they look you up in the Yellow Pages." Ace advertises in the Yellow Pages under legal services, videotaping, and audiovisual equipment.

Once you get an attorney's attention, delineate the advantages of video: For example, you can tape patients who are too sick to appear in court. If there's reason to suspect a will may be contested, an attorney might suggest a video version. The judge can decide whether he or she was competent when making the will by seeing and hearing the deceased.

In addition, "Most [legal] videographers say the best way to get started is by associating yourself with a court reporting service" that takes depositions, says Charlene Canape. "Most lawyers still insist that a written record be kept in addition to the video record."

Video Bartering

In the beginning, you may have to tape a few events for free so you'll have sample videotapes to show. Why not offer your services to professionals whose help you could use? For example, tape the accoutrements and handiwork of a caterer who might recommend your services. Record a party for an advertising company executive who will help you design your brochures.

When taping an event, Canape recommends that you get specific orders from the person who commissioned the tape. "Are there certain activities (a toast, arceiving line, the arrival of an important guest) that you must be sure not to miss? Are there certain people who should be photographed more than others?" Visit the scene ahead of time to see what lighting is needed. If you're shooting a wedding, check with the church to make sure your equipment is permitted.

Since video equipment is easy to use, many people will tape their own events. But "a video involves more than just letting the camera roll," says Jerry Fried, referring to "script writing, setting up scenes, adding titles in the editing, setting up locations." Just as shutterbugs who squeeze off millions of shots turn to professional photographers for formal portraits, it's a sure bet that video hobbyists will call on professional videographers.

57

Franchising Abroad Regulations on Indian Master Franchisor

The Indian rupee is still not fully convertible and the Reserve Bank of India (RBI) has continued to maintain records of all principal financial transactions that an Indian company or business makes abroad. Although the Foreign Exchange Restrictions Act 1973 (FERA) was replaced by the Foreign Exchange Management Act 1999(FEMA), which came into force in June 2000, it has not removed the requirement of obtaining a number of RBI permissions.

Further, the RBI still regulates and limits any foreign exchange outflow. So it is still easier for a business to get permission for release of foreign exchange if it has been a foreign exchange earner. The amount of foreign exchange available is much higher and more realistic under the new regime.

Initial start-up costs

Initially, Indian franchisor abroad will have to spend foreign exchange to investigate the market and find suitable franchisees, use the services of foreign retail consultants and lawyers, and comply with the regulations of the country involved (such as completing disclosure documents, registering the franchise, registering trademarks etc...).

Then it will be a foreign exchange earner through franchise fees, royalties, fees to consultants, dividends etc. subject to paying the tax in the country where it has received such payments. Unless, the franchisor wants to be a developer and make sizeable investments and keep control over the business.

Whether the franchisor spends on initial start-up costs or becomes a developer, it still has to go through the authorised dealer in foreign exchange who makes the application to the RBI whenever foreign exchange is required. All documents have to be retained for inspection by the RBI.

In the past certain franhised outlets in the US of Indian businesses had to be shut down due to FERA violations and not due to any franchisee problems abroad.

Regulations to be adhered to

The Indian regulations that an Indian Master franchisor would have to keep in mind are given below:

BUSINESS SET-UP:

Joint Venture agreement between Indian Master franchisor and foreign business to form Master franchisee company in the foreign country.

REGULATIONS:

- ❑ FEM (Transfer or Issue of any Foreign Security) Regulations 2000, Specifically nos 3 and 5.
- ❑ Indian party's direct investment in JV abroad has restrictions:

- Total financial commitment cannot to exceed US$ 50 million in three years.*
- Foreign party involved in JV must be in the same core activity as Indian party;
- Indian party must have earned net profit in last 3 years*
- Drawal of foreign exchange from bank must not exceed 25% of net worth of Indian party as on the date of the last balance sheet;
- All transactions to be routed through one dealer in foreign exchange;
- Indian party must not be in RBI's caution list or under investigation.

- Obligations of the Indian party include:
  - Production before the RBI share certificates and documents relating to the investment within 6 months.
  - Repatriate to India dividends, royalties, other fees within 60 days of its falling due.
  - Production of audited accounts every year within prescribed time.
- *New budget seeks to allow $50 million annual investment without 3 year profitability rule.

BUSINESS SET-UP:

Simple franchisor-franchisee relationship.

REGULATIONS:

- RBI permission for transactions above $25,000, through authorised dealer/bank.
- If goods have to be exported to the franchise outlets abroad then FEM (Export of Goods and Services) Regulations 2000 would apply.
- Exporter would need to furnish declaration on full export value of goods or software. (Forms GR/SDF, PP or SOFTEX as appropriate)
- Payment for goods have to be realised and repatriated to India within 6 months from the date of export. If goods are going to a warehouse then payment can be realised 15 months from date of shipment of goods.
- RBI may seek to see irrevocable letter of credit in favour of Indian party for export of expensive items.

  Trade sample are exempted.

BUSINESS SET-UP:

Distribution Agreements involving direct investment

REGULATIONS:

- Foreign Exchange Management (Current Account Transactions) Rules 2000, Schedule III-RBI permission required to provide any credit to overseas office.
- Section 6 FEMA restriction on capital account transactions.
- RBI approval would be required for transactions such as:

- transfer or issue of foreign security by a person resident in India;
- deposits between a persons resident in India and persons resident out of India;
- Giving of a guarantee or security in respect of debt, obligation or other liability incurred by a resident in India and owed to a resident outside India.

❑ FEM(Acquisition and Transfer of Immovable Property Outside India) Regulation 2000 would apply. If Indian developer seeks to acquire or transfer property abroad RBI permission would be required.

The FEM (Foreign Currency accounts by a Person Resident in India) Regulations 2000 identifies two types of accounts that an Indian master franchisor can hold for its business and possibly get exemptions from requiring permission for using foreign exchange below $25,000; namely:

- Resident Foreign Exchange Account
- Exchange Earner's Foreign Currency Account

The Indian party can also make investment through utilization of the proceeds of ADR/GDR issues.

Unfortunately, Indian master franchisors would still have to deal with the formidable red tape at home, apart from worrying about their business abroad.

However, Indian private businesses are at least able to take the step of doing business abroad, which was practically impossible prior to 1991.

58

49 Fantastic Money-Spinning Opportunities @ e - biz

If you have a computer, a modern and connected to the Internet, then you are all ready to become a significant player in the global digital landscape with your own online business.

Of course, before setting out on your venture you need to study the market, generate small business ideas, go online, have your own e-mail address and get ready to launch your own website to promote your business venture.

once that is done you can go right ahead and pick one of these 49 business to launch yourself into the making of a successful business owner.

49 e-commerce enterprises for you to consider.

1. Sell Advertisement :

Sells ads for others on their web-sites. Engage sponsors. You will be starting your very own online advertising agency. You can sell ads on your own website too, but consider helping others get ads for their websites. Study their business, develop a target list of potential advertisers and begin by selling both banner ads that will run across the topic of their website, boxes and consider sponsorship.

2. Profit From Net Affiliations :

Make money via commissions from your network affiliations. This is the charming business that enables one to make thousands of rupees a month while sleeping. This is how it is done: you develop a website businesses. Amazon.com is probably one of the most well known net affiliations. Every time your visitor goes to Amazon.com directly from your website-and buys a book-you receive a commission from the sale. There's no bookkeeping involved; you will just receive a cheque at the end every month. There are dozens of net affiliations that you can use. to find them, search through Affiliations that you can use. To find them, search through Affiliate Sales programme Directories.

Here are some for you:

www.associate-it.com,

www.associateprograms.com'

www.clickquick.com,

wwwsitecash.com

3. Build An Online Store :

Build an online store and sell products from other enterpreneurs. Do you know a lot of crafts enterpreneurs who could benefit by reaching a worldwide audience? Organise them and offer their products for sale on your website shop.

4. Become An InternetTutor :

Conduct internet tutor workshops for students, other small business owners and anyone who wants to become a "webizen" if not a webpreneur. you can teach your classes privately or you can set up classes which are much more cost effective.

5. Design Website :

Launch you own service designer. you can follow software that exists if you are already websavvy, or take a course to really hone your talents and skills.

6. Start A B2B Business :

Sell services and products related to online ventures. See them over your own website. You will research and compile ways to help businesses use their online capabilities and sell them support services and products to help them conduct business in a way that is compititive, faster, cheaper and much better.

7. Launch An Online Zine :

Select a topic you are interested in and launch a website about it. it will be your online zine and you can make money selling ads. If you love what you do the money will follow. The internet is open to all types of interests so do not hold back because you fell zine on surfboards that were shaped from 1955 to 1961. If you build it, they will come!

8. Compile Mailing Lists :

Put together e-mailing lists for other small business owners. Your clients will be small business, organisation, hospitals, charity groups, fund raisers, clubs, and others who need to compile specific lists for an event or ongoing project.

9. Start Special Interest Services :

Start a service website that contains listings for events, concerts and other activites that will attract a dedicated group of followers. Sell ads to companies that are compatible with your product and service listings. For example, if you are developing a website of holiday parties and planning, contact appropriate companies who might be interested in advertising on such a specific site.

10. Offer Piggyback Web Space :

Visit existing business in your area and ask them if they have website. If they do not invite them to piggyback on your website for a fee, of course.

11. Sell Your Product :

Sell your product via an online cyberstore. You do not even have to have your website to sell your wares online. You can tie in with a cybermail or cyberstore by contacting one of the many existing online stores. One of the biggest and most popular is store.yahoo.com. For about $100 (approx Rs. 4,500) a month, you can list up to 50 items for sale using their website and technology. You can design the store yourself, but they will help you build a storefront for your new internet shop.

12. Start A Talk Show :

Host discussions and Question and Answer session with guest on your website. Banner ads that scroll through the conservations could be worth a nice income. This could be a serious endeavor or a fun, kitsch enterprise that develops a worldwide cult following.

13. Offer Credit Card Know-How :

Become familiar with the formats of electronic payment methods and help other entrepreneurs achieve merchants card status. Once a company or individual decides to start a business online, they will reach the fast conclusion that they must accept credit card in order to function and conduct a business. Many are under the misconception that it is extremely difficult to achieve merchant credit card status. You can investigate the many options and develop a business owners achieve this merchant credit card status.

14. Edit A Website :

Become a web editor and manage the website of the company or individual. You do not have to have been the designer or creator to manage a website and keep it current and up-to-date for your clients. You will be the webmaster. Many businesses and individual have a website, but do not have the time to keep it updated. This is where you come in selling the convenience of your time saving service.

15. Become A Web Development Manager :

Start your own business as an internet business development manager and help other small business owner investigate moneymaking options online. Develop a list of your service and start marketing your new business to other small business owners and to individuals who are contemplating staring their own online business.

16. Start A Data Tracking Venture :

Start a data-tracking venture for online biz. You can help your clients conduct research, analysis surveys and develop new products and services based on your data tracking capabilities.

17. Start A Data Mining Biz:

Launch you own business in data mining. You will be analysing sales information to increase effectiveness of your client's website.

18. Sell Your Creative Wares :

Start a website to specifically sell your own CD, designer outfit, accessory or book. Dozens need a record or a book deal. Estimate in the music business say it use to cost tens in thousands of rupees to make a CD and market it via mail order and through local shops and stores. Now, it costs much less thanks to the promotional methods of the web.

19. Establish A Research Company :

Start your own research service for customers who do not have the time or the inclination to use the internet. Book travel for client's order books they need, organise data and information. You can conduct research on a wide variety of topics for your clients and even help them to learn how to do it, too.

20. Open An Import Shop :

You can start your own import shop online. Find a product from another part of the world that you want to import and sell via your website. You can specialise in one product or develop an online catalogue. This is an exciting business for you to consider, as the possibilities are endless. Pick a topic that you love and figure out how to setup a online shop and get paid for your passion.

21. Turn Trash To Cash :

Visit e-Bay and other auction sites and start your own business turning your junk into treasure.There are so many options sites available, but you have to do some research and some reading on the online auction action so you can avoid the pitfalls.

22. Begin a Promotional Biz :

You can start a business helping others establish different types of promotion-lotteries, sweepstakes and contest on their website.Trivia contest and promotional gimmicks keep customers returning to a website for more fun and playful times. These visits are record as "hits" and more hits one has, the more they can charge for advertising. Develop several fun tricks that will keep client's coming back and try to sell them to business for use on their websites or start your own promotional website and keep the traffic coming back for your advertisers. You will need to update the trivia on a regular basis.

23. Conduct Translations :

Start a translation service for companies that want to have their website in a variety of languages. You can be the translation agent hiring others to do the actual translations if you are not proficient in the language.There are plenty of software programmes that will help you translate documents, etc. for your clients that do not want to be bothered with what they perceive as a hassle.

24. Direct Selling :

Take your direct selling products or line of multilevel marketing products and sell them online via your very own website. If you are involved in any type of multi-level marketing programme, develop a website to further extend your reach and market penetration. Check with the headquaters to make sure starting your own website will not jeopardise your relationship with the corporate bigwigs. They might have a corporate website to the market products for each distribution. It could be worth a bundle to take this business into cyberspace. Remember that you will be reaching a global audience, so make sure you determine shipping figures for international orders.

25. Write For Others :

Write articles for companies that need to create material for their websites that change frequently in fact, daily. Companies need a lot of material to keep their websites fresh and you can work on a complete repertoire of choices, graphs, contests, interviews and photo stories to keep their websites active and build traffic.

26. Help Entrepreneurs Get Online :

You will investigate all the internet Service Providers and help get your clients online. You can even help pick out a computer if they need that, too. You will educate yourself and become a savvy shopper before launching this business. Make sure you have patience, as some clients might resist change and need to be carefully coaxed along.

27. Go Cyber In Your Current :

And online capabilities to your existing business. If you have a coffee bar, install few terminals and rent them to your customers by the hour. If you have any type of business, conduct a survey to see if your clients would like it if you added a terminal so they could go online - for a fee, of course - while hanging out in your shop, store, cafe.

28. Perform Pr Services :

Start a business that specially targets online business as your clients. You will be their public relation, publicity and marketing communications centre and help publicise their websites and web related activites. Develop contests and other interesting promotion to keep their websites "sticky".

29. Manage E-Mail For Clients :

Some business, and even individual, get 100 e-mails a day. Many are junk, but a significant number might have to be answered even with a short, polite response. You can start your own business offering to manage the e-mail for your clients.

30. Create Online Scrapbooks :

Thanks to scanning technology, it is very easy to store hundreds of photographs on a disk. And, thanks to many fonts available it is to wrap text around the photographs and create interesting, witty or sentimental scrapbook for a variety of events. You can start an online scrapbook business that provides a wide range of books, or that specialise in one type say weddings, for example. You will contact couples who are about to tie the knot and ask them to e-mail you photos, the invitation, etc. from the wedding scrapbook and then e-mail it to all of their guests that attended the wedding.

31. Publish Newsletter For Yourself Or Other Biz :

Newsletters are wonderful vehicles to keep people informed of what you are doing. You can develop e-mailing lists to promote your newsletter and distribute it to greatest number of people you possible can. Offer top stories, photos, include a Q&A about your particular business and ask recipients to send you a special requests. You might just develop an entire new market and client base that will be generated from your e-mail newsletter. You can start a newsletter for small-to-medium sized business in your community, but do not ever limit yourself geographically with the internet. You can create a newsletter for a small company in Port Blair even if you live in Srinagar providing you understand the business, the topic of interest and know how to communicate to their target market.

32. Promote Local Events & Celebrities :

If you want to help your community, but again do not limit yourself geographically, start a fun tabloidstyled promotional website for celebrities, politicians and events in your region. You can offer interviews with politicians, publish photographs of upcoming theatrical events, and much more.

33. Sponsor A Sports Site For Community Teams :

Local sports teams in your area - everysthing from the national and state-level teams to the high school girl's badminton team - would love to be immortalised on the web. They might not have a website, but you can create a roving sports reporter website that will include regional activities of all the teams. You will include scores, tournaments, events and photographs thanks to your scanner. You can charge teams a fee to be included on your website, or you can generate revenue exclusively from the advertising you will sell to local sports stores, batting ranges, golf courses and local tennis club.

34. Become A Cyber Assistant :

You can launch a personal or corporate concierge business right from your kitchen table. Work for others conducting research, putting together mailing lists, ordering tickets, and more.

35. Open An Auction House :

You can use e-Bay and some of the other online auction houses to sell goods and old treasures for others. Specialise in one type of item-sports, collectibles, for example - or generalise and sell just about anything, anywhere, anytime. You take a profit of the sales.

36. Start On Line Art Gallery :

Contact local artists in your community and scan photos of their artwork sculpture, and photography into your computer. Post it on various auction websites or start your own website selling their artistic efforts. You can sell advertisements from local art supply stores, local farmers, etc. on your website to make even more cash from your new online business.

37.Teach Class :

Contact local learning seminars and adult education course directors and propose a crash course on the internet. You can even sell a guide to accompany your lecture series. Teach netiquette, e-mail, marketing and the nuts-and-bolts of getting online.

38. Launch A Travel Service :

Are you an expert in one part of the world? Do you love Shillong or Goa and know lots of its very special spots, cafes, walks, and parks? Do you know the best way to tour Himachal Pradesh? Then start a travel website on your obession and develop advertisements bulletin boards, chat rooms and have a really good time in the process making money for something about which you are passionate. You can also sell ads to airlines,travel bookstores, travel product catalogue, the local luggage stores and limo services. Think big!

39. Arrange Events For Senior Clubs & Groups :

There are plenty of senior citizen groups and clubs all over the country and because of our aging demographics, these groups are growing. but the activites that senior in the next few years will crave will probably be a lot more adventurous than what current crop of 80-year-old want to do. You can start a website that will attract the activity directors of senior citizen clubs from all over the country. They will e-mail you with requests for activites, ideas for trips and party plans for special events holidays. You can provide than with a list of local resources or start your own business not only providing the party planning ideas, but actually hiring local party planner to help implement these great festive ideas.

40. Publish A Local Online Magazine :

How many residents in your community are online? If you determine that you have thousands of folks with online status, consider starting your own online magazine. You'll write about local events, affairs, politics, publish articles on upcoming shows, plays and community happenings along with letters to the editor, essays and more. You will also carry advertisments from local business who want to reach a very targeted market. If you are web savvy, this is an easy business to establish and run. You can change your magazine on a weekly, biweekly or monthly basis.

41. Start An Online Catalogue :

You can sell products created by others on your website. You do not need to develop any products or invent the next pet rock. Sell what others have -such as their products, kitchen gadgets, creative artwork, practical offerings and much more. You can even help local schools sell their items with your every own online store.

42. Start Your Own Survey Biz :

You can use the internet to create your own surveys and polls of Internet users for businesses and others and you will also conduct them for fun on a wide variety of topics - sometimes wild and wacky - just to attract visitors to your site.

43. Publish Articles, Features Offline :

You can become a writer specialising in various aspects of the internet and have your articles, features and columns published in newspapers and magazines. many newspapers around the country do not yet have staff writers to develop Internet-related copy, so you can carve yourself a nice niche doing this. If you are a web designer or have an Internet business, consider offering bylined articles to editors at no cost. You will receive some nice publicity having your byline published. These bylines and clients that could be generated from the articles are worth more than the freelance fee you would receive.

44. Online Sales For Businesses :

You use your website as a cyber superstore to promote and sell goods for businesses that do not actively use their websites to build their business and sell their goods and services. promote local and regional businesses. You charge a monthly fee for the service and take a cut of products sold via your website.

45. Nod To Nostalgia :

The whole world is excited about collectibles and nostalgia items and you can set up a web business informing your visitors about trade shows, publications, books, other websites, collectors, shops, stores, and centers that deal in collectible goods. Remember, your audience is now global so do not forget to mention that little shop in Jaipur that sells those terrific collectible figurines made by men and women all over the state.

46. Teach A Class Online :

Do you posses a special talent or skill? Could you teach it to others online? If you are determine that the answer is 'yes' then write up your course as succinctly as possible and start a website "teaching" your talent or skill.

47. Engage In Online Trading :

Proceed with caution, but dabble if you have some disposable income and want to start your own business trading stocks. Make sure you are working with capital that you do not need to rely on for other uses or any significant expenditure. begin by examining the option with E-Trade, Ameritrade, DLKDIRECT, Datek and American Express.You can learn about online investing and the stock market in general by visiting the sites of such online financial gurus as: Motley Fool, No Load Fundx, Low Priced Stock Surevy, Zacks Advisor and the financial section of major daily newspaper.

48. Become An Online Organizer :

There are a lot of people out there who are eager to get into the Internet but do not know how to organise their favorite sites into "Bookmarks" or do not want to take the time to research some of the options that will be most helpful and valuable to them.This is Where you come in and charge for your services.You can develop a questionnaire that you will have your clients fill out that will help you understand their needs and interest and you will be able to determine what they really need from the tremendous resources of the Internet.You will help them organise and focus their wants and needs. After the initial consultation, you will return home and surf the net their interests and return to your client's home or office to set it all up. Do not forget to send a direct mail piece to various community groups in your region who might need your services too.

49. Evaluate Online Needs For Others :

You can establish a small business helping other entrepreneurs figure out what value the Internet holds for them. You can help them determine whether or not they would profit with an active website, or if they merely require an e-mail address to keep in touch with their customers and offer a means by which potential customers from all over the globe can contact them.You can also most likely establish an online cosultancy helping small business owners get online and manage their online businesses and website presence.

117. MANUFACTURE OF TIN CONTAINERS
118. MANUFACTURE OF STORAGE TANKS, PRESSURE VESSELS, HEAT EXCHANGERS
119. MARK II HAND PUMPS
120. MARUTI WORKSHOP CUM - SERVICE STATION
121. MECHANICAL JACKS
122. METAL CUTTING DIE DESIGN
123. METAL CUTTING OF AND GRINDING WHEELS (ABBRASIVE CUTTING WHEELS)
124. METAL HOOKS & CLIPS
125. METAL SEPARATION (COPPER, TIN, LEAD) FROM SPENT WASH ACID
126. METALLIC RING JOINTS
127. METALLIC GASKET (SPIRAL WOUND)
128. MICROVEE & ABSOLUTE FILTER
129. MICROWAVE OVEN
130. MILD STEEL INGOTS
131. MINI STEEL PLANT
132. MODERN VEHICLE WORKSHOP
133. MOPED
134. M.S.HINGES
135. M.S.INGOT AND HR. STEEL STRUCTURALS
136. M.S.INGOT BY INDUCTION FURNACES
137. M.S.PIPES
138. M.S. WELDING ELECTRODE
139. MUFFLERS & SILENCERS FOR THREE WHEELERS
140. NAIL CUTTER WITH FILER & MANICURE
141. NICHROME WIRE
142. NICKEL LINED SCREENS
143. NON-FERROUS ALLOY ROLLING
144. NON-FERROUS FORGING
145. NON-FERROUS FOUNDRY
146. NON PRESSURE
147. INCANDESCENT LAMP
148. NUMBER COMBINATION LOCKS FOR LUGGAGES
149. NUTS & BOLTS
150. PAPER COATED ALUMINIUM AND COPPER WIRE
151. PETROMAX CONTAINER
152. PHOTO ETCHING OF STAINLESS STEEL PLATES
153. PIPE GALVANIZING PLANT
154. PISTON RING-AUTOMOBILE
155. PLANT PROTECTION EQUIPMENTS
156. PLATINUM LABORATORY APPARATUS
157. PRESSURE COOKER & ALUMINIUM UTENSILS
158. PRESSURE COOKER (ALUMINIUM)
159. PRESSURE DIE CASTING
160. PRINTED ALUMINIUM COLLAPSIBLE TUBES
161. PRINTED TIN CONTAINERS
162. PRINTING PRESS (CYLINDER MACHINE)
163. PUMPS FOR CHEMICAL INDUSTRY (SPECIAL)
164. RAILWAY SLEEPERS (M.S.)
165. RAZOR TWIN BLADE
166. R.C.C SPUN PIPES
167. RECONDITIONING OF M.S. DRUMS/BARRELS
168. RE-ROLLING COPPER AND BRASS SHEET AND RODS
169. RE-ROLLING MILLS
170. RESIN COATED SAND
171. RESIN CORED SOFT SOLDER WIRES
172. ROLLING MILL (BY INDUCTION FURNACE) & MANUFACTURE OF BARS, ANGLES, SQUARES, TUBES AND OTHERS
173. ROLLER BEARING & FORGING
174. ROLLING OF STAINLESS STEEL PATTA
175. RUBBER INSULATED PLIERS (HAND TOOLS)
176. RUBBING COMPOUND FOR AUTOMOBILES
177. SCIENTIFIC LABORATORY EQUIPMENTS
178. SCOOTER ASSEMBLING
179. SECONDARY LEAD EXTRACTION BY SCRAP BATTERY PLATES,PIPES & SHEET
180. SEAMLESS M.S. TUBES & PIPES
181. SELF TAPPING STEEL SCREW
182. SEWING NEEDLES
183. S.G. IRON & ALLOY STEEL
184. SHEET METAL PRODUCTS, (FERROUS/NON-FERROUS)
185. SHIP/MARINE CONTAINER
186. SHOCK ABSORBERS
187. SHOE EYELETS
188. SHOT AND GRITS BY AUTOMIZATION PROCESS
189. SHOVELS
190. SILICO MANGANESE ALLOYS
191. SILENCERS (MUFFLERS) EXHAUST & TAIL PIPE FOR ALL TYPES OF VEHICLES
192. SINTERED BEARING
193. SINTERED BUSHES
194. SINTERED METAL PRODUCTS
195. SOFT AND HARD FERRITES
196. SPANNERS
197. SPARK PLUGS
198. STEEL PLANT (ELECTRIC ARC FURNACE BASED- EAF)
199. SPHERIODAL GRAPHITE CAST IRON
200. SPRAY DRYER
201. STAINLESS STEEL HINGES
202. STAINLESS STEEL SHEET ROLLING TO PRODUCE STAINLESS STEEL UTENSILS
203. STAINLESS STEEL UTENSILS
204. STAPLE PINS,PAPER PIN , GEM CLIPS ETC.
205. STEEL CASTINGS
206. STEEL CHAIN
207. STEEL FOUNDRY
208. STEEL FURNITURES AND ELECTRICAL APPLIANCES
209. STEEL PLANT (MINI)
210. STEEL RODS AND COILS FROM SCRAPS
211. STEEL ROLLING MILL
212. STEEL STRIPS (COLD ROLLED) SILICON WITH GRAIN RIENTED FOR ELECTRIC USE
213. STEEL TRANSMISSION LINE TOWERS & ROLLING MILL TO PRODUCE STEEL SECTION
214. STEEL FURNITURES AND ELECTRICAL APPLIANCES
215. STEEL WIRE DRAWING AND GALVANIZING
216. STEEL WOOL
217. SUBMERGED ARC WELDED PIPES
218. SUBMERSIBLE PUMP MANUFACTURING
219. SUPER ENAMELLED COPPER WIRE
220. THREE WHEELERS
221. TIE-ROD ENDS
222. TIN CONTAINERS
223. TOOLROOM AND SHEET METAL PRODUCTS
224. TRACTOR TRAILERS
225. TRANSMISSION POWER FITTING
226. TUBULAR POLES
227. SUPER ENAMELLED COPPER WIRES
228. TUBULAR POLES FOR ELECTRICAL TRANSMISSION (BY FABRICATION PROCESS)
229. TUBULAR POLES OF M.S. & HIGH TENSILE STEEL
230. VACUUM CLEANERS
231. VACUUM FLASK (STAINLESS STEEL)
232. VALVES FOR REFRIGERATION AND AIR-CONDITION
233. VEHICLE WELDING & PAINTING
234. VENETION BLIND
235. WASHING MACHINES (AUTOMATIC & COMPUTERISED)
236. WATER CONTROLLER (AUTOMATIC)
237. WATCH STRAPS/CHAINS/ BRACELETS/BELT BRASS & STAINLESS STEEL
238. WATER COOLERS
239. WELDED WIRE MESH
240. WELDING ELECTRODES
241. WICK STOVES
242. WIND MILL WINDOW FRAME (FERROUS & NON-FERROUS)
243. WRIST WATCH

359. DI ETHYL OXALATE
360. DI METHYL ORTHOPHTHALATE
361. DI-METHYL PHTHALATE
362. DICLOFENAC GEL
363. DIOCTYL PHTHALATE (DOP)
364. DI PHENYL GLYCERINE
365. DI PHENYL OXIDE
366. DINITRO-CHLORO BENZENE
367. DISTILLED WATER
368. DODECYL BENZENE SULPHONATE
369. DUSTLESS CHALK
370. EDTA & ITS SALTS
371. ELECTROLESS NICKEL PLATING ON PLASTICS
372. ENDOSULFAN
373. EPOXY RESIN BASED COMPOUND
374. ETHYL ACETATE
375. EHTYL ETHER
376. ETHYL ALCOHOL (POTABLE LIQUOR)
377. ETHYL HEXANOL
378. EXTRACTION OF ESSENTIAL OILS BY SUGAR CRITICAL FLUID (CARBON DIOXIDE) METHOD FROM FLOWERS, HERBAL & SPICES
379. FERRIC ALUM
380. FERRO CHROME LIGNO SULPHONATE
381. FERRO MANGANESE
382. FERRO SILICONE
383. FERRO VANADIUM FROM VANADIUM SLUDGE
384. FERROUS SILICATE
385. FERROUS SULPHATE
386. FERTILIZER FROM ANIMAL BLOOD & LEATHER WASTE
387. FLUORESCENT TUBE LIGHT POWDER
388. FOAMED PVC COMPOUNDING & ITS PRODUCTS
389. FORMALDEHYDE
390. FRACTIONAL DISTILLATION OF D.M.O (DEMENTHOLIZED OIL)
391. FRACTIONAL DISTILLATION OF ESSENTIAL OIL & MEDICINAL PLANT EXTRACT
392. FRICTION DUST (LIQUID & POWDER) FROM CNSL
393. FRUIT FLAVOURS
394. FURFURAL FROM RICE HUSK
395. GARLIC ACID
396. GASKET SHELLAC COMPOUND
397. GEAR OIL
398. GIBBERELLIC ACID
399. GLASS PUTTY
400. GLYCERINE
401. GOSSYPOL (POLY PHENOL) FROM COTTON SEED OIL
402. GUAR GUM POWDER
403. HAIR FIXER (HAIR GEL TYPE)
404. H - ACID
405. HENNA PASTE MAKING
406. HEPTAL DEHYDE
407. HIGH CARBON FERRO CHROME
408. HYDRATED CALCIUM SILICATE BRICK
409. HYDRATED LIME FROM SEA SHELL
410. HYDROCHLORIC ACID
411. HYDRO FLUORIC ACID
412. HYDROGEN PEROXIDE (BY AUTO-OXIDATION PROCESS)
413. ICE PACKS (SOLUTIONS TYPE, WHITE GEL TYPE, VIOLET SEMI SOLID POLYMER TYPE)
414. IMPROVING DROP POINT PARAFFIN WAX FROM 45-50°C TO 75-80°C
415. INDUSTRIAL ALCOHOL
416. INTEGERATED COMPLEX OF EASTER & ALLIED PRODUCTS (D.O.P, D.B.P, ETHYL ACETATE WIRE ENAMEL & CABLE JELLY)
417. IMFL (WHISKY) & COUNTRY LIQUOR
418. IRON OXIDE FOR MAKING FERITTE
419. IRON SULPHIDE
420. JUTE BATCHING OIL
421. KESH KALA TEL (HAIR DYE LOTION) (VASMOL 33, BLACK NITE TYPE)
422. L-LYSINE MONOHYDROCHLORIDE
423. LACTIC ACID FROM WHITE SUGAR BY FERMENTATION PROCESS
424. LDPE GRANULES FROM VIRGIN (LDPE RESIN)
425. LEAD EXTRACTION FROM BATTERY SCRAP
426. LEAD OXIDE (A) LEAD MONOXIDE (B) LEAD TETRA OXIDE (C) GREYLEAD OXIDE
427. LIQUID GLUCOSE & ITS BY PRODUCTS
428. LIQUID OXYGEN BOTTLING PLANT
429. LIQUID SHOE POLISH
430. LIQUID FLOOR POLISH
431. LUBE OIL VISCOSITY IMPROVED FOR P.P.G/P.E.G.
432. LUBRICANTS ASHLESS 100% COMBUSTION
433. MAGNESIUM CARBONATE AND MAGNESIUM BICARMONATE
434. MAGNESIUM HYDROXIDE POWDER
435. MAGNESIUM SILICATE
436. MAGNESIUM SULPHATE
437. MALACHITE GREEN
438. MALEIC ANHYDRIDE
439. MANGANESE SULPHATE
440. MANUFACTURING OF CARBON MONO-OXIDE WATER GAS
441. MENTHOL BOLD CRYSTALS FROM FLAKES
442. MENTHOL CRYSTAL & MENTHA OIL
443. MERCURIC OXIDE
444. METAL PRE-TREATMENT CHEMICALS
445. METHANE GAS BY SODIUM ACETATE & SODA LIME
446. METHYL ACETYL RICINOLATE
447. METOL
448. METOL FROM HYDROQUINONE & METHYLAMINE
449. MICANITE
450. MICRO NUTRIENT MIXTURE
451. MINERAL WATER
452. MINERAL WATER AND PET BOTTILNG PLANT
453. MINERAL WATER IN BOTTLES, GLASS AND POUCHES
454. MINI CEMENT PLANT (BY ROTARY KILN PROCESS)
455. MIXED FERTILIZER
456. MOSQUITO & FLIES REPELLENT AGARBATTI (INCENSE STICKS)
457. MONO CHLORO ACETIC ACID
458. MONOCROTOPHOS (TECHNICAL)
459. MOSQUITO COIL
460. MOSQUITO COIL & MAT
461. MOSQUITO MAT
462. MOTHER TINCTURE & BIO CHEMIC MEDICINES
463. NAPHTHALENE & PHENYL (INTEGRATED UNIT)
464. NATURAL MINERAL WATER BY REVERSE OSMOSIS PROCESS
465. NICKEL PLATING BRIGHTNER (PRIMARY OR CARRIER BRIGHTNER & SECONDARY BRIGHTNER)
466. NICKEL SULPHATE
467. NICOTINE FROM TOBACCO WASTE
468. NICOTINE SULPHATE FROM TOBACCO WASTE
469. NITRO BENZENE
470. NITRO CELLULOSE SANDING SEALER/LACQUER
471. NITRO MUSK
472. NITROGEN & OXYGEN GAS PLANT
473. NON-IONIC SURFACTANT (WETTING AGENT)
474. NO-CARB PASTE
475. OCTANOL
476. ORTHO NITRO PHENOL
477. OXALIC ACID FROM MOLASSES
478. OXALIC ACID FROMRICE HUSK
479. OXALIC ACID FROM TREE BARK
470. OXALIC ACID FROM WASTE VEGETABLES
471. OXYGEN GAS PLANT
472. OXYGEN GAS PLANT (AIR SEPERATION METHOD)
473. PARA-AMINO BENZOIC ACID
474. PARA-AMINO PHENOL
475. PARA TOLUENE SULPHONIC ACID
476. PECTIN FROM RAW PAPAYA
477. PERFUME (LEMON & OTHERS)

CRUDE NAPHTHA
570. TRIMETHYL AMMONIUM CHLORIDE
571. TRIPHENYL PHOSPHITE (T.P.P)
572. ULTRAMARINE BLUE (LIQUID)
573. UREA FORMALDEHYDE & MELAMINE FORMALDEHYDE POWDER
574. UNDECYLINIC ACID
575. VINYL ACETATE MONOMER
576. VITAMIN C
577. VITAMIN E
578. WASTE WATER TREATMENT PLANT FOR INDUSTRIAL SECTOR IN INDIA (ONLY MARKER SURVEY)
579. WIRE DRAWING LUBRICANT
580. WIRE ENAMEL
581. XANTHATES
582. YELLOW DEXTRIN
583. ZINC CHLORIDE
584. ZINC OXIDE
585. ZINC PHOSPHATING BY COLD PROCESS
586. ZINC SILICATE
587. ZINC STEARATE
588. ZINC SULPHATE
589. ZINC SULPHATE MONOHYDRATE
590. ACID BLACK
591. AURAMINE'O'
592. AZO DYES STUFF
593. DYE & DYE INTERMEDIATE
594. DYE INTERMEDIATES
595. MALACHITE GREEN
596. METHYLENE BLUE
597. PHTHALOCYANINE BLUE
598. PHTHALOCYANINE BLUE & GREEN
599. REACTIVE DYES
600. SULPHUR BLACK DYE
601. VAT DYES
602. WATER CHILLING PLANT
603. WADDING OIL (100%) FOR WADDING OF COTTON HOSIERY CLOTH IN THE DYEING PROCESS
604. WHITE OIL
605. WAX FLOOR POLISH

ELECTRICAL, ELECTONICS, COMPUTERS AND INFOTECH/IT PROJECTS

606. AIR CONDITIONING
607. ALUMINIUM ALLOY CONDUCTOR
608. ALUMINIUM CABLE
609. ALUMINIUM ELECTROYTIC CAPACITORS
610. AUDIO CASSETTE ASSEMBLING & RECORDING
611. AUDIO CASSETTES DUPLICATING RECORDING
612. AUDIO CASSETTES & AUDIO STUDIO
613. AUDIO CASSETTES PLANE & RECORDED
614. AUDIO MAGNETIC HEADS
615. AUDIO MAGNETIC TAPE
616. AUDIO/VIDEO CASSETTES
617. AUTO BULB/LAMPS
618. AUTOMATIC VOLTAGE STABILIZER
619. BATTERY PLATES
620. BACK OFFICE (Rs. 5000/-)
621. B/W TV & COMPUTER MONITOR PICTURE TUBE
622. BREAD BOARDS
623. CALL CENTRE
624. CAMERA (35 MM)
625. CAPACITORS
626. CARBON ELECTRODE USED FOR BATTERY CELL
627. CARBON POTETIOMETERS
628. CEILING FAN
629. CERAMIC INSULATOR
630. CHILDREN INFOTECH TRAINING INSTITUTE (Rs. 5000/-)
631. CHOKE AND PATTI
632. CHOKE AND STARTER
633. CHOKE USED FOR FLUORESCENT LAMPS
634. COLOUR TELEVISION
635. COLOUR AND BLACK & WHITE TELEVISION
636. COMPACT DISC
637. COMPACT DISC PLAYER (AUDIO/VIDEO)
638. COMPUTER EDUCATION INSTITUTE
639. COMPUTER ASSEMBLY
640. COMPUTER HARDWARE
641. COMPUTER KEYBOARD
642. COMPUTER PERIPHERALS
643. COMPUTER PRINTERS
644. COMPUTER RIBBON
645. COMPUTER RIBBON REINKING OR REFILLING
646. COMPUTER STATIONERY
647. COMPUTER STATIONERY &

IMPORTED HARDWARE PARTS
648. COMPUTER TERMINALS
649. COMPUTERISED WASHING MACHINE (AUTOMATIC)
650. COMPUTER SOFTWARE
651. CONDENSER FOR MOTOR USING MPP FILM
652. CONTENT DEVELOPMENT CENTRE (EOU) (Rs. 5000/-)
653. CONTROL PANEL BOARD
654. COOLING COIL FOR AIR CONDITIONERS
655. COPPER STRIP COIL FROM SCRAP
656. CORDLESS TELEPHONES
657. CYBER CAFE
658. CYBERKIOSK (Rs. 5000/-)
659. DATA PROCESSING CENTRE (Rs. 5000/-)
660. D.C. MICRO MOTORS
661. D.G.SETS
662. DISH ANTENNA AND CABLE T.V. NETWORK EQUIPMENT
663. DISTRIBUTION TRANSFORMERS & REPAIRS
664. DOMESTIC ELECTRICAL APPLIANCES- ROOM COOLER, WASHING MACHINE, WATER HEATER, ELECTRIC ROOM HEATER
665. E-SCHOOL
666. E-COMMERCE/BUSINESS
667. ELECTRIC ENERGY METER
668. ELECTRIC FANS
669. ELECTRIC HORN FOR AUTOMOBILE
670. ELECTRIC LAMP/GLS (INCANDESCENT LAMP)
671. ELECTRIC MIXER
672. ELECTRIC MOTORS UP TO 10 HP. REWINDING OF ALL TYPES OF MOTORS WATER PUMPS
673. ELECTRIC MOTOR WINDING (FOR FAN, MIXIES, ETC.)
674. ELECTRIC STEAM IRON
675. ELECTRICAL APPLIANCES
676. ELECTRICAL FIXTURES
677. ELECTRICAL STAMPING
678. ELECTROLYTIC CAPACITORS
679. ELECTROMAGNETIC RELAY
680. ELECTRONIC BALAST/CHOK
681. ELECTRICAL CHOKE
682. ELECTRONIC DIGITAL WATCHES
683. ELECTRONIC DIGITAL WEIGHING MACHINE
684. ELECTRONIC FIRE ALARM
685. ELECTRONIC GAS STOVE LIGHTERS
686. ELECTRONIC PRESSURE INDICATORS, ELECTRICALS, ELECTRONIC LIQUID LEVEL INDICATORS, ELECTRONIC TEMPERATURE INDICATOR, DIGITAL TACHOMETER
687. ELECTRONIC TELEPHONE INSTRUMENTS
688. ELECTRONIC TOYS
689. ELECTRONIC WATCHES & CLOCKS
690. FAX MACHINES
691. F.H.P MOTORS
692. FLOPPY DISKETTES
693. FLUORESCENT LAMP STARTER
694. FLUORESCENT TUBULAR

LAMPS WITH INTRODUCTION TO MERCURY VAPOUR LAMP
695. FRANCHISEE COMPUTER EDUCATION CENTRE (Rs. 5000)
696. GAS DETECTOR (L.P.G)
697. GENERATOR SET & PUMP SETS
698. GENERATOR (BATTERY OPERATED)
699. GIS SERVICE CENTRE (GEOGRAPHICAL INFORMATION SYSTEMS)
700. HARDWARE FITTING FOR TRANSMISSION LINE OVERHEAD LINE MATERIAL
701. HEADERS FOR TRANSISTOR ICS SEMI CONDUCTOR
702. H.T & L.T INSULATORS
703. H.T & M.V INDUSTRIAL CUBICAL SWITCH BOARD
704. INFORMATION MOVING DISPLAY (L.E.D TYPE)
705. INSURANCE CLAIM PROCESSING CENTRE (EOU) (Rs. 5000/-)
706. INTEGRATED CIRCUITS
707. INTERNET BASED STOCK TRADING (Rs. 5000/-)
708. INTERNET SERVICE PROVIDER (I.S.P.)
709. JELLY FILLED TELEPHONE CABLES
710. LAP TOP COMPUTERS
711. LEAD ACID BATTERIES
712. LEAD ACID BATTERY PLATES AND ASSEMBLING OF BATTERY
713. LEGAL TRANSCRIPTION & SECRETARIAL SERVICES CENTER (EOU)(Rs. 5000/-)
714. LIGHT EMITTING DIODES (L.E.D)
715. LINEAR ICS TRAINER KIT
716. LOUD SPEAKER
717. L.T TRANSFORMER REPAIRING
718. MEDICAL TRANSCRIPTION CENTRE
719. METAL FILM RESISTORS
720. METALLISED POLYPROPYLENE, POLYESTER FILM CAPACITOR
721. MICA BASE ELECTRONIC COMPONENTS
722. MICA PAPER WASTE PAPER FROM MICA WASTE
723. MICRO PROCESSORS TRAINER KITS BASED ON MICRO PROCESSORS
724. MINI COMPUTER (PERSONAL COMPUTER)
725. MINIATURE CIRCUIT BREAKER (M.C.B)
726. MINIATURE WATCH BATTERIES (BUTTON CELL)
727. MIXER/GRINDER (MIXI)
728. MONO CHROME COMPUTER MONITOR
729. MOTOR START ELECTROLYTIC CAPACITOR
730. MULTI LAYER P.C.B
731. MULTIPLE RELAY FOR LOW VOLTAGE
732. NEON INDICATOR
733. NEON SIGN MANUFACTURE
734. OPTICAL FIBRE CABLES
735. ON LINE SHOPPING MALL (Rs. 5000/-)
736. OPTO MECHANICAL & ELECTRICAL EQUIPMENTS
737. PHOTO COLOUR LAB
738. PICTURE TUBE (B/W)
739. PLAIN PAPER COPIER
740. PLASTIC FILM CAPACITORS
741. POLYESTER CAPACITORS
742. PORTABLE GENERATOR SET
743. PORTAL
744. PORTABLE TELEVISION(TV)
745. POWER CAPACITORS
746. POWER INVERTERS
747. POWER PLANT
748. POWER TRANSFORMERS UP TO 600 KVA
749. PRINTED CIRCUIT BOARD
750. PVC WIRES & CABLES
751. RE-CONDITIONING OF PICTURE TUBE
752. RESIN CAST CT & PT (1 KV)
753. SEMI CONDUCTOR DEVICE
754. SEMI CONDUCTORS FOR TRANSISTORS & DIODES
755. SETTING UP OF A VIDEO STUDIO
756. SMOKE DETECTORS
757. SOLAR CELLS
758. SOLAR MODULES
759. SOLAR PHOTO VOLTAIC SYSTEM
760. SOLDER FLUXES
761. SOLAR WATER HEATING PANELS
762. STEEL FURNITURE & ELECTRICAL APPLIANCES
763. STEREO AMPLIFIERS
764. STEREO CASSETTE RECORDERS/PLAYERS
765. STREET LIGHT FITTINGS SURGE SUPPRESSOR
766. TANTALUM CAPACITORS
767. TEFLON COATED ELECTRIC CABLE
768. TELEMEDICINE (DISTANCE HEALTH CARE) (Rs. 5000/-)
769. TELEPHONE CORD/CABLE
770. TELEPHONE (PUSH BUTTON TYPE)
771. TELEPHONE (PUSH BUTTON & CORDLESS)
772. TELEVISION (CTV & B/W)
773. TELEVISION (3-D)
774. TELEVISION DEFLECTION COMPONENTS
775. TELEVISION SIGNAL BOOSTERS
776. TELEVISION TUNERS
777. TRACTION BATTERIES
778. TRAINING INSTITUTE OF MEDICAL TRANSCRIPTION
779. TRANSFORMER FOR B/W TV
780. TRANSFORMER FOR VOLTAGE STABILIZER & E.H.T
781. TRANSMISSION POWER LINE FITTING
782. TRANSMISSION TOWER FITTING
783. TV AUDIO EQUIPMENT CABINETS & THEIR ASSEMBLING UNIT
784. UN-INTERRUPTED POWER SUPPLY (U.P.S)
785. VARIABLE FREQUENCY
786. VARIABLE VOLTAGE A.C. DRIVE
787. VIDEO CASSETTES (COMPLETE MANUFACTURING & ASSEMBLING)
788. VIDEO CASSETTES RECORDER (V.C.R)
789. VIDEO FILM STUDIO
790. VOLTAGE REGULATOR FOR AUTOMOBILES
791. VOLTAGE STABILIZERS
792. VOLTAGE STABLIZER & T.V. GAIN BOOSTER
793. WAX AND CHEMICAL COATED, BRAIDED TINSEL WIRE
794. WEBSITE DESIGN & E-MAIL REGISTERING
795. WELDING ELECTRODES
796. WIND ENERGY POWER PROJECT (10 MW)
796A WIRES (METAL)

FOOD, AGRO FOOD, PROCESSED FOOD, AGRO PLANTATION, CULTIVATION, FARMING, DAIRY/MILK, TOBACCO/PAN MASALA, BREWERY & DISTILLERY, EDIBLE OILS, EOU FOOD PRODUCTS AND ALLIED PRODUCTS

797. ALCOHOLIC BEVERAGES & VENEGAR FROM COCONUT WATER
798. ALCOHOL DRINKS FROM ETHYL ALCOHOL BY MIXING OF VARIOUS FLAVOURS
799. ANTI SCALE COMPOUND FOR ADDING INTO SUGAR JUICE BOILING
800. APPLE JUICE CONCENTRATED & DEHYDRATED FRUIT & VEGETABLES
801. ARTIFICIAL FISH MEAL FOR POULTRY FEED
802. AUTOMATIC BISCUIT PLANT
803. BABY CEREAL FOOD AND MILK POWDER
804. BACTERIA FOR CANE JUICE
805. BAKER'S YEAST
806. BAKERY INDUSTRY
807. BANANA PUREE
808. BEER & WINE
809. BEER PLANT (BREWERY)
810. BIDI
811. BIDI & CIGARETTE
812. BISCUIT PLANT

813. BREAD (AUTOMATIC PLANT)
814. BLACK PEPPER (SPICES)
815. BREAD AND BISCUITS
816. BREEDING FARM
817. BROILER CHICKEN
819. BUTTON MUSHROOM CULTIVATION & PROCESSING
820. CANNING OF RASAGULLAS IN METAL CANS
821. CAFFEIN FROM TEA WASTE
822. CANNING OF FRUITS & VEGETABLES
823. CASEIN AND BY-PRODUCTS
824. CASHEW FRUIT JUICE FROM CASHEW FRUIT APPLE
825. CASHEWNUT KERNEL EXTRACTION FROM CASHEWNUT FRUIT
826. CASHEWNUT SHELL LIQUID & KERNEL PROCESSING
827. CASHEW FENI
828. CATECHEU (BY CHEMICAL PROCESS)
829. CATTLE FEED FROM TAPIOCA
830. CHEWING & BUBBLE GUM
831. CHICKEN/SHEEP MEAT PROCESSING
832. CHOCOLATE (MILK)
833. CIGARETTE AND BEEDIES
834. COCOA BUTTER FROM COCOA MASS
835. COCONUT PRODUCTS & BY PRODUCTS PROCESS COMPLEX
836. COLD/SOFT DRINKS
837. COLLECTION OF MILK AND MILK MAKING POWDER
838. COLLECTION OF MILK AND PACKING IN POLYTHENE POUCH (1/2 KG.1 KG. & 2 KG.)
839. CONDENSED MILK (SWEETNED)
840. CONFECTIONERY INDUSTRY (TOFFEE & CANDY, SEMI-AUTOMATIC PLANT)
841. COUNTRY LIQUOR FROM MOLASSES
842. CIGARETTE
843. DAIRY FARM AND DAIRY (MILK) PRODUCTS (PASTEURISED MILK, BUTTER, GHEE, PANEER)
844. DAIRY FARM TO PRODUCE MILK & PACKING IN POUCHES (50%) & CAN(50%)
845. DAIRY FOR MILK PROCESSING
846. DAIRY FARM (BUFALO)
847. DAL (PULSE) MILL UNIT
848. DEHYDRATION OF CARROT & GARLIC
849. DEHYDRATION & CANNING OF FRUITS & VEGETABLES
850. DEHYDRATION OF FIGS
851. DEHYDRATION OF FRUITS AND VEGETABLES
852. DEHYDRATED ONIONS AND ONION POWDER
853. DRY ICE BY BREAKING OF AIR
854. DRYING OF RED CHILLIES, HALDI, DHANIA, AND GREEN PEAS
855. EGG POWDER (40,000 EGGS PROCESSING PER DAY)
856. EXPORT OF PROCESSED FOODS AND MARINE PRODUCTS
857. FISH CANNING & POUCHING
859. FISH FARMING (PRAWN & OTHER MARINE PRODUCTS)
860. FISH MEAL
861. FLOUR MILL AND MUSTARD OIL
862. FOOD COLOUR & ORASTED GROUNDNUT GRAM PEAS, ETC IN POUCHES
863. FROG LEGS PROCESSING
864. FROZEN MEATS PROCESSING
865. FOOD FLAVOURS (WHISKY) VODKA, GRAPE, BUTTER SCOTCH)
866. FOOD PRODUCTS COMPLEX (DEHYDRATED ONIONS, GARLIC POWDER & FLAKES, CATTLE FEED, TOMATO POWDER, TOMATO PRODUCTS, CANNED FRUITS & VEGETABLES, TOMATO PURE, GROUN NUT OIL, REFIND OIL, DEHYDRATED GRAPES, BANANA POWDER & WAFFERS)
867. FRUIT JUICE, JAM, JELLIES & ALLIED PRODUCTS
868. FRUIT JUICE, PICKLES PROCESSING AND CANNING
869. FRUIT JUICE MAKING & PACKING IN PLASTIC CONTAINER/POUCHES
870. FRUIT PROCESSING (JAM & JELLIES)
871. FRUIT PULP & JUICE CONCENTRATES
872. FRUIT & VEGETABLE DRYING (FREEZE DRYING METHOD)
873. GOAT & SHEEP FARMING
874. GRAM DALL/PULSE MILL
875. GRAPE DEHYDRATION
876. HARD BOILED CANDY (TOFFEE & CANDY)
877. HERBAL CIGARETTES
878. HONEY PROCESSING & PACKAGING
879. ICE CREAM OF DIFFERENT FLAVOURS
880. ICE CREAM STABILIZER
881. ICE MAKING PLANT
882. INDIAN MADE FOREIGN LIQUOR (I.M.F.L)
883. INSTANT FOOD (IDLI MIX, DOSA MIX, GULAB JAMUN MIX)
884. INSTANT FOOD (INSTANT FOOD & FAST FOOD PARLOUR)
885. INSTANT NOODLES
886. INSTANT TEA
887. INSTANT TEA FROM BLACK TEA
888. INTEGERATED STARCH BAKING POWDER/YEAST INDUSTRY
889. IODIZED SALT
890. IODIZED SALT (ORDINARY MOISTURE-LESS/FREE FLOWING IN PLASTIC BAGS AND CONTAINERS)
891. JAM, JELLIES, FRUIT JUICE & ALLIED PRODUCTS
892. KATHA AND CUTCH
893. KHANDSARI SUGAR
894. KHANDSARI SUGAR & IMFL
895. LACTIC ACID FROM WHITE SUGAR BY FERMENTATION PROCESS
896. LACTOSE & BY PRODUCTS PROCESSING FROM MILK
897. LIQUID GLUCOSE AND ITS BYE PRODUCTS
898. MACRONI AND VERMICILLI
899. MALT EXTRACTION FROM BARLEY
900. MANGO PROCESSING (MANGO PULP, JUICE & SLICES)
901. MAYUR BRAND TYPE CHEWING TOBACCO
902. MINERAL WATER
903. MILK PRESERVATION & MARKETING TO WHOLE SELLERS (INPOUCH PACKING BY UHT TECHNOLOGY)
904. MILK PROCESSING AND PACKAGING OF MILK PRODUCTS
905. MILK PRODUCTS (CASEIN, LACTOSE, GHEE & WHEY POWDER)
906. MILK TOFFEE
907. MINI FLOUR MILL
908. MINI SUGAR PLANT
909. MISRI (PEARL SUGAR CANDIES)
910. MODERN RICE MILL
911. MURABBA
912. MUSTARD OIL EXTRACTION & REFINING
913. MUTTON TALLOW
914. NAMKEEN INDUSTRY (BHUJIA, CHANA CHUR ETC.)
915. NAMKEEN & SWEETS
916. NON-BASMATI RICE FROM PADDY
917. OLEORESIN, ESSENTIAL OIL, DYES & POWDER OF SPICES
918. OLEORESIN EXTRACTION FROM DIPTERO-CARPUT TURMINATUS AND PINUS KHASYANA
919. OLEORESIN EXTRACTION FROM CHILLI
920. PAN MASALA AND POUCH

1059. BUFFALO HORN TIP, HOOF
1060. BANQUET HALL
1061. BUTTON
1062. CALCINED PETROLEUM (C.P) COKE
1063. CANVAS SHOES
1064. CANVAS SHOES, JUNGLE BOOTS
1065. CARBON BRUSH, BRUSH HOLDER & SLIP RING
1066. CEMENT SHEETS WITH COIR FIBRE & OTHER SEGMENTS
1067. CERAMIC TILES (GLAZED) BY DOUBLE FIRING/HEATING
1068. CHILDREN RECREATION CENTRE
1069. COAL BRIQUETTES
1070. COLD STORAGE & ICE
1071. COLD STORAGE FOR FRUITS AND VEGETABLES
1072. COMPRESSOR (HERMETIC) FOR AIR CONDITIONER
1073. COSTUME JEWELLERY/ IMITATION JEWELLERY
1074. DECORATIVE LAMINATED SHEET (SUNMICA)
1075. DIAMOND CUTTING & EXPORTS
1076. DRINKING STRAW FROM PROPYLENE
1077. ENGINEERING COLLEGE
1078. ENTERTAINMENT CLUB
1079. FASHION TECHNOLOGY INSTITUTE
1080. FAST FOOD PARLOUR
1081. FAST FOOD (INSTANT FOOD & FAST FOOD PARLOUR)
1082. FIRE EXTINGUISHERS (SODA ACID TYPE)
1083. FISH NET
1084. FLORICULTURE (CUT FLOWER ROSE) WITH GREEN HOUSE
1085. FLOOR COVERING SHEET
1086. FILM STUDIO (VIDEO)
1087. FLUSH DOOR, CHIP BOARD, WOOD WOOL & OTHER INSULATING BOARDS
1088. GAS DETECTORS OF L.P.G
1089. GEMS MANUFACTURING
1090. GLASS BOTTLE BY SCRAP
1092. GOAT & SHEEP FARMING
1093. GOLD ELECTROPLATING
1094. GOLD JEWELLERY (E.O.U)
1095. GOLD PLATED SILVER JEWELLERY & CUTLERY
1096. GRANITE SLAB AND TILES
1097. GREEN HOUSE
1098. HARD CHROMIUM PLATING
1099. HEALTH CLUB AND BEAUTY PARLOUR CUM HAIR SALOON WITH SONA BATH
1100. HEALTH CLUB CUM BEAUTY PARLOUR TRAININGINSTITUTE
1101. HORN TIP,HOOVE BUTTON
1102. HOSPITAL
1103. HOSPITAL (100 BEDS)
1104. HOSPITAL (200 BEDS)
1105. ICE MAKING PLANT
1106. IMITATION AND COSTUME
1107. JEWELLERY (NECKLACE, EARRINGS EAR TOP ETC.)
1108. INITMATE SCENT CHEMICALS FROM ALL TYPES OF FLAVOUR
1109. INVESTMENT CASTING
1110. JUTE, COIR, GLASS ROPE/ SUTLI
1111. JUTE TWINE
1112. L.P.G BOTTLING PLANT
1113. L.P.G REGULATOR (DOMESTIC PURPOSE)
1114. LAMINATED PARTICLE BOARD & HARD BOARD
1115. LAMINATED SAFETY AND TOUGHENED GLASS
1116. LEASING & HIRE PURCHASE
1117. LICHEN (CHARILA)
1118. MANILA ROPES
1119. MEDICAL COLLEGE
1120. MATCH UNIT FROM WAXED PAPER
1121. MEDIUM DENSITY FIBRE BOARD
1122. MELAMINE CROCKERY
1123. MINERAL WATER
1124. MINI CEMENT PLANT
1125. MIRROR SILVER, GOLDEN, PINK, BLACK & SMOKES
1126. MODERN ADVERTISING AGENCY WITH DTP & FILM STUDIO
1127. MOTEL/SMALL HOTEL
1128. MULTI COLOUR PRINTING
1129. MULTI STOREY COMMERCIAL COMPLEX ALONGWITH RESIDENTIALAND DELUX FLATS FOR FOREIGN TOURISTS & REVOLVING RESTAURENT AT THE TOP
1130. MULTIPLE LAMINATION INDUSTRY
1131. MUSHROOM GROWING AND PROCESSING (BY DEEP FREEZING METHOD)
1132. NEWS PAPER PRINTING
1133. NICKEL LINED INDUSTRIAL SCREEN
1134. OFFSET COLOUR PRINTING PRESS (SIX COLOUR)
1135. OFFSET PRINTING PRESS
1136. P.C.C ELECTRIC POLES
1137. PHOTOGRAPHIC DEVELOPER & FIXER
1138. PVC EXTRUSION PROFILE (DOOR & WINDOWS)
1139. POP-CORN
1140. PHOTO ETCHING OF S.S.
1141. PRE STRESSED CEMENT CONCRETE PIPES
1142. PILFER PROOF CAPS
1143. PILFER PROOF CAPS AND CROWN CAP
1144. POUCH MAKING & GRAVURE PRINTING (ROTO PRINTING)
1145. POULTRY & FISH FARMING (INTEGERATED UNIT)
1146. PRINTING OF TIN SHEETS
1147. READYMADE GARMENTS
1148. RESTAURANT
1149. ROSE PLANTATION AND ROSE OIL EXTRACTION
1150. ROTOGRAVURE PRINTING
1151. SAFETY BELTS
1152. SAFETY MATCHES
1153. SHOE LACES
1154. SILK COCOON CULTIVATION (GROWING OF SILK COCOON WARM)
1155. SILK SCREEN PRINTING FORMULATIONS FOR PLASTIC, PAPER & CLOTH
1156. SPIKENARD (JATAMANSI)
1157. STENCIL COATING SOLUTION
1158. SUGAR CANDY (MISRI)
1159. SUGAR CANE PLANTATION
1160. SUGAR CANE JUICE PRESERVATION
1161. SURAT ZARI
1162. SYNTHETIC SHOES & SOLES
1163. TEA PACKAGING INDUSTRY
1164. TENNIS BALLS
1165. THREE STAR HOTEL
1166. TRAVELLING AGENCY
1167. TRAYS, TROLLEYS FOR HOSPITAL WITH SCRATCHLESS COATING
1168. WAX EXTRACTS (TANNING POWDER)
1169. WIRE ROPE SLINGS
1170. WOOD WOOL SLAB
1171. WOODEN CANE FURNITURE WITH EXPORT POTENTIAL
1172. WOODEN FURNITURE
1173. WOODEN PANEL INCLUDING KILN SEASONING
1174. WOODEN FURNITURE
1175. WATCH CASE BUFFING
1176. WATCH DIAL
1177. WRIST WATCHES
1178. WATCHES (ELECTRONIC)
1179. ZEDOARY (KACHUR)

EDIBLE OILS, ESSENTIAL OILS LURICATIING OILS, GREASES, VEGETABLE OILS, WAXES, CAMPHOR, PERFUMES & PERFUMERY COMPOUNDS AND REFINED OILS ETC.

1180. AROMATIC PERFUMERY COMPOUND
1181. AEROSOL
1182. AGARBATTI PERFUMERY COMPOUND
1183. BEES WAX MANUFACTURE
1184. CAMPHOR
1185. CARDANOL FROM CASHEW NUT SHELL LIQUID
1186. CASTOR OIL
1187. CASTOR OIL DERIVATIVE OLEORESINS
1188. CHILLI OIL
1189. CITRONELLA OILS
1190. CLOVE OIL
1191. CONCENTRATE OF ROSE JASMINE & LILY ETC.
1192. COLOURED FLAME CANDLE

1193. CANDLES (SEMI-AUTOMATIC)
1194. CORN OIL (MAIZE OIL)
1195. DEHYDRATED CASTOR OIL
1196. EUGENOL FROM CINNAMON LEAF OIL
1197. EXTRACTION OF ESSENTIAL OIL (CARDAMON, JEERA, AJOWAN, GINGER OILS ETC. & PACKAGING OF GROUND SPICES)
1198. EXTRACTION OF JASMINE ESSENCE
1199. EXTRACTION OF ESSENTIAL OILS BY SUPER CRITICAL FLUID METHOD FROM FLOWERS, HERBS & SPICES
1200. EUCALYPTUS OIL
1201. EXTRACTION OF OIL FROM OIL SEED EXPANDEREXTRUSION TECHNOLOGY)
1202. FAT LIQUOR SULPHATED OIL
1203. FLAVOURS FOR FOOD
1204. GARLIC OIL & POWDER
1205. GINGER OIL, SANDALWOOD OIL AND NAGARMOTHA OIL
1206. GINGER OIL
1207. GINGER OIL & GINGER DUST
1208. INTEGERATED WAX COMPLEX
1209. IONONE FROM LEMON GRASS OIL
1210. JASMINE & LILLY FLOWER OIL
1211. LEMON GRASS OIL
1212. LIQUID PARAFFIN
1213. LUBE OIL & GREASE
1214. LUBRICATING OIL
1215. MENTHOL CRYSTALS
1216. MENTHOL OIL & CRYSTAL
1217. MICRO CRYSTALLINE WAX
1218. MUSTARD OIL (EDIBLE OIL)
1219. OIL FROM ARTEMISIA HERBS
1220. PALM OIL CRUSHING UNIT
1221. PAN MASALA
1222. PARAFFIN WAX
1223. PARAFFIN WAX FROM SLACK WAX
1224. REFINED OIL-SUN FLOWER OIL, GROUNDNUT OIL, STAFF FLOWER OIL & COTTON SEED OIL
1225. REFINED VEGETABLE OIL
1226. RECLAMATION OF USED ENGINE OIL
1227. RICE BRAN OIL (R.B.O)
1228. ROSE OIL EXTRACTION
1229. SMOKE LESS CANDLE
1230. SPICE OIL & OLEORESINS
1231. SOLVENT EXTRACTION PLANT (OIL CAKE BASED)
1232. SYNTHETIC ALMOND OIL
1233. SYNTHETIC TALLOW
1234. SYNTHETIC GHEE
1235. VEGETABLE OIL EXTRACTION & REFINING
1236. WADDING OIL (100%) FOR WADDING OF COTTON HOSIERY CLOTH IN DYEING PROCESS
1237. WAX EMULSION FOR TEXTILE
1238. WAX FLOOR POLISH

PAINT, ENAMEL, SOLVENTS, THINNERS, INKS & VARNISH

1239. ACRYLIC EMULSION PAINTS
1240. ALUMINIUM PAINT
1241. AUTOMOBILE PAINTS
1242. BALL POINT PEN REFILL INK
1243. BITUMINIOUS ROAD EMULSION
1244. BITUMEN
1245. BITUMINIOUS FELTS FOR WATER & DAMP PROOFING
1246. BITUMINIOUS ROAD EMULSION RAPID MEDIUM & SLOW SETTING
1247. BUFFING & POLISHING
1248. CEMENT PAINT FOR WHITE & GREY CEMENT

1249. DISPERSANT
1250. DRY DISTEMPER
1251. DRY DISTEMPER & CEMENT PAINT
1252. DUPLICATING INK BLACK FOR GESTNER DUPLICATOR
1255. EMULSION PAINTS (WATER BASED)
1256. HAMMERTONE PAINT
1257. INSULATING VARNISH & WIRE ENAMEL
1258. IRON OXIDE PIGMENTS
1259. INSULATING VARNISH (POLY VINYL BUTYRAL BASED, FFC GRADE)
1260. LIME COLOUR (CEMENT COLOUR)
1261. SYNTHETIC RED OXIDE FOR FLOORINGS
1262. SOLVENT & THINNERS
1263. MARKING INKS (WATER PROOF)
1264. METAL NAPHTHANATE (AS DRIER FOR PAINTS)
1265. N.C.PUTTY
1266. OFFSET PRINTING INK
1267. OIL BOUND DISTEMPER PAINT
1268. PAINT BRUSHES
1269. PAINT REMOVERS
1270. PAINT INDUSTRY
1271. PAINT & VARNISH
1272. PICTURE VARNISH
1273. POWDER COATING PAINT
1274. PRINTING INKS (OFFSET, FLEXO & ROTO GRAVURE)
1275. PRIMER PAINT & ENAMEL PAINT
1276. PUTTY & WATER PROOFING PAINT
1277. PRINTING INKS (FLEXO-GRAPHIC INK)
1278. PUTTY (METAL CASEMENT)
1279. RED OXIDE PRIMER (ANTI CORROSIVE)
1280. REFRACTORY PAINT (GRAPHITE BASED)
1281. SCREEN PRINTING INKS
1282. SILK SCREEN PRINTING INK FORMULATION FOR PLASTIC, PAPER, CLOTH
1283. STAMP & PAD INK
1284. STOVING PAINT
1285. SPIRIT SOLUBLE MALEIC RESIN
1286. TEXTURE PAINT
1287. THINNERS AND ITS ALLIED PRODUCTS
1288. TONER INK
1289. VARNISH THINNER (SOLVENT)
1290. VACUUM METALLIZING LACQUERS
1291. WOOD PRIMER

PHARMACEUTICAL, DRUGS, AYURVEDIC/HERBAL COSMETICS & MEDICINES, HOMOEOPATHIC MEDICINES, DISPOSABLE SYRINGE, DENTAL COLLEGE & FINE CHEMICALS ETC.

1292. AROMATIC PILLS
1293. ASPIRIN
1294. AYURVEDIC PAIN BALM OINTMENTS
1295. AYURVEDIC CHURAN AND TABLETS
1296. AYURVEDIC TABLETS (HAJMOLA TYPE)
1297. AYURVEDIC/HERBAL PHARMACY
1298. AYURVEDIC SHERBATS
1299. AYURVEDIC PRODUCTS
1300. BULK DRUGS (E.O.U)
1301. BLOOD BAGS
1302. CALCIUM GLUCONATE
1303. CAPSULE, TABLET & INJECTION WITH MODERN INSTRUMENTS
1304. CASHEW FENI
1305. CHLOROQUINONE PHOSPHATE (BULK DRUGS)
1306. CLINICAL THERMOMETER
1307. DENTAL CLINIC

Above all the Detailed Project Report are available at *"ENGINEERS INDIA RESEARCH INSTITUTE"*. 4449, Nai Sarak (D), Main Road Delhi - 110 006
● Ph : 91-11-23918117, 2391 6431, 2392 0361, 31082370 ● Fax : 91-11- 2391 6431
● E-Mail : eirisidi@bol.net.in

1308. DENTAL COLLEGE
1309. DENTAL GRADE EUGENOL
1310. DEXTROSE MONOHYDRATE, LIQUID GLUCOSE
1311. DEHYDRATED ONION & ONION POWDER
1312. DEXTROSE POWDER (ANHYDROUS FROM STARCH)
1314. DEXTROSE SALINE SOLUTION
1315. DISTILLERY (I.M.F.L)
1316. DISPOSABLE NEEDLES FOR SYRINGES
1317. DISPRIN
1318. DISTILLED WATER
1319. EMPTY HARD GELATINE CAPSULES
1320. FILLING & PACKING OF CAPSULES
1321. GLUCOSE - D - POWDER
1322. GLYCERINE
1323. HERBAL COSMETICS
1324. HERBAL SHAMPOO
1325. HERBAL HAIR OILS (AYURVEDIC)
1326. HOMOE & BIO-MEDICINES WITH MOTHER TINCTURE
1327. HOMOEPATHIC MEDICINES
1328. HYPODERMIC NEEDLES
1329. I.V. FLUIDS
1330. IBUPROFEN
1331. INFUSION & TRANSFUSION SETS (I.V. SET)
1332. INJECTABLE FOR PHARMACEUTICALS
1333. INJECTION AMPOULES PACKAGING BOX
1334. INTEGERATED SURGICAL COTTON
1335. ICE MAKING PLANT
1336. ICE & COLD STORAGE
1337. LACTOSE & BY PRODUCTS PROCESSING FROM MILK
1338. LICHEN (JATAMANSI CHARILA)
1339. LIQUID GLUCOSE AND ITS BY-PRODUCTS
1340. L-LYSINE MONOHYDRO CHLORIDE
1341. LIQUID GLUCOSE FROM POTATOES
1342. MEDICAL COLLEGE
1343. NICOTINE FROM TOBACCO WASTE
1344. OINTMENT-AYURVEDIC (YELLOW & WHITE)
1345. PHARMACEUTICAL AND FOOD GRADE GELATINE
1346. PHARMACEUTICAL INDUSTRY (TABLETS, CAPSULES, LIQUID, GEL, OINTMENT POWDER INJECTABLE)
1347. PHARMACEUTICAL UNIT (EOU) WITH FORMULA TIONS, INJECTABLES, ETC. PYRIDINE & DERIVATIVES
1348. SALT (IODIZED SALT)
1349. SALINE & INJECTION WATER
1350. SALINE WATER & DEXTROSE SOLUTION (I.V.FLUID IN PLASTIC BOTTLES)
1351. SORBITOL
1352. STARCH (MAIZE)
1353. SURGICAL ADHESIVE PLASTER
1354. SURGICAL BANDAGES
1355. SURGICAL GLOVES
1357. SURGICAL COTTON
1358. SURGICAL COTTON AND BANDAGE
1359. SYNTHETIC CAMPHOR POWDER
1360. TABLETS & CAPSULES
1361. TISSUE CULTURE
1362. TINCTURE FROM RECTIFIED SPIRIT
1363. TRIMETHOPIME
1364. VETERENARY MEDICINES (ONLY FORMULATIONS)
1365. VITAMIN 'C', SORBITOL' ANHYDROUS DEXTROSE, STARCH

PULP, PAPER, STRAW/GREY BOARD, KRAFT PAPER, PACKAGING, PAPER CARRY BAGE, PAPER FROM AGRO WASTE & STATIONERY ETC.

1366. AMMONIA PAPER
1367. AUTOMATIC BOOK BINDING
1368. ADHESIVE (FEVICOL TYPE)
1369. ALL PIN & GEM CLIPS
1370. CARBON PAPER
1371. CARD BOARD
1372. CARBON LESS PAPER
1373. CELLPHANE PAPER
1374. COMPUTER FORMS & SECURITY PRINTING PRESS
1375. CORRUGATED BOARD & BOX (PRINTED & LAMINATED)
1376. CORRUGATED BOARD AND BOXES FROM FROM CARD BOARDS
1377. CORRUGATED CARTONS FROM PLAIN PAPERS
1378. CORRUGATRED PACKING & MATERIAL (BULB & TUBES PACKING)
1379. DESK TOP PUBLISHING
1380. DEFOAMING AGENT FOR PAPER PLANT
1381. DRINKING STRAW PAPER
1382. D.T.P CUM OFFSET PRESS
1383. EGG TRAYS
1384. EXERCISE NOTE BOOK, REGISTER AND PAD
1385. FLEXOGRAPHIC INK
1386. GREETING CARD BY OFFSET PRESS
1387. HAND MADE PAPER FILTER PAPER
1388. HARD BOARD
1389. INJECTION AMPOULES PACKAGING BOXES
1390. INSULATIING PAPER
1391. KRAFT PAPER
1392. KRAFT PAPER FROM BAGASSE
1393. LAMINATED PACKAGING PAPER WITH PRINTING
1394. LAMINATION & COATING ON PAPER
1395. M.G. PAPER FROM WASTE PAPER
1396. MILL PAPER FROM WASTE PAPER
1397. MILL BOARD FROM RICE & WHEAT STRAWS
1398. MILL BOARD FROM WASTE PAPER
1399. MINI PAPER PLANT FROM SISAL
1400. MINI PAPER PLANT
1401. MULTI WALL PAPER SACKS
1402. NEWS PAPER FOR CHILDREN
1403. NEWS PRINT PAPER FROM RICE STRAW BAGASSE
1404. NEWS PAPER CHILDRENS
1405. NEWS PRINT PAPER
1406. OFFSET AND TREADLE TYPE PRINTING PRESS
1407. MILL BOARD BASED ON RICE STRAW
1408. PAPER AND BOARD FROM STRAW
1409. PAPER & PAPER PRODUCTS
1410. PAPER ENVELOPES
1411. PAPER CARRY BAGS
1412. PAPER BOARD CARTON
1413. PAPER CONES FOR LOUD SPEAKERS
1414. PAPER FROM AKRA
1415. PAPER FROM BAGASSE WITH CORRUGATED BOARD & BOXES
1416. PAPER FROM BAMBOO
1417. PAPER GLASSES FOR BEVERAGES
1418. PAPER FROM RICE HUSK & WHEAT HUSK
1419. PAPER FROM TREE BARK, EUCALYPRUS WOOD
1420. PAPER PRODUCTS
1421. PAPER PLANT (WHITE WRITING & NEWS PAPER FOR PULP & WASTE PAPER)
1422. PAPER PLATES, PAPER GLASS
1423. PAPER CONES & TUBES
1425. PAPER PLANT WITH DTP & PRINTING & PUBLISHING UNIT
1426. PAPER BASED PHENOLIC SHEET
1427. PAPER CUP FOR ICE CREAM
1428. PAPER TUBES SPIRAL WINDING COMPOSIT CONTAINER
1429. PAPER LABLE FOR BEER BOTTLES
1430. PARTICLE BOARD & BLACK BOARD WITH SANDING & LAMINATION OF PARTICLE BOARD
1431. PARTICLE BOARD FROM RICE HUSK
1432. POUCH FILLING & MAKING FOR TOMATO SAUCE
1433. POUCH MAKING &

GRAVURE PRINTING
1434. PROCESSING OF PAPER FOR FEEDING IN COMPUTER
1435. PULP FROM BAMBOO & WOOD
1436. PAPER FILES
1437. PLAYING CARDS
1438. ROSIN SIZING AGENT (FOR PAPER PLANT)
1439. SAND PAPER
1440. SANITRY NAPKINS
1441. SILICON COATED PAPER
1442. STENCIL PAPER
1443. STRAW BOARD AND GREY BOARD
1444. STRAW BOARD & MILL BOARD
1445. STRAW BOARD AND PAPER BOARD
1446. TISSUE PAPER FACIAL
1447. TISSUE MOIST TOILETERY CLEANSING TISSUE AND RELATED PRODUCTS
1448. TISSUE PAPER ROLLS
1449. TETRA PACK FOR MILK PACKAGING, GHEE & OTHER LIQUIDS
1450. TOILET PAPER ROLLS
1451. TOILET PAPER & NAPKINS
1452. WAX COATED PRINTED PAPER
1453. WET FACE FRESHNER TISSUE
1454. WHITE WRITING & PRINTING PAPER
1455. WRITING & PRINTING PAPER (PAPER MILLS)

PLASTIC, B.O.P.P, ACRYLIC, DISPOSABLE PLASTIC PRODUCTS, PET PRODUCTS, P.V.C, H.D.P.E, P.P, L.D.P.E., P.U, A.B.S, THERMOFOARMING, MASTER BATCHES, & POLYMER AND RUBBER PRODUCTS, TYRE, TUBE, ADHESIVE, SHEET, COIR & MANY OTHERS

1456. ABS GRANULES FROM ABS SCRAPS FROM OLD T.V. CABINETS, WHITE GOODS ETC.
1457. ACRYLIC BEADS
1458. ACRYLIC COPOLYMER EMULSION
1459. ACRYLIC LATEX
1460. ACRYLIC SHEET
1461. ACRYLIC SHEET & MOULDED PRODUCTS
1462. ACRYLIC TEETH
1463. AUTO TUBES
1464. AUTO FLAPS FOR TRUCKS & BUSES
1465. AUTO TYRES & TUBES
1466. BABY BOTTLES (PLASTIC) WITH WHITESILICON RUBBER NIPPLES
1467. B.O.P.P. FILM
1468. B.O.P.P. PRESSURE SENSITIVE SELF ADHESIVE TAPE
1469. BABY NIPPLE (SILICON)
1470. BABY NIPPLE (BIG SIZE)
1471. BALLOON PLASTIC ADVERTISING
1472. BLISTER FILM PVC
1473. BLISTER PACKAGING & POUCH PAKAGING
1474. BLOW MOULDING PLASTIC CONTAINER
1475. COATING ON METALIZED POLYESTER FILM/METALISED PAPER/ ALIMINIUM FOIL
1476. COATING ON PLASTIC (ELECTROLYSIS) & GLASS
1477. COIR FOAM (RUBBERISED)
1478. COLOUR COATING ON PLASTICS
1479. COLOUR MASTER BATCHES FOR VARIOUS PLASTICS
1480. CYCLE TYRES AND TUBES
1481. DISPOSABLE PLASTIC CUPS GLASSES, ETC.
1482. DISPOSABLE PLASTIC SYRINGES & NEEDLES
1483. DISPOSABLE PLASTIC SYRINGES
1484. DOUGH MOULDING COMPOUND (D.M.C)
1485. EPOXY RESIN
1486. EXPANDED POLYESTRENE MOULDING (THERMOCOLE)
1487. F.R.P AUTO,SCOOTER ROOFS & CEILINGS
1488. F.R.P PRODUCTS (HELMET, WASHBASIN SHEETS, ROOFING SHEETS)
1489. FIBRE REINFORCED PLASTIC (HIGH PRESSURE MOULDING WITH SMC BMC AND DMC)
1490. FIELD RUBBER CONVERTED TO THE 60% LATEX RUBBER
1491. FLEXIBLE P.U. FOAM
1492. FORMALDEHYDE CROCKERY & OTHER ITEMS
1493. FORMALDEHYDE RESIN (UREA, PHENOL,MELEMINE)
1494. GASKET SHEET
1495. GUM BOTTLE (PVC)
1496. GLASS BEADS
1497. HDPE COATED PAPER SACK
1498. H.D.P.E. BAGS
1499. H.D.P.E. CONTAINERS (BLOW MOULDING)
1500. H.D.P.E. CONTAINER, POLY JARS BY INJECTION MOULDING (FOOD GRADE)
1501. H.D.P.E. JERRY CANS
1502. HDPE MANUFACTURING FROM ETHYLALCOHOL
1503. H.D.P.E PIPE AND FITTINGS
1504. H.D.P.E. PIPES
1505. H.D.P.E PRINTED BAGS
1506. H.D.P.E TWINES AND ROPES
1507. H.D.P.E. & L.D.P.E PIPES AND FITTINGS
1508. H.D.P.E/PP BOX STRAPPING
1509. H.D.P.E/PP WOVEN SACKS USING PLAIN LOOMS
1510. HOLOGRAM STICKERS-3D
1511. H.M BAG PLANT WITH PRINTING UNIT
1512. HAWAI CHAPPALS (RUBBER)
1513. I.V PLASTIC BOTTLE
1514. ICE CREAM CUP (PLASTIC)
1515. INJECTION MOULDED AUTO COMPONENTS
1516. INJECTION & BLOW MOULDED PLASTIC PRODUCTS
1517. INJECTION MOULDED PLASTIC PRODUCTS
1518. INTEGERATED COMPLEX ESTER'S & ALLIED PRODUCTS (D.O.P,D.B.P, & ETHYL ACETATE, BUYTL ACETATE, WIRE ENAMELS, JELLY CABLE COMPOUND)
1519. L.D.P.E. (LOW DENSITY POLY ETHYLENE) GRANULES FROM VIRGIN (L.D.P.E. RESIN)
1520. INTEGERATED SURGICAL RUBBER GOODS INDUSTRY
1521. INJECTION MOULDED PLASTIC BALLS
1522. L.D.P.E FROM ETHYL ALCOHOL
1523. LDPE MOULDED PRODUCTS
1524. LAMINATION OF COEXTRUSION MULTILAYER FILM IN ROLL FORM
1525. LATEX RUBBER
1526. LATEX RUBBER CONDOM
1527. MASTER BATCHES (COLOURED, P.V.C, L.D.P.E, H.D.P.E, ETC.)
1528. MELAMINE FORMALHYDE RESIN
1529. MOULDED LUGGAGE
1530. MULTI-LAYER (3 LAYER BAGS)
1531. MULTI-LAYER (3 LAYER) FILM WITH LAMINATION & PRINTING
1532. OIL SEAL
1533. PET BOTTLE/CONTAINERS
1534. PET BOTTLES FROM PRE FORM
1535. PET BOTTLE & MINERAL WATER
1536. PET PRE-FORM FROM PET RESIN
1537. PET PRE-FORM CUM PET BOTTLES
1538. PET PRE-FORM PET BOTTLES CUM MINERAL WATERS
1539. POLY CARBONATE RESIN
1540. PTFE COMPONENTS
1541. PU/PVC SOLE FOR SPORT SHOE BY IMPORTED M/C.
1542. PVC BATTERY SEPARATOR
1543. P.V.C COMPOUNDS (FRESH)
1544. P.V.C COMPOUNDS (SCRAP)
1545. P.V.C ELECTRICAL INSULATING TAPE
1546. P.V.C. EXTRUSION PROFILES
1547. P.V.C FITTINGS
1548. P.V.C FLEXIBLE FUSIBLE POWDER HEAT FUSIBLE POWDER
1549. P.V.C GRANULES (FOR

INSULATION & SHEETS GRADES)
1550. P.V.C GRANULES FROM PVC SCRAPS (WITH POLLUTION CONTROL)
1551. P.V.C HOSES
1552. P.V.C LEATHER CLOTH
1553. P.V.C FLEXIBLE PIPES
1554. P.V.C PIPES AND FITTINGS
1555. POLYTHENE BAGS (PRINTED)
1556. PVC PLASTICS FILM SHEET SOFT/RIGID
1557. PVC RESIN AND COMPOUND
1558. PVC RULAR
1559. PVC STABLIZERS (SINGLE PACK SYSTEM)
1560. PVC WIRE AND CABLES
1561. PAPER BASED PHENOLIC SHEET FOR ELECTRICAL
1562. PHENOL FORMALDEHYDE RESIN
1563. PHENOLIC RESIN
1564. PLASTIC BEADS FROM PLASTIC SCRAPS
1565. PLASTIC BUTTONS
1566. PLASTIC CANS
1567. PLASTIC COLLAPSIBLE TUBE
1568. PLASTIC CORRUGATED SHEET & BOXES
1569. PLASTIC FILM AND SHEETS WITH PRINTING FLEXO & ROTO/LDPE/HDPE/PP/HM/PVC
1570. PLASTIC FILTER MASTER BATCH & OTHER MASTER BATCHES FOR VARIOUS PLASTICS
1571. PLASTIC JERRY CANS
1572. PLASTIC GRANULES OR POWDER FROM PLASTIC SCRAP
1573. PLASTIC INJECTION MOULDED T.V. CABINETS
1574. PLASTIC ITEMS MANUFAC TURE FROM POWDER MELAMINE
1575. PLASTIC GOODS
1576. PLASTIC PIPES & TARPAULINES
1577. PLASTIC SHEET FROM SCRAP
1578. PLASTIC PLANT (BLOW MOULDING & INJECTION MOULDING)
1579. PLASTIC PRODUCTS (GOLD, SILVER, NICKEL)
1580. PLASTIC TOYS
1581. POLYESTER BEADING
1582. POLYESTER FILM
1583. POLYTHENE BAGS & AUTOMATIC PRINTING
1584. POLYTHENE PRINTED BAGS
1585. POLYURETHANE FOAM AND ITS PRODUCTS
1586. PROPYLENE FILM (PRINTED) & BAG MANUFACTURING
1587. PLASTIC MATS
1588. RAINBOW COLOUR ON PVC FILM & SHEET
1589. RED MUD PVC PIPES AND FITTINGS
1590. RE-RUBBERISED OF SOLID TYPE
1591. RESIN COATED SAND REXINE
1592. REXINE CLOTH & ALLIED PRODUCTS
1593. RUBBER ADHESIVE
1594. RUBBER AUTO PARTS
1595. RUBBER BELTING
1596. RUBBER MOULDING UNIT INCLUDING LINING RUBBER SHEETING
1597. RUBBER RECLAIMING
1598. RUBBER ROLLERS FOR TEXTILE MILLS & PAPER INDUSTRIES
1599. RUBBER & PLASTIC SHEETS, MATS & FLAPS
1600. RUBBER SHEET AND ALLIED HOSPITAL RUBBER GOODS
1601. RUBBERIZED PVC GASKET
1602. RUBBERISED COIR
1603. RUBBER COMPOUND FOR AUTOMOBILES
1604. SAFETY BELTS
1605. SILVER AND GOLD PLATING ON PVC AND NYLON-6
1606. SILICONE RUBBER NIPPLES/ TEATS
1607. SPECTACLE FRAMES (PLASTIC)
1608. SPUNGE RUBBER
1609. SURGICAL EXAMINATION GLOVES
1610. SYNTHETIC PEARL COATING ON POLYSTYRENE BEADS
1611. SYNTHETIC RUBBER ADHESIVE
1612. TEFLON MANUFACTURING
1613. TEFLON TAPE
1614. TEFLON TAPES & CABLES
1615. THERMOCOLE SHEET AND MOULDED PRODUCTS EXPANDED POLYESTERENE EXTRUSION PROFILES
1616. THERMOFORMED PACKAGING (BLISTER PACKAGING & POUCH PACKAGING)
1617. THERMOPLASTIC POLYURETHANE
1618. THERMOFORMED CUPS, PLATES & GLASS WITH HIPS SHEET
1619. THERMOCOLE
1620. THERMOCOLE BASED DISPOSABLE GLASS, CUPS & PLATES
1621. TOOTH BRUSHES
1622. TOY BALLOON, DECORA TIVE & INDUSTRIAL BALLOONS
1623. TREAD RUBBER
1624. TYRE RETREADING (HOT)
1625. TYRE RETREADING BY COLD PROCESS
1626. TYRE TUBES & FLAPS
1627. TYRE & TUBES
1628. UNSATURATED POLYESTER FOR REXINE
1629. V-BELT AND FAN BELT
1630. VINYL ASBESTOS AND PVC WALL PAPER
1631. VITON (FLUORO ELASTOMER)

SOAP, COSMETICS & PERFUMS

1632. ACID SLURRY, SYNTHETIC DETERGENT POWDER
1632. ACID SLURRY
1633. AGARBATTI SYNTHETIC, PERFUMERY COMPOUND
1634. AFTER SHAVE LOTION
1635. ANTISEPTIC CREAM
1636. BETA IONONE
1637. BLEACHING POWDER
1638. BLUE DETERGENT POWDER
1639. CLEANING POWDER (VIMTYPE)
1640. COLD CREAM
1641. COLOURED FLAME & PERFUMED CANDLES (RED, BLUE, GREEN FLAME)
1642. COSMETIC INDUSTRY (MODERN)
1643. COSMETIC INDUSTRY (SHAMPOO, SPRAY PERFUME, TALCUM POWDER
1644. DETERGENT POWDER (ARIEL TYPE)
1645. DETERGENT POWDER (NIRMA TYPE) FULLY AUTOMATIC PLANT
1646. DETERGENT WASHING POWDER
1647. FISH OIL SOAP
1648. GLYCERINE TRANSPARENT SOAP
1649. HAIR REMOVING CREAM
1650. HERBAL COSMETICS
1651. HERBAL SHAMPO & CREAM
1652. HERBAL/AYURVEDIC COSMETICS
1653. INCENSE POWDER,INCENSE STICKS & INCENSE CAKE
1654. OPTICAL WHITENERS
1655. ROSE OIL EXTRACTION
1656. SHAMPOOS (COCONUT OIL BASED COLD PROCESS)
1657. SHAVING CREAM
1658. SINDUR (KUMKUM)
1659. SOAP COATED PAPER
1660. SPRAY DRIED DETERGENT POWDER
1661. STAIN REMOVER
1662. TALCUM POWDER (FACE & TOILET POWDER)
1663. TOILET AND HERBAL SOAP
1664. TOOTH PASTE & POWDER
1665. WASHING DETERGENT POWDER AND WASHING SOAP
1666. WASHING POWDER LIQUID DETERGENTS,LOTION & SHAMPOO

TEXTILE INDUSTRIES, READYMADE GARMENTS, COTTON, DYEING, BLEACHING, CLOTH, HOSIERY, POWER LOOM, HAND LOOM, WOOLLEN, SILK, SOCKS, SURGICAL COTTON & MANY OTHERS

1667. ANGORA RABBIT WOOL
1668. BUCKRAM
1669. CANVAS SHOES, JUNGLE BOOT, BOOT RUBBER KNEES & BOOT COMBAT
1670. CARPET FROM COTTON WASTE
1671. CERAMIC THREAD GUIDE
1672. COTTON BUDS/SWABS
1673. COTTON FROM WASTE YARN
1674. COTTON ROLLS
1675. COTTON SPIDERS FOR LOUD SPEAKERS
1676. DENIM CLOTH
1677. DENIM CLOTH (INTEGERATED UNIT WITH BLEACHING, DYEING AND PRINTING)
1678. DISPERSENT FOR TEXTILE
1679. DYEING & BLEACHING
1680. DYEING OF HANK YARN
1681. EMULSIFIER FOR WOOL BATCHING OIL
1682. EMBROIDERY ON FABRICS
1683. GARMENT DYEING, WASHING & STITCHING (JEANS, JACKETS, SKIRTS & SHIRTS)
1684. GOVES KNITTING
1685. GUNNY BAGS
1687. HDPE WOVEN SACKS
1688. HDPE TARPAULINS USING PLAIN LOOM WITH LAMINATION
1689. HDPE/PP WOVEN SACKS USING CIRCULAR LOOMS
1690. HOSIERY CLOTH (COTTON) PROCESSING (BLEACHING, DYEING, FINISHING OF CLOTH)
1691. HOSIERY INDUSTRY
1692. HOSIERY MERCERISING
1693. HOSIERY PRODUCTS LIKE VEST, BRIEF, T-SHIRTS & SOCKS
1694. JACQUARD FABRICS
1695. JUTE COIR, GRASS ROPE/ SUTLI MAKING
1696. JUTE FELT
1697. JUTE TWINES
1698. KNITTED FABRICS
1699. LAMINATED JUTE BAGS
1700. LAMINATION OF HDPE WOVEN CLOTH (JUTE,COTTON, PAPER)
1701. NYLON YARN CRIMPING, DOUBLING AND BLEACHING
1702. PIGMENT BINDER FOR TEXTILE PRINTING
1704. POLYESTER RESIN FOR WIRE ENAMEL
1705. POLYESTER RESIN
1706. POLYESTER YARN FROM WASTE POLYESTER ZIP FASTENERS
1707. POWER LOOM
1708. READYMADE GARMENTS & HOSIERY
1709. READYMADE GARMENTS MERCHANDISE
1710. READYMADE GARMENTS & COVERS
1711. READYMADE GARMENTS & EMBROIDERY OF GOWNS, SHIRTS, BLOUSES, T-SHIRTS ETC. (ONLY LADIES)
1712. READYMADE SALWAR SUIT
1713. RECOVERY OF NYLON FROM NYLON WASTE
1714. ROTARY PRINTING AND DYEING ON COTTON, SYNTHETIC TEXTILE
1715. SANITARY NAPKINS
1716. SCREEN PRINTING ON COTTON CLOTH
1717. SEWING THREAD REELS & BALLS MAKING INDUSTRIES
1718. SCREEN PRINTING ON COTTON, POLYESTER & ACRYLIC
1719. SHAWLS (WOOLLEN)
1720. SHOE LACES
1721. SILK FABRICS ON HANDLOOM
1722. SOCKS KNITTING
1723. SPINNING, DOUBLING DYEING MERCERISING & BLEACHING OF COTTON YARN
1724. SPINNING & CARDING OF WOOL INTO YARNS
1725. STARCH BOOK BINDING CLOTH
1726. SURAT JARI
1727. SURGICAL COTTON & BANDAGE
1728. SYNTHETIC TEXTILE INDUSTRY(SUITING, SHIRTING, SAREES) TERRY CLOTH
1729. T-SHIRTS
1730. TOWELS, BED SHEET COVERS
1731. TERRY TOWEL
1732. TERRY FABRICS WEAVING UNIT
1733. TEXTILE AUXILLIARIES & CHEMICALS
1734. TEXTILE BLEACHING, DYEING & FINISHING & PRINTING OF COTTON FABRICS
1735. TEXTILE (HOSIERY)
1736. TEXTILE MILL
1737. TEXTILE DYEING & PRINTING
1738. TEXTILE PRINTING (JOB WORK)
1739. TEXTILE PIGMENT PRINTING BINDER
1740. TOWEL (TERRY)
1741. VELVET CLOTH BY FLOCKING PROCESS
1742. VISCOSE STAPLE FIBRE
1743. WADDING OIL (100%) FOR WADDING OF COTTON HOSIERY CLOTH IN THE DYEING PROCESS
1744. WEAVING OF DASUTI CLOTH WITH PRINTING, DYEING, EMBROIDERY & FINISHING
1745. WASHING OF JEANS & OTHER GARMENTS
1746. WORSTED WOOLLEN YARN CLOTH
1747. ZARI GLITTER SALMA SITARA OF PLASTIC FILM

INFOTECH/IT, HOSPITALITY, HOSPITAL, COLLEGE, SCHOOL, MEDICAL, ENTERTAINMENT CLUB, WARE HOUSING & REAL ESTATE, PROJECTS

1748. AMUSEMENT PARK
1749. AMUSEMENT PARK CUM WATER PARK
1750. BANQUET HALL
1751. CALL CENTER (DOMESTIC)
1752. CALL CENTER (INTERNATIONAL)
1753. CHILDREN RECREATION CENTRE
1754. COLD STORAGE
1755. COMMUNITY HALL
1756. COMPUTER EDUCATION INSTITUTE
1757. COMPUTER SOFTWARE
1758. COLLEGE
1759. CYBER CAFE
1760. DENTAL CLINIC
1761. DENTAL COLLEGE
1762. DIAGONOSTIC CENTRE
1763. E-COMMERCE/BUSINESS
1764. E-SCHOOL (Rs. 5000/-)
1765. ENGINEERING COLLEGE
1766. ENTERTAINMENT CLUB
1767. ENTERTAINMENT CLUB, HOLIDAY RESORT, 4 STAR HOTEL, AMUSEMENT PARK CUM WATER PARK, MUSHROOM & ITS PRODUCTS, FISH FARMING, LAKE FOR BOATING, DEER PARK
1768. FASHION TECHNOLOGY INSTITUTE
1769. FAST FOOD PARLOUR
1770. FIVE STAR HOTEL
1771. FOOD PARLOUR
1772. FRANCHISE TRAINING PROGRAMME FOR IIT & ENGINEERING ENTRANCE EXAMS.
1773. GOLF COURSE
1774. HEALTH CLUB, BEAUTY PARLOUR
1775. HEALTH CLUB AND FITNESS CENTER
1776. HEALTH RESORTS
1777. HOLIDAY RESORTS
1778. HOLIDAY RESORT CUM

ENTERTAINMENT CLUB WITH 4 STAR HOTEL
1779. HOSPITALS
1780. ICE CREAM PARLOUR
1781. INTERNET SERVICE PROVIDER (I.S.P.)
1782. MEDICAL COLLEGE
1783. MEDICAL COLLEGE, HOSPITAL & RESEARCH INSTITUTE
1784. MEDICAL TRANSCRIPTION CENTRE
1785. MENTAL RETARDATION HOSPITAL & CEREBRAL PALSY
1786. MOTEL/SMALL HOTEL
1787. MULTISTOREY COMMERCIAL COMPLEX
1788. MULTISTOREY RESIDENTIAL COMPLEX
1789. NURSERY SCHOOL
1790. NATURE CARE CENTRE
1791. NURSING HOME
1792. ONLINE SHOPPING MALL (RS. 5000/- REPORT)
1793. PORTAL
1794. REHABILITATION CENTRE FOR AGED & NEEDY PERSONS
1795. RESIDENTIAL CUM COMMERCIAL COMPLEX
1796. RESTAURANT
1797. RESTAURANT WITH PUB
1798. SCHOOL (PRIMARY)
1799. SCHOOL (HIGHER SECONDARY)
1800. THREE STAR HOTEL
1801. TOURIST CLUB
1802. TRAINING INSTITUTE FOR MEDICAL TRANSCRIPTION
1803. VIDEO FILM STUDIO
1804. WARE HOUSE
1805. WEBSITE DESIGN & E-MAIL REGISTERING

AGRO BASED INDUSTRIES

1806. COAL BRIQUETTES FROM AGROWASTE
1807. FURFURALFROM RICEHULL
1808. MUSHROOM CULTIVATION & PROCESSING (BUTTON)
1809. MUSHROOM GROWING & PROCESSING WITH AIR CONDITIONING
1810. MUSHROOM CULTIVATION & PROCESSING UNIT DEHYDRATION & PACKAGING OF OYSTER & PADDY STRAW MUSHROOMS
1811. ORGANIC MANURE
1812. PAPAYA CULTIVATION
1813. PAPAYA & TOMATO CULTIVATION
1814. PROCESSING & UTILISATION OF COCONUT
1815. PROCESSING OF SHEEP HAIR TO PRODUCE WOOL

BAKERY, CONFECTIONERY & FOOD PRODUCTS

1816. AGROLACTOR SOYA MILK
1817. APPLE FRUIT JUICE WITH CANNING BOTTLING
1818. AYURVEDIC SHARBAT
1819. BAKERY UNIT (PASTRIES, BREAD, BUNS, CAKE, TOFFEE ETC.)
1820. BAKING POWDER
1821. BANANA & ITS BY PRODUCTS
1822. BANANA POWDER
1823. BANANA WAFERS
1824. BANANA CULTIVATION
1825. BEER INDUSTRY
1826. DEHULLING OF JAUN FOR BEER
1827. BEER & WINE
1828. BEER, ALCOHOL, IMFL
1829. BESEN PLANT
1830. BISCUIT PLANT
1831. BREAD & BISCUIT PLANT
1832. BOTTLING PLANT COUNTRY LIQUOR FROM RECTIFIED SPIRIT
1833. BRANDY
1834. BREAD RUSKS
1835. CANNED FRUITS & VEGETABLES
1836. CANNING & PRESERVATION OF MEAT
1837. CANNING & PRESERVATION OF VEGETABLES
1838. CANNING OF MANGO PULP & MANGO SLICES
1839. CARBONATED BEVERAGS
1840. CASHEW FENI
1841. CASHEW NUT (DRIED & FRIED)
1842. CATTLE BREEDING
1843. CATTLE BREEDING & DAIRY FARM TO PRODUCE MILK
1844. CATTLE FEED FROM TAPIOCA
1845. CHEWING GINGER & AMLOKI
1846. CHEWING GUM
1847. CHILLI SAUCE
1848. CHILLI POWDER
1849. CHOCOLATE
1850. CIDER PLANT
1851. COCOA POWDER
1852. COCOA BUTTER & COCOA POWDER
1853. COCONUT SHELL POWDER
1854. COCONUT WATER
1855. COCONUT SWEET (WATERY)
1856. COCONUT MILK POWDER (DEHYDRATED)
1857. COCONUT PRODUCTS & BY PRODUCTS (INTEGRATED PLANT)
1858. COLD DRINK
1859. CURRY POWDER
1860. DAIRY FOR MILK PROCESSING (GHEE, BUTTER & PANEER)
1861. DAIRY PRODUCTS
1862. DAIRY PRODUCTS MILK PACKAGING IN POUCH (GHEE, BUTTER, ETC.
1863. DAIRY FARM TO PRDUCE MILK WITH PACKAGING (COW)
1864. DAIRY FARM TO PRDUCE MILK WITH PACKAGING (BUFALLOE)
1865. DAIRY FARM & MILK PRODUCTS
1866. DAL MOTH, CHANACHUR & BHUJIYA
1867. DEHYDRATION OF FRUITS & VEGETABLE
1868. DESICCATED COCONUT POWDER FROM COCONUTS
1869. DEHYDRATION & CANNINGOF FRUITS & VEGETABLES
1870. DRY FRUIT ROASTING & PACKAGING
1871. DRYING OF RED CHILLIES, HALDI, DHANIYA, PEAS & GROUND NUT
1872. EGG POWDER
1873. FISH CANNING IN TIN & POUCHES
1874. FISH DEHYRATION (DRYING OF FISH)
1875. FISH MEAL
1876. FISH PROCESSING (BEAST FREEZING PROCESSES)
1877. FLAVOURS FOR FOOD INDUSTRIES
1878. FLOUR MILL (ROLLER)
1879. FROZEN MEAT
1880. FOOD DEHYDRATION (FRUITS & VEGETABLES)
1881. FRIED & ROASTED GROUND NUT, GRAMS, PEAR ETC.
1882. FRUIT JUICE MAKING & PACKAGING IN PLASTIC CONTAINER
1883. FRUIT JUICE IN TETRA PACK (DRINKS)
1884. FRUIT JUICE, SQUASHES, SAUCE & KETCHUP, JAM, JELLY, VINEGAR ETC.
1885. GARLIC FLAKES
1886. GARLIC POWDER
1887. GHEE & BUTTER
1888. GINGER (PULVERISED)
1889. GINGER GLAZING & PRESERVATION
1890. GINGER STORAGE
1891. GINGER PROCESSING
1892. GINGER OIL & GINGER DUST
1893. GINGER POWDER (DRY) & OLEORESIN
1894. GRAPE DEHYDRATION
1895. GRAPE CULTIVATION
1896. GRAPE JUICE
1897. HONEY PROCESSING & PACKAGING
1898. ICE CREAM & ICE CANDY
1899. ICE CUBE
1900. INVERT SUGAR
1901. IDLI MIX, DOSA MIX SAMBHAR MIX, VADA MIX, GULAB JAMUN MIX
1902. INSTANT COFFEE & INSTANT TEA

1903. INSTANT NOODLES
1904. INSTANT SOUPS
1905. IODIZED SALT FROM CRUDE SALT
1906. JAM CHUTNEY PICKLES & SQUASHES
1907. KATHA MANUFACTURING
1908. LECITHIN (SOYA BASED)
1909. LEMON & ITS PRODUCTS
1910. MACARONI MANUFACTURING
1911. MACARONI, SPAGHETTI, VERMICELLI & NOODLES
1912. MAIZE & ITS BY PRODUCTS MALTING PLANT
1913. MANGO PAPPAD (AAM PAPPAD)
1914. MANGO POWDER RIPE
1915. MANGO POWDER
1916. MANGO PROCESSING & CANNING (MANGO PULP)
1917. MEAT PROCESSING (CHICKEN MUTTON)
1918. MEAT PROCESSING (BUFFALO)
1919. MENTHOL BOLD FROM MENTHOL FLAKES
1020. MILK POWDER
1921. MILK POWDER & GHEE
1922. MILK POWDER, GHEE & SPICES
1923. MILK PRESERVATION & MARKETING TO WHOLE SELLERS
1924. MILK PRESERVATION & MARKETING TO WHOLE SELLERS (IN POUCHES)
1925. MILK TOFFEE MANUFACTURES
1926. MINERAL WATER
1927. MINERAL WATER IN POUCHES
1928. MINI FLOUR MILL ATTA MAIDA, SUJI & WHEAT BRAN
1929. MITHAI/HALWAI (SWEET & NAMKEEN)
1930. MUTTON PROCESSING
1931. PAN MASALA (MEETHA, SADA, ZARDA) MAKING & PACKING
1932. PAN MASALA AND POUCH MAKING
1933. PANEER (CHEESE)
1934. PAPAD & BARIYAN
1935. PAPAD PLANT
1936. PEPSICOLA IN POLYTUBES
1937. PETHA PACKAGING
1938. PICKLES
1939. PIGGERY/MEAT/CHICKEN PROCESSING
1940. PINE APPLE JUICE CANNING
1941. POTATO & ONION POWDER
1942. POTATO & ONION FLAKES
1943. POTATO CHIPS
1944. POTATO GRANULES
1945. POUCH FILLING FOR SAUNF SUPARI ILAICHI ETC.
1946. PRESERVATION OF RAWS MANGO JUICE
1947. PROCESSED CHEESE & MARINE PDTS.
1948. PULP FROM TARMARIND
1949. READYMATE PROCESSED FOOD
1950. RICE & CORN FLAKES
1951. RICE BASMATI (TRADING)
1952. RICE POLISHING & PACKAGING IN POUCH
1953. ROASTED/SALTED/MASALA/ CASHEW NUTS ALMONDS & PEA NUT
1954. ROLLER FLOUR MILL

INFOTECH/IT PROJECTS

1955. MEDICAL TRANSCRIPTION
1956. E-COMMERCE
1957. CYBERCAFE
1958. INTERNET SERVICE PROVIDER (ISP)
1959. COMPUTER EDUCATION CENTRE
1960. PORTAL (WEBSITE DESIGN)
1961. CALL CENTRE

TERMS AND CONDITIONS

FOR INDIA

1. Please ask for Quotations of Each *Market Survey Cum Detailed Techno Economic Feasibility Report.* Payable in advance through Draft/M.O./Cash in favour of 'ENGINEERS INDIA RESEARCH INSTITUTE', Delhi. Delivery by Regd.post within 2 Days. (Postage Free)

2. Ask for the Hi-Tech Projects Monthly magazine. Each Magazine covers many Project Profiles for selection of Industry.

FOR OVERSEAS

1. Please ask for Quotations in US $ of Each *Market Survey Cum Detailed Techno Economic Feasibility Report.* Payable in advance through Draft/M.O./Cash in favour of 'ENGINEERS INDIA RESEARCH INSTITUTE', Delhi. (Payable in India) Delivery by Regd.post within 4 Days.

2. Ask for the Hi-Tech Projects Monthly magazine. Each Magazine covers many Project Profiles for selection of Industry.

ENGINEERS INDIA RESEARCH INSTITUTE

4449, Nai Sarak (D), Main Road, Delhi - 110 006 (India)
Ph:. 91-11-23918117, 23916431, 23840361, 31082370
Fax: 91-11- 23916431 E-Mail : eirisidi@bol.net.in
Website:www.startindustry.com
Also at : 4/27, Roop Nagar, Near Roop Nagar No. 1 School, Delhi - 110 007 (India) Ph:. 23840361

JUST PUBLISHED-NEW BOOKS

HAND BOOK OF CONFECTIONERY WITH FORMULATIONS

By : EIRI BOARD

ISBN. 81-86732-35-7 + Rs. 600/-

The book is covering Confectionery Processes & formulations, Caramels Toffees, Butterscotch Fudge, Chocolates, Supari, Nougat, Soft Nougat, Milk Toffee, Chocolate & Confectionery Spreads Chocolates Syrups, Multiple Confectionery Bars, Project Profiles, Details of Plant & Machinery,Addresses of Suppliers of Machinery, Raw Materials & Packaging Materials etc. Actual photographs of Plant and Machineries used to manufacture Confectionery items.

HAND BOOK OF BAKERY INDUSTRIES

By : EIRI BOARD

ISBN. 81-86732-8-7 + Rs. 350/-

Book covers Bakery Raw Materials, Bread Making Processes, Biscuits, Cookies & Crackers, Sponge Cakes, Pies & Puff Pastries, Sweet Yeast Dough Products, Bakery Machinery, Confectionery, Process, Packaging for Biscuits, Project Profile of Bakery, Cofectionery, Bubble Gum Plant etc., Manufacturers & Suppliers of Plant & Machineries, Manufacturers & Suppliers of Raw Materials and many other relevant details for new comers in this field.

PLASTIC COMPOUNDING MASTERBATCHES, PET AND OTHER PLASTIC PROCESSING INDUSTRIES

By : EIRI BOARD

ISBN. 81-86732-49-7 + Rs. 750/-

The book covers almost all the basic and advanced details to setup own Plastic Processing Industry. The new edition of the book is covering latest technology including Polyethylene, Extrusion, Injection Moulding, Blowmoulding, Polyester Terephthalate (PET), Rotational Moulding, Post Extrusion Process, Vacuum Metallizing, Identification of Plastic Materials, Thermosetting Plastics, Recycling, Additives for Polymers, Virgin Quality from Reprocessed, Specialty Additives and Masterbatches, PVC Compounding with Formulations, Automobile Injection Moulded Plastic Components, Colour Master Batch for various Plastics, Compact Disks, Co-Extruded Multilayer Film and Laminated Multilayer Film, Egg Trays from Plastics, Ethylene Vinyl Acetate Sheet and Sole, Polypropylene Multifilament Spinning Yarn, Plastic Films and Sheets with Printing, Plastic Granules from Fresh Resin, Plastic Injection Moulding Products, Plastic Mats, PET Bottles from Pre-form, PET Pre-form from PET Resin, PVC Pipes and Fittings, PVC Extrusion Profiles, Computer Ribbon Cartridges, HDPE/PP Woven Sacks (Bags), Semi-Conductive Compounds and Masterbatches, Plastic Sutli, Disposable Plastic Syringes, Plastic Water Storage Tanks, Thermocole Based Disposable Glass, Cups and Plates, Plastic GranulesCross Linked Polyethylene (XLPE) Compound for XLPE Cables, Suppliers of Plant, Equipments & Machineries, Suppliers of Raw Materials etc.

ENGINEERS INDIA RESEARCH INSTITUTE Mobile : 9811437895

4449, Nai Sarak, Main Road, Delhi - 110 006 (INDIA) Ph./Fax : 91-11- 23918117, 23916431, 23840361